THE OLYMPIC GAMES EFFECT

How Sports Marketing Builds Strong Brands

THE OLYMPIC GAMES EFFECT

How Sports Marketing Builds Strong Brands

JOHN A. DAVIS

John Wiley & Sons (Asia) Pte. Ltd.

Other Wiley Editorial Offices
John Wiley & Sons, Inc., 111 River Street, Hoboken, NJ 07030, USA
John Wiley & Sons, Ltd., The Atrium, Southern Gate, Chichester, West Sussex P019 8SQ, UK
John Wiley & Sons (Canada), Ltd., 5353 Dundas Street West, Suite 400, Toronto, Ontario
    M9B 6H8, Canada
John Wiley & Sons Australia Ltd., 42 McDougall Street, Milton, Queensland 4064, Australia
Wiley-VCH, Boschstrasse 12, D-69469 Weinheim, Germany

Library of Congress Cataloging-in-Publication Data
ISBN: 978-0-470-82366-8

Typeset in 11/13 point, Palatino by *eYES! Impressions*
Printed in Singapore by Saik Wah Press Pte. Ltd.

10 9 8 7 6 5 4 3 2 1

DEDICATION

To Leo Long—a World Class

Track & Field Coach and Motivator

CONTENTS

SECTION IV
Winning Marketing Gold: Work Like Crazy

SECTION V
Training for Olympic Marketing Victory

ACKNOWLEDGMENTS

Sports have been an important part of my life since I was a little boy growing up in the San Francisco Bay Area. Of course, the list of personal influences from my youth is far too long to mention here. Suffice to say that Stanford University, the San Francisco 49ers, the San Francisco Giants, the Oakland Raiders and, oddly enough (since they are at the other end of the country), the Boston Red Sox and Boston Celtics were among the teams that captured my imagination as a kid. As I grew older, my sports interests expanded beyond North America to include Manchester United, Real Madrid, the New Zealand All Blacks, and Australian Rules Football. I love sports and, fortunately, a large portion of the world does as well. Most of all, I am a fan of the Olympic Games. As a high school track athlete who ran the 880-yard run (now the 800 meters), I dreamed of making the Olympic team. But I never made it—not even close. In fact, I was only the third-best half-miler on my high school team (our high school teams were always loaded with talent and we were coached by a great guy named Leo Long, to whom this book is dedicated). But in researching the winning times in the 800 since the modern Olympics began, I was thrilled to see that my best time would have won the gold medal in both the 1896 and 1900 Olympiads. While this knowledge does make me feel a bit better about my Olympic dreams, it is tempered by the fact that there are thousands of non-Olympic athletes who can make similar claims.

I have had terrific students the past few years in my Sports Marketing course and they have conducted excellent research on sports organizations around the world, from clubs to leagues to companies and, of course, the Olympics, providing a solid foundation in the latest trends in sports marketing. I would like to thank them all because their energy and enthusiasm in the classroom makes my job very enjoyable.

I would also like to thank the following people for their support— I greatly admire their work: David Haigh, CEO of Brand Finance; David Shaw, Director of Brand Marketing and Marketing Communications at Lenovo Asia Pacific; George Foster of Stanford Business School; Rod Beckstrom, co-author of the best-selling book *The Starfish and the Spider: The Unstoppable Power of Leaderless Organizations* (and my former college roommate); Glenn Hubbard, Dean of Columbia Business School; Earl Taylor, Chief Marketing Officer of MSI (Marketing Science Institute); and Oon Jin Teik, CEO of the Singapore Sports Council.

I would also like to thank the intrepid John Wiley & Sons (Asia) team: Nick Wallwork, CJ Hwu, Janis Soo, Joel Balbin, Louise Koh, and Cynthia Mak. They are becoming like family, which is probably not what they want to hear. Finally, Nicole Frank was my editor this time around and it was delightful working with her.

John A. Davis
Singapore
August 2008

INTRODUCTION

The Olympic Games, at their core, are about athletes and athletic competition. But the Olympics have evolved into a much larger phenomenon that extends beyond the boundaries of sport. Propelled by the Olympic Movement, the term that describes the interrelationship among athletes, local/national Olympic committees, and related international federations (which are responsible for specific sports around the world), the Olympics have come to represent hope and prosperity—hope in the sense of a peaceful, better world energized by sport; and prosperity in the economic, social, and political contexts.

Each Olympic Games is a substantial undertaking involving economic and infrastructural resource commitments by the host city and nation. One city, dozens of new venues, hundreds of companies (with thousands of employees), millions of volunteers, and billions of dollars are combined to make the Olympics happen every two years. No other sporting event unleashes such a complex array of activities.

Companies invest $200–$300 million to be TOP (TOP = The Olympic Partner Program, the name of the highest level of Olympic sponsorship that gives companies the right to sponsor one quadrennial cycle of both the Winter and Summer Games—see Exhibit I-1) sponsors for an event that lasts just over two weeks. While this is an enormous amount of money, such an investment can make sense when it is properly conceived, executed, and reviewed. To be fair, the $200 million figure is an estimate of the total investment in sponsoring the Olympics, since neither the International Olympic Committee (IOC) nor individual sponsors release official figures. But an

---

Exhibit I-1
TOP Program[1]

TOP stands for The Olympic Partner Program. Created in 1985, the TOP program, managed by the IOC, is the only sponsorship with the exclusive worldwide marketing rights to both Winter and Summer Games.

As an event that commands the focus of the media and the attention of the entire world for two weeks every other year, the Olympic Games are one of the most effective international marketing platforms in the world, reaching billions of people in over 200 countries and territories throughout the world.

Sponsor support is crucial to the staging of the Games and the operations of every organization within the Olympic Movement. Commercial partners also provide vital technical services and product support to the International Olympic Committee (IOC), Organizing Committees (OCOGs) and National Olympic Committees (NOCs).

---

approximate breakdown shows that TOP sponsors pay a sponsorship fee of over $70 million each, then spend an additional three to four times that amount in activation expenditures. Activation expenditures refer to the specific marketing programs and tactics in which a sponsor invests to bring the sponsorship to life. These include investing in creative development, media placement, execution/promotion, support services, and post-event review.[2] When one considers that Coca-Cola, Lenovo, GE, Johnson & Johnson, McDonald's, Visa, Samsung, Omega, Kodak, Atos Origin, Manulife, and Panasonic are the 12 TOP sponsors for the 2008 Olympic Games in Beijing, then one may also assume these companies did not invest their money incautiously or collude in a fit of collective foolishness.[3] In fact, companies that become TOP sponsors have exclusive rights to market in both the Summer and Winter Olympic Games, reaching a cumulative total viewing audience of over 44 billion people.[4, 5] Using more conventional figures, the total number of viewers for the 2004 Olympic Games in Athens was 3.9 billion.[6] While the Olympics are a unique and potentially highly beneficial sponsorship opportunity, not everything associated with the Olympics turns gold, as this book will point out. Both the sponsors and the IOC make mistakes. But on balance, an Olympics sponsorship can be rewarding to sponsoring companies and their shareholders, as well as customers. We will look at what TOP sponsors are doing to make their Olympic investments productive and value adding.

The first part of the book's title is *The Olympic Games Effect*—hinting at the potential for a positive brand halo casting a profitable glow over those that are part of such a unique, historical event. And yes, there is a great deal of risk as well—risk that scandal or other significant problems might arise that could tarnish your investment. Common sense says that a company's shareholders might be a bit upset at management if $250 million were spent and the result was zilch. Interestingly, many companies have repeatedly sponsored the Olympics, or some portion of it, to great effect. After all, they wouldn't do this if they weren't getting results.

Of course, not everyone or everything related to sports illustrates common sense (such as the penchant for some athletes to use performance-enhancing drugs that give them an athletic edge yet with unfortunate side-effects, like a larger head, smaller genitals, shorter life spans, hair in weird places, and a generally grumpier disposition. Not to mention the fact that, when caught, they have to give their medals back, suffer public humiliation, and be banned from the sport for life). For companies, part of the allure of sponsoring sports in general, and the Olympics in particular, is knowing that the unexpected could and does happen, bringing added attention and interest to that event and their efforts associated with it. I teach a course in sports marketing at Singapore Management University. The course is popular with students, partly because the subject is fascinating due to all the reasons people love sports, and partly because the industry is huge—estimates range from $100 billion to $500+ billion—and growing 4–8% per year.[7] For example, NPD Group, a global research firm, estimated in 2006 that the global sports industry was $256 billion, a 4% increase over 2005. Interestingly, this estimate focused on four segments (footwear, apparel, equipment, and bikes and accessories) and did not include spectator-sports statistics such as professional sports leagues, teams, or the economic impact of fan support around the world.[8]

Sports are an industry that develops some of the world's most innovative products and offers an amazingly diverse array of events, teams, and contests around the world in different, exotic locales. Sports fans are in every country, making sports a form of universal language.

In many societies success is associated with distinction and greatness, by the people and organizations within, based on cultural standards. We look to those who have achieved as role models, figuratively hoisting their accomplishments aloft as the standards to which the rest of us should aspire. As individuals, many of us work hard so that we are "noticed" and seen as "valuable" by those who can influence the course of our career. Our societal organizations, whether business, not-for-profit, or government, seek visibility and awareness while also striving to be seen as highly valued by their customers. Of course, our assessments of each other are often the result of perception born from reputation, to actual experiences with that person or organization, which ultimately determine whether the perception matches reality. More simply, we try to create a positive image and act accordingly so that others see us favorably. This is where marketing has gotten itself into trouble over the years since some have misconstrued the intent to create a positive image into an effort to communicate a ridiculous or misleading image. The more pejorative aspects of "hype" usually spring to mind with misleading claims inducing people to buy a product because it is "the greatest product in the history of products," or some such nonsense. Hype is not the same as marketing. Hype usually fails because those who promise it can't deliver and those who buy it won't do so twice.

For companies, developing a positive image involves a complex, dynamic, and ongoing set of activities well beyond having an office with a desk, chair, and telephone. Management has to have some sense of what they want to sell and to whom to sell it. Selling includes building awareness by letting the market and customers within know you exist, and creating distinction to show why your offerings are unique (this requires more than merely stating "new and improved" or "we're better"). To build awareness, marketers use a myriad of marketing techniques, including marketing communications, products, distribution, pricing, and well-trained, customer-oriented employees, all engaged in an effort to educate the market about the company and its products. As awareness transitions to growth, companies must shift the marketplace's perception away from general recognition and toward differentiating their offerings from those of the competition. To accomplish this, marketers must tailor their marketing activities to appeal as specifically and relevantly as possible to the target audiences that are most attractive to their company. The idea of communicating clearly to customers seems utterly simple, bordering on simple-minded. Yet too many companies communicate poorly with ill-conceived marketing campaigns and equally bad products and execution. For those companies unwilling to take the time and thoughtfulness needed to plan their businesses properly to avoid mediocrity, a marketing investment such as sponsoring the Olympics would be a stupid idea because they would be embarrassed on an epic scale. But for companies that see marketing as a strategic asset, having a sharp focus on what they expect to gain from sponsoring the Olympics, communicated properly, can help them win customers and grow profits for years. This book will show the lessons of many companies that have benefited from sponsoring the Olympics, as well as the pitfalls. Furthermore, many of these lessons can be applied to other sports sponsorships as well.

Developing recognizable distinction includes associating your company with other prestigious organizations and events, and few are as powerful or meaningful as the Olympic Games. The Olympics epitomize prestige and distinction, qualities associated with the rare and unique. They are held only every four years (each Summer and Winter Olympics is four years apart but they alternate every two years.) The Games' infrequency heightens demand, inspiring the most ambitious athletes to schedule their entire training program around this quadrennial event. They are analogous to a limited edition, exclusive luxury item, never to be offered twice in exactly the same way. Olympic athletes undertake a rigorous, multi-year preparation regimen with no guarantee they will qualify for the Olympics, let alone win their event. Therefore, those who win are seen as extraordinary, heroic individuals who won in an exclusive, even rare, form of international competition against the very best competitors from around the world. The exclusive appeal of the Olympic Games, combined with the unique, even daunting challenges athletes undertake, creates a compelling, irresistible quality that motivates companies to support the Olympics in the hope of benefiting from the associated halo effect.

A more frequent annual schedule would diminish part of the charm and mystique attached to the Olympic Games.

Beyond this generalized halo are innumerable factors that inspire each of us to watch the Olympics. It is not just the infrequency of the Games or the determination of the athletes that creates the appeal of the Olympic Games. After all, there are plenty of events with dedicated participants, but that have poor fan followings. The Olympics have succeeded in capturing the popular imagination around the world, and this broad-based appeal is attractive to companies for obvious commercial reasons. There is also deep credibility attached to the Olympics that creates a particularly intoxicating appeal. Part of this appeal is witnessing athletes pushing their abilities to the limit, coupled with the element of surprise. No matter how formidable an athlete appears, usually due to dominating performances in competitions leading up to the Olympics, there is always the chance of an unexpected outcome. Physical preparation is crucial to competitive success against rivals, but psychology plays an important role as well. There are many instances in sports where a supposed underdog ends up the victor, vanquishing a foe previously considered indomitable. The gold-medal-winning 1980 U.S. Olympic ice hockey team is one such example. Such surprises are part of the allure of any sport. As fans, we know that underdogs may win, no matter how unlikely, because we understand that athletic competitions have numerous complex variables interacting in unique ways, creating unpredictable outcomes. We are inspired by such surprises just as we are awed by the performance of dominating teams, even if we do not personally like the result. In the case of both the underdog and the favorite, we know that both competitors (whether individuals or teams) worked hard prior to the event and that both also want to win. If an underdog wins, the psychological impact may change the dynamics of future competitions simply because the victor feels more confident, stirring the rest of us to improve our own efforts with the hope that similar outcomes happen for us. If the favorite wins, then we often aspire to reach the same level of consistent dominance, pushing ourselves to improve yet again.

People strive for improvement throughout life. As kids we always competed. Whether playing in the streets or at school, our goal was to be better than the other kids. Every year we followed our favorite teams, from high school to college to pros, usually those from the city in or near where we grew up, debating how our team would beat the others in the league and, most importantly, our rivals. As adults, our competitions often shift to encompass business and other professional interests, but the theme of besting a rival, or our own performance, lies close to the surface. Throughout life, competition serves as an energizing force, helping us define who we are while also guiding our objectives (beat my time, this person, this team, or this record next year). If someone chooses not to compete, then we often see that person as weaker and lacking ability. Indeed, we learn to compete on so many levels so often that we attach significant value to the act of competing itself, making almost any competition a vital ingredient of determining worth. We admire competitions that pit one dedicated person or team against another, especially when the commitment is long-standing and reputations have been built accordingly. While rigorous training comprised of relentless practice and repetition is important, indeed vital, to success in any sport, this commitment is motivated by the athlete's ambition to be the best and reach the top of their sport. Winning their sport's premier/championship competitions is the athlete's ultimate goal. Whether it is the NBA (National Basketball Association), EPL (English Premier League), or NFL (National Football League), the end-of-season championship is considered the pinnacle event and those who compete in it qualified by enduring a rigorous schedule of training and regular-season matches, competing at the highest level most consistently, and winning more contests than losing. As fans, we know that a given sport's championship crowns the victor—a status the athlete or team retains for a year until the next championship. As fans, we know and understand that our favorite athletes may have only one chance to compete in the Olympics and that the odds of them winning are quite small, even if their past achievements suggest superior abilities compared to opponents. TOP sponsors understand this as well and recognize the unique and massive audience of nearly four billion people that each Olympic Games attracts—which, in today's globalizing business world, makes the Games even more commercially valuable and attractive. The challenge for TOP sponsors is determining how to take full advantage of the global exposure afforded by associating with the Olympic Games in a way that enhances their company brand, excites consumers, and grows their business over the long term, yet does not cheapen or undermine the prestigious reputation of the Olympic Games themselves.

How This Book is Organized

There are five sections. Each section is important because the size and scope of large-scale, sports-sponsorship investments require a deep and knowledgeable understanding of the event being sponsored. Deciding to become a corporate sponsor for the Olympics costs a great deal of money well before any effort is put into the activities that actually activate the sponsorship. Imagine buying another company without knowing anything about it and then ignoring it after the purchase—one would not do so. Companies considering a sports sponsorship are well advised to approach it much as one would approach launching a new company or a major product offering. There are significant operating and marketing complexities, and coordinating them is a 24/7 job. The good news is that the Olympic Games are a global stage, reaching one of the largest audiences of any event in the world, providing a unique opportunity to create a positive, lasting, and economically valuable relationship with consumers.

Section I: 2,700 Years of Olympic Tradition, 100 Years of Olympic Marketing – There is more to the Olympics than the media spectacle with which we are all familiar today. The Olympics are also more than a sport (or a collection of sports). Learning about the early circumstances and context surrounding an organization's formative years (or a company's, for that matter) can provide both profound insights and competitive leverage when evaluating the attractiveness of an investment. This section presents a short history of the Olympics and the sociocultural influences that shaped the event at the time of the ancient Greeks. There is a richness to the Olympics that is unlike any other sports event in the world, and much of it is due to the historical legacy from the ancient Greeks. The Games have a formidable reputation as a powerful force for good for people everywhere, and understanding how this reputation was built is instrumental in understanding why they are still revered to this day. There are also interesting parallels between the ancient and modern Olympics that may surprise people.

Section II: When Things Go Well... – Part of the explanation for the ongoing success and popularity of the Olympics lies in the fact that more good things happen than bad. When things go well, whether it an expected or unexpected performance, people celebrate and the halo effect casts a wide glow over those associated with success. While modern society has placed a premium on winning and relegated anything but first as a "loss," the Olympics stand for a higher definition of success. When an athlete becomes an Olympian, they have already achieved something few others can ever experience. Of course, when they are a medal winner, their performance attains a loftier status, and gold- medal winners often become icons. For companies, associating with Olympic success can have an obviously positive and long-lasting impact on their image. This section will discuss the benefits to associating with the Olympics.

Section III: When Things Go Wrong... – With success comes visibility. The Olympics have become one of the best-known brands in the world, which attracts a wide range of interest groups that know the Games are a useful platform for their own message. Political issues are often intertwined with the Olympics, despite the Olympic Charter's statements to the contrary. Athletes, too, sometimes find themselves in untenable situations. When controversy hits, the negative impact on all involved can be enormous. We will discuss examples of controversies and the potential risks for corporate sponsors.

Section IV: Winning Marketing Gold: Work Like Crazy – There are still no shortcuts to success. Whether one is an athlete with the dream of Olympic glory or a corporation with ambitions to increase value to stakeholders, rigorous preparation every day for years is required. The IOC has developed a series of revenue-generating programs designed to maximize corporate associations while also providing significant funding to support the Olympic Movement. The best results come with time, and this section provides details on four select TOP sponsors (TOP is the acronym for "The Olympic Partner" program, which is discussed in this section as well) and the sponsorship programs they have developed over the length of their association with the Olympics.

Section V: Training for Olympic Marketing Victory – This section guides sponsors through how to design their sponsorship-program plans based on a clear understanding of customers, creative execution, and marketing communications.

"At the end of each section is a chapter of Sponsorship Preparation Questions," based on the theme of the section and designed to be asked both of the corporate sponsor and the sports event. These questions will help corporate sponsors evaluate their understanding of their own organization and of the sports event. The Sponsorship Preparation Questions will be useful to companies considering sponsoring a wide range of sports events, whether it is Olympic-scale or not. Finally, all figures are in US$ unless otherwise indicated.

I

2,700 Years of Olympic Tradition, 100 Years of Olympic Marketing

CHAPTER 1

The Olympic Dream

Marketing, if nothing else, is about developing, building, and sustaining a positive reputation for the entity being marketed in the hopes that others will find the entity compelling enough to support. In the modern era, this support is in the form of profitable, loyal customers. The Olympic Games of the ancient Greek world built a remarkable legacy of reputable success that lasted for 1,200 years, yet they were not marketed, at least not in the modern sense of marketing. The Games were an integral part of Greek life, known for attracting the best athletes to compete and represent their home city-state for the honor and glory of Olympic champion. Victors received rewards, including free food for life, new homes, and tax-free status. Victory and the ensuing fame, therefore, were certainly sought. Olympic success, and the subsequent notoriety, undoubtedly helped foster positive reputations for those involved, spreading the Olympic message through an ancient form of viral marketing—word of mouth. The stories of Olympic competition provided instructive lessons on the virtues of dedication to cause, translated through the tradition of storytelling in which tales of Olympic athletic achievement were spread from one generation to the next, inspiring images of victory and dreams of eternal glory.

"Holding an Olympic Games means evoking history," said Baron Pierre de Coubertin, the founder of the modern Olympics.[1] This is a grand, perhaps even a daunting, sentiment. Evoking history implies a significant responsibility and, less majestically, a great burden is placed on those who attempt to carry out such lofty ambitions. Failure by any city and its Olympic planners to recognize the importance of the Olympic Games and then organize resources to ensure success risks eternal historical infamy. Given this risk, why do so many companies and cities today vie for a chance to be involved with the Olympic Games? The answer lies partly in understanding the origins of the Olympic Games, since even a rudimentary review will provide a better sense of the traditions and historical context that have helped shape the Olympic reputation as it exists today. Additionally, there is the magnetic attraction of the Olympic Dream—a concept loaded with imagery and associations such as *authenticity, mythology, mystique, and the pinnacle of sport* that are simultaneously positive, motivating, and virtuous. Thomas B. Shepard, executive vice president, Global Merchant Partnerships & Sponsorship, Visa International, offered this explanation for the appeal and benefits of sponsoring the Olympic Games:

> *If you look at the Olympics, it is a perfect fit for us. Olympic brand equities include being at the pinnacle of its category; having universal appeal; standing for excellence; having broad-based consumer awareness and acceptance; having global reach with local impact and participation; and standing for leadership. Visa's brand equities of industry leadership; global yet local; accepted everywhere; innovative and modern; and service excellence parallel Olympic brand equities. Visa could probably work on innovativeness, though, because we're not known as the most innovative brand.[2]*

Shepard's rationale goes beyond assessing benefits based on return on investment analysis by revealing the strategic rationale and qualitative linkages between the Olympics and Visa. Shepard even describes Visa's weaknesses compared to the Olympics when he discusses the company's need to be more innovative, perhaps implying that an association with the Olympics might provide the catalyst Visa needs to improve its innovativeness.

For host cities and corporate sponsors, the premier status of the Olympics offers a unique and highly credible event that captures the imagination of the world and casts a remarkable halo effect over the stakeholders involved. This is not to suggest that the Olympics are without fault, as there are well-documented examples of scandals and improprieties that violate the Olympic spirit and rules of conduct that, as a consequence, risk tarnishing the event's reputation and harm the commercial interests of the IOC's key corporate sponsors, as will be discussed later in the book. But interestingly, the scandals have not caused irreparable harm (yet), which suggests that the Olympics enjoy such an exalted status in the eyes of the public that they are willing to forgive short-term transgressions if the integrity of the actual athletic competitions themselves remains intact. Of course, ongoing scandals would be increasingly hard to overcome, so the onus is on the International Olympic Committee (IOC) to ensure the highest possible integrity and rules of conduct for all involved.

Authenticity

There is little doubt that the Olympic Games are exciting, unpredictable events, providing fans and competitors with a rich set of experiences. Beyond the excitement, part of the appeal of the Olympics is due to its image of authenticity, born from centuries of tradition around the purity of honest athletic competition. We expect and trust that the Olympics overall and the competitions within will be conducted fairly, with athletes having prepared using legitimate training techniques, building their reputations through rigorous and varied competitive events. This simple set of expectations is central to our belief in the Olympics as a pure event free from manipulation, as opposed to, say, professional wrestling, where there is an implicit and explicit understanding between the wrestling stars and the fans that the entire event is scripted, complete with far-fetched storylines and outsized personas. If the Olympics were ever to resort to rigging or scripting, the entire foundation of the Games would be eroded and thousands of years of credibility would be wiped out.

The ancient Olympics were a revered religious rite—a celebration and homage to the Greek gods, especially Zeus. Pindar, a famous Greek poet, said in his First Olympian Ode,

> *Water is best, and gold, like a blazing fire in the night, stands out supreme of all lordly wealth. But if, my heart, you wish to sing of contests, look no further for any star warmer than the sun, shining by day through the lonely sky, and let us not proclaim any contest greater than Olympia.*[3]

Begun in 776 BC, the first Games consisted of one event called the "stade," a 192-meter foot race. The term "stade" evolved over the centuries into the modern word "stadium." The stade pitted individual runners against each other, with the outcome determined by physical and mental preparedness and nothing else, suggesting an authentic, unpolluted combination of virtues. Competitors were all male, as women were forbidden from competing in, or even watching, the Games. If women were caught, they faced the possibility of death. However, a separate and related women-only set of races called the Heraea were held, which historians believe were conducted before each men's Olympics. The men wore a simple covering, often just a loincloth, until Orsippus of Megara lost his covering during his Olympic race in 720 BC, yet still went on to win his event naked. Legend says his victory inspired other competitors and, thereafter, nudity was a common theme for Olympic athletes.[4] The ancient Olympics were remarkable in another respect: no awards were given for those who lost. While there was public honor and affection bestowed on victors as described by Pindar, "they showered leaves and flowers on the victors,"[5] there was little sympathy nor the pat on the back suggesting "nice try, better luck next time," or similarly supportive sentiments for those that did not win. Losers often suffered shame, humiliation, and social ostracism, as Dion Chrysostomos, a Greek philosopher, observed in contrasting public reaction to victors versus losers, "The shouts of sections of the crowd differ so much between those which are made with heartiness and praise from the others which are accompanied by irony and often with antipathy."[6]

There were no teams or team events in the ancient Olympics, only individual athletes with their coaches, if they were fortunate enough to have one. Coaches had to accompany their athlete without a cloak, which may seem like an odd requirement, but it was a practice established after Pherenike, a boxing coach, celebrated her athlete's victory a bit too vigorously, causing her cloak to drop and revealing her gender in front of the surprised male fans and athletes. Her winning athlete was her son Pisodorus and she herself was the daughter of a famous Olympic boxing champion Diagoras, who competed in the Games of 464 BC. Ancient Greek tradition punished women who violated the rules of sport by throwing them to their death from Mount Typaeum, but her family's famous athletic accomplishments (her three brothers and a nephew were also Olympic champions) persuaded the judges to pardon her, saving her life. Thereafter, she was called Callipateira, Greek for "Mrs. Good Father."[7]

With Olympic victory being important for social status, the athletes of the ancient Olympics often sought any advantage they could, from medicinal treatment to financial inducement. They consulted magicians prior to events, seeking spells and potions that might give them an edge, certainly an effort similar in intent to that of today's steroids users. Eupolus of Thessaly, a boxer in the Olympic Games of 388 BC, bribed his opponents to lose. Several hundred years later, the Roman Emperor Nero also bribed Olympic officials to include poetry as an official Olympic event (he admired Greek culture and apparently saw his own poetic abilities in a favorable light) and also bribed officials to declare him the victor of the chariot race, even though he fell off his chariot and never finished the event.[8] Athletes who cheated in the ancient Olympics faced beatings, fines, or both. The fines were used to pay for statues that lined pathways leading to the competition venues. The statues were inscribed with a description of the guilty athlete's transgression, serving as a clear, visible reminder to competitors of the penalties they face should they cheat.

Such simple themes are simultaneously quaint and hard to imagine given today's plethora of scientific training techniques (sometimes including the use of performance-enhancing substances), armies of handlers, larger-than-life personas, and commercial incentives. Yet despite the commericialization of Olympic athletes, there is little doubt that a key appeal for the Olympic Games remains, at its core, this notion of authenticity rooted in simple athletic ability.

Such challenges and historical legacies aside, the Olympic Games are still seen as a force for good with athletes competing on the basis of preparation, strategy, and determination, perpetuating the credibility of a several-thousand-year-old brand. Despite the controversies, the power of the Olympic *ideal* drives our perceptions of the Games even as problems continue to occur, pushed along by an overriding sense of hope that the world can set aside its differences for two weeks and come together in a show of community and support for the purity of athletic competition. As long as athletes focus on achievement through honest, ethical means, then the integrity of the Olympic Games should remain intact, even as companies and officials occasionally mar this prestigious event with the odd bribe, political favor, and revelations of impropriety.

Companies keen on building and reinforcing an image of trust and integrity invest in sponsoring the Olympics because the event's very authenticity can confer similar credibility on the sponsoring company due to the visibility resulting from the association, not unlike when a person has their photograph taken with a famous person—suddenly, that average Joe gets the notoriety. The sheer novelty of the occasion elevates the unknown temporarily. The challenge is translating this one-time event into longer-term success and benefits. For smart companies, the real advantage of Olympic sponsorship lies in the long-term commitment and associated activities, and not the temporary excitement of two weeks of Olympic events. This rationale of supporting a long-term marketing investment is vital to effective and successful marketing efforts. Stopping sponsorship after one Olympics does not enable a company to leverage its investment and/or contribute to a longer-term growth plan. Senior management will always be tempted to cancel any program that does not demonstrate direct contribution to company performance. Yet, as successful marketers know, one run of an ad campaign, or any other communication, is too limited to gain a complete understanding of the long-term impact. Conversely, switching marketing tactics frequently can confuse the market, undermine company positioning and reputation, and embolden competitors to take advantage of weakness. Think of it from an athlete's point of view: if a top athlete trains for months, or years, and then races once to see whether the training paid off, but retires if he or she loses, then there is little learned. The real benefit comes from altering race techniques and competing repeatedly to see what nuances are required to achieve consistent success.

Mythology and Mystique

The Olympics inspire mixed emotions and trans-regional loyalties, fomented by centuries of myth and mystique. Greek city-states vied for the top athletes, offering inducements to persuade top performers to abandon their allegiances.[9] Victory in an Olympic event was a high honor, bestowing riches and virtue upon the winner, and potential ruin upon the losers. The ancient Olympics spanned a period of nearly 12 centuries, from roughly 776 BC to 393 AD when Roman Emperor Theodosius banned the Games because he viewed them as a pagan cult. Theodosius's ban may have been political, but it was by no means the only evidence of politics asserting its influence in the Olympics. The Olympics stand out over the ages as a memorable, even mythical, event partly because each Olympiad reveals the stories of athletic success and heroism. Such stories of legendary athletic achievement are passed from one generation to the next, developing society's shared notions of character and virtue, which serve to reinforce the Olympic mythology. We want athletes from our own country to win, but we also want our favorite athletes in specific sports to win, even if they are from another country. The Olympics are unique because they are about the athlete and transcending national boundaries, although nationalism certainly plays an important role as well. Fans around the world look forward to the Olympics because of their reputation, unique structure, and values. Images of the ancient Greek athletes competing purely for honor permeate our collective psyche and ignite our expectations every four years (note: until 1992, the Winter and Summer Olympics were held in the same year, every four years. The Winter Olympics were subsequently separated from the Summer Olympics by two years beginning in 1994. The four-year interval between each Winter and each Summer Olympics remains, however). The Olympic Dream, while inspiring virtue in the form of athletic competition, is also an insightful guide to broader social mores and codes of acceptable conduct. We *implicitly* understand what is meant by "sportsmanship" and "fair play"— understanding that is common across cultures. Consequently, we look forward to the Olympic Games because they bring the world together for two brief weeks, reminding us of the importance of harmony and peace as seen through the lens of athletic achievement. In fact, the Olympics can serve as a positive substitute for international conflict, allowing countries to set aside political differences and elevating sports into the role of settler of disputes. These noble associations of sportsmanship and fair play are central to the mystique of the Olympics.

From a business perspective, an important determinant of a marketing program's success is whether the company's own image retained or gained a stronger mystique with its customers. Do not misinterpret the intent here. Mystique is not meant to suggest that companies should strive to be obscure or mysterious. Being understandable and accessible to customers is still important if a company wishes to reduce obstacles to market acceptance. Instead, companies should endeavor to delight their customers with their ability to convey and reinforce uniqueness. As awkward as it may sound, we often attach a vague sense of mystery to success, asking ourselves "what are the secrets to that company's success?" even though those secrets may be painfully obvious (such as superb, high-quality products; clever communications; extraordinary services). But a key for any successful company versus its less-successful competitors is the very fact that it has found a way to more effectively attract customers and convince the market of its uniqueness, often even if the competitor's products are known to be similar if not equal. There is no hidden mystery or deep secret, other than the weight of market expectations motivating company management to focus on consistent, successful delivery of promises made. In this sense, well-conceived and executed marketing activities, including event marketing, can and should serve not just to win more business and reinforce distinctiveness, but also to create competitive *disadvantage* for rivals. By associating with the Olympic Games, company marketers believe they increase the likelihood that their company will be seen as both positive and different vis-à-vis the competition. Since the Olympics often produce stories of amazing athletic prowess and success, the by-product for sponsoring companies is success by association. Such connections add to a company's image, traditions, and history, all of which are quite visible to millions of people around the world. Better yet, the countless conversations and viral marketing effects can benefit sponsoring companies well after the Olympic Games have ended.

Pinnacle of Sport

While winning may be an important goal of any athletic competition because it is a common measure of success, the Olympic Games stand for something even greater: they represent an *idea*. The idea, particularly from the earliest days of the ancient Greek Olympics, is simply that achievement is not limited to how one finishes a competition, but how one competes. What is their reputation? What is their strategy? What is their philosophy? What is their character? The present-day equivalent is captured by a popular sports sentiment, "It's not whether you win or lose, it's how you play the game." Today it is easy to reduce the Olympics to financial gain—after all, the athletes who win have the potential to earn millions of dollars in endorsement fees and the companies that support them stand to gain by association. But the financial gain does not define the outcome. Instead, the athlete's single-minded determination in pursuit of the *idea* and the dream that the Olympics represent are the true measure of success. Both in ancient times and since 1896, when the modern Olympic era began, the Olympic Games have been considered the pinnacle of sports because they represent athletic competition at its purest level, free from politics, focusing only on the skills of the competitors. Interestingly, this notion of apolitical purity is part of the Olympic mythology, yet it is not entirely accurate historically. According to Stephen Miller, author of *Ancient Greek Athletics*[10] despite popular belief to the contrary, the Games were not pure apolitical contests between amateur athletes. Competitions between cities carried the subtext that victory equaled superiority, perhaps more crudely known today as bragging rights. Furthermore, the ancient Greek athletes were not amateurs, at least as we understand the term today. The winners often found themselves the beneficiary of free meals for life, tax exemption, and substantial monetary rewards (in 600 BC a winning athlete from Athens would be given 500 drachmai which was an enormous sum on which one could live comfortably for the rest of his life).[11] Certainly these rewards are analogous to the benefits accorded today's athletes, although the magnitude of the riches thrust upon today's athletes arguably reflects an even greater largesse. The issue of amateur versus professional athlete did not exist for the ancient Greeks because rewards and prizes were normal for athletes to receive, much as a salary or wage is common today for most jobs.

The idea that the ancient Greeks were beacons of amateur virtue was partially a contrivance of the nineteenth-century, Victorian era, a historical revision of sorts from a period of time during which there was a significant amount of social and industrial change, with Great Britain the leading influence in the world. In the nineteenth century, many sports were the purview of the wealthy aristocracy, who could afford to spend time competing without worrying about compensation. They believed that for sports to be pure and untainted, one must participate for the love of competing and the thrill of besting another. But the real agenda was to snub the working classes since they were "professionals" in that they earned a wage for a specialized skill. An organization was started by English aristocrats called the Amateur Athletic Club (AAC), which established guidelines for amateur athletes. David Young, a professor of classics at the University of Florida, is a well-respected Olympic historian. He delivered a speech prior to the 2004 Olympic Games in Athens in which he discussed the origins of the modern Olympics and the AAC's efforts to exclude the working class from sports: "It declared that men who were 'mechanics, artisans, or laborers' were de facto 'pros,' barred from all amateur contests, which were reserved for 'gentlemen,' that is, people who did no labor for a living."[12]

Young's speech is fascinating, revealing that the first Olympics of the modern era actually preceded the 1896 Athens Olympics by several decades, but did not resemble the Games as we now know them. There were separate efforts, first proposed in Greece in 1835, which ultimately inspired an English-led movement in the mid-1850s—a movement that worked initially, but which also sparked resentment among select members of the aristocracy, who led the rival formation of the aforementioned AAC. By the mid-1860s, England's Olympic movement dissipated. Interest reemerged in Greece, taking a circuitous route that eventually led to the Games of 1896.

The image of Olympic purity confers a certain image of prestige and higher status, an image that sponsoring companies want to promote since such a perception can further separate them from their competitors. Certainly, idealism may play a role in management decisions to sponsor the Olympics, since linking direct results to an Olympic sponsorship can be problematic (for reasons we will discuss later). Idealism suggests that companies want to associate with the Olympics because doing so is "the right thing to do" and promotes an image of corporate social responsibility—not a bad outcome, certainly. But sponsoring companies still need to grow and generate profits, so altruistic intentions are likely a minority percentage of the overall decision calculus to support the Olympic Games. Therefore, if a company can convey to the market that it is successful and unique, like the Olympics, then logic dictates that, of the millions of viewers and customers around the world, some percentage of them will increase their purchase of the sponsoring company's products, accelerating that company's performance compared to its competitors, including increasing market share (among other measures). Therefore, the appeal of being directly associated with an event considered the pinnacle of sport offers an important potential impact for sponsoring companies since they, too, may be seen as the pinnacle equivalent in their markets.

CHAPTER 2

How the Olympics Make Us Feel

The Thrill of Competition

In the United States, ABC Television once had a popular Sunday sports show called *ABC's Wide World of Sports*, which showed highlights of recent sporting events from around the world. The opening narrator, who was also one of the show's anchors, was Jim McKay, and he intoned over dramatic sports scenes in the opening introduction, "Spanning the globe to bring you the constant variety of sport, the thrill of victory, and the agony of defeat." The video footage, of course, showed celebrations of victory, such as World Cup goals, coupled with images of sports disasters, including Yugoslavian ski jumper Vinko Bogataj's stunning crash as he came down the ski ramp at the World Ski Flying Championships in West Germany in 1970. Fans around the world relate to these kinds of images because of the unpredictable nature of each competition. With any given event, we don't know who will win, even if there is a clear, dominant performer. We don't know what surprises may occur that alter the competition directly. We don't know which strategy an athlete or team might employ in their efforts to achieve victory. We don't know how athletes might act when faced with the pressure of the Olympic spotlight. Will they be motivated? Terrified? Sluggish? What we do know is that we will see thousands of well-trained athletes with ambitions to win a gold medal.

The size and scope of the Olympics have changed dramatically over time, as has the composition of the athletes, creating an increasingly dynamic and thrilling mix of competitors and events. While precise figures are not known for the ancient Olympics, Games held during the fifth century BC had roughly 300 male athletes from neighboring Greek city-states compete in a total of 14 events. The 1896 Olympic Games in Athens, Greece, featured 43 events with 241 male athletes from 14 nations. The 1900 Olympics were held in Paris, France, and featured 997 athletes from 24 nations. Women also competed for the first time, although their status was considered unofficial. In the 1912 Stockholm Olympics, women were officially allowed to compete in swimming events, and they began competing in all track and field events at the 1928 Olympics in Amsterdam.

From 1896 to 1924, there were no Olympics devoted to winter sports. Instead, the early Olympics of the modern era were held in the summer, and while figure skating was scheduled as part of the 1900 Summer Olympics in Paris, the event was never actually held.[1] It wasn't until the 1908 London Olympics that figure skating finally appeared. In 1924 the Winter Olympics were introduced in Chamonix, France (in fact, these games were originally called "International Sports Week 1924," partly related to objections by modern Olympics founder Baron Pierre de Coubertin. Following the success of this event, it was retroactively renamed the first official Olympic Winter Games and included 16 medal events in 7 sports and 200 athletes from 7 countries).[2] By the 2006 Winter Olympics in Turin, Italy, the breadth and depth of the Winter Olympics encompassed 2,508 athletes from 84 nations competing for 84 medal events in 15 disciplines and 7 sports (for example, the sport of skiing comprises the disciplines of Alpine skiing, freestyle skiing, cross-country skiing and snow boarding. Then, the discipline of Alpine skiing has several medal events: downhill, slalom, super G, giant slalom, and the combined).[3]

The growth of the Winter Olympics has been remarkable. As we will see, the ancient Greeks had their Olympic heroes, but none of them was an accomplished downhill skier or a triple-axel figure skater. Three primary themes help explain the growth:[4]

- The Olympic *brand*
- The Olympic *experience*
- Olympic *myths and heroes*

The Olympic Brand[5]
Definitions of "brand" have evolved significantly in recent years, as companies and marketing have grown more sophisticated. In the best

performing companies, the concept of brand is distilled simply and concisely into: *The entire organization as seen through the eyes of stakeholders.*

In effect, "brand" encompasses every activity and each touchpoint[6] across both tangible and intangible dimensions. It is useful to think of brand in this way because one is forced to consider external points of view, beyond our own understanding of who we are. "Do others see us as we see ourselves?" is a common question. A trap into which companies can fall is to believe their own PR—being so internally focused that leaders assume the market sees them the same way. As individuals, we try to create a positive outward image. Success is typically predicated on whether such a portrayal is genuine to whom we are. But when we receive indications that we are not what we think, then we seek ways to adjust (or ignore it at our own peril). The adjustment is inspired by a combination of external perceptions and disconnects with our own internal sense of self. As organizations, successful brands operate much the same way, working hard to authentically reflect their best qualities so that they deliver on their promises, enhancing the company's reputation as a result. When a brand has a positive reputation, almost anything associated with it (from imagery to products) benefits.

Part of the larger Olympic Games appeal is their reputation for goodwill and also for inspiring a sense of optimism and hope. The feeling of shared experience, while characteristic of many sports, is particularly acute with the Olympics, partly because the sports within are so varied that they appeal to a diverse audience virtually everywhere, even if many of the fans have never tried the sport. As John Furlong, head of the Organizing Committee of the Olympic Games (OCOG) for the Vancouver 2010 Winter Olympics and Paralympics, said,

> *I think people everywhere believe that Olympic values are values to live by. I think through the Olympics people get a sense of hope that they could be better than they are... Everybody's equal, there are certainly great moments where people achieve hero status but for a brief period of time—people of the world are the same.*[7]

The Olympic brand as we know it today was not invented recently. Its reputation is the result of thousands of years of traditions supported by societies passing on heroic stories from one generation to the next, giving the Olympic brand its meaning. Over time, this "meaning" has shaped our appreciation for Olympic values and transformed the Olympics into a global event on an epic scale. Baron Pierre de Coubertin's vision came to fruition in 1896, although not without trepidation:

> *...although the IOC's eager embrace of private enterprise, sponsorship and commercial marketing techniques to fund the games in the latter part of the twentieth century ultimately thwarted his wish to see the Olympics "purify" sport of the "commercial spirit" that he recognized was developing.[8]*

Coubertin was animated by the idea of sports as a driver of social good:

> *Sport is not a luxury activity, or an activity for the idle, or even a physical compensation for cerebral work. It is, on the contrary, a possible source of inner improvement for everyone.[9]*

> *Olympism may be a school of moral nobility and purity as well as physical endurance and energy.[10]*

Of course, as the Games evolved in the twentieth century, it became increasingly hard to pursue a broad social agenda without accompanying resources to support such a complex undertaking. As more countries and athletes were involved, a more professional organization and management structure was required. The Olympics' brand strength and value today are supported by the activities and behaviors of six key influencers:[11]

1. Members of the Olympic Movement (anybody connected to the Olympics, volunteers or otherwise, who promotes Olympic values)
2. The IOC (International Olympic Committee)
3. The OCOG (Organizing Committee of the Olympic Games), which works in association with the NOCs (National Olympic Committees)

4. Athletes
5. Broadcasters
6. Consumers

The Olympics are unique because their reputation is known around the world, across countries and cultures. Football (soccer in the United States) is the world's biggest and most popular sport, culminating every four years in the World Cup. Its traditions are also well known. But the Olympics still have broader appeal overall due to the variety of events and the many brand associations attached to the Games. People everywhere rally around the Olympics, from volunteers assisting with each Olympiad to kids with dreams of being an Olympian to fans cheering for their favorite athletes. The modern Olympics thrive because of the ongoing interaction among these six factors.

Richard Pound, former vice president of the IOC, describes the Olympic Movement's enormous influence, from informal to formal relationships among people and groups around the world, before, during, and after every Olympiad: "There are hundreds of millions of people involved at various levels. Not everybody involved is going to turn into an Olympic athlete. Some are going to be able to play in the street, some are going to play in schools, some on city teams, some on provincial teams."[12]

His comments are not unique. They reflect a common understanding around the world about what the Olympics are and represent. Any organization, at its core, offers hope in various forms. It is the promise of something better that inspires people to become loyal customers. In the case of the Olympics, that sense of hope ascends far beyond the athletic competitions themselves and toward a world filled with potential in which differences are temporarily set aside. These brand associations are not easily developed and they are certainly not manufactured. They are embedded deep within the DNA of the Olympic Games, distinguishing them from every other sporting event.

The Olympic Experience[13]
Experiential marketing has received increasing academic attention since the mid-1990s, although it has been practiced far longer by

leading companies such as Nike (its Niketown stores), Nordstrom (an upscale American department store known for its exceptional service), and leading hoteliers such as Ritz-Carlton and Four Seasons. The concept is simple: engage consumers by actively involving them with your brand using multiple touchpoints such as physical environments, products, services, and atmospheric stimulation of the five senses to create a positive and memorable experience. When a customer has a great experience, then the organization has delivered on the promises it has made. Of course, with sports, the element of surprise is fundamental to enjoying the experience even if the surprise doesn't always favor our athlete or team, whereas as consumers the surprises we prefer are those that delight us. True sports events are unpredictable (as opposed to scripted events, such as professional wrestling). One cannot know an outcome for certain, which is a central tenet of fan attraction. Sports in general, and the Olympics in particular, embody the sense of hope that a team or an athlete can rise to the occasion and win, even against formidable odds. Fans are also attracted to the possibility of inevitability—the likelihood that a dominant performer will continue to dominate, much as the golf world is watching Tiger Woods as he pursues Jack Nicklaus's record for major victories. While there is no guarantee that Tiger will beat Nicklaus's career majors record, most fans and sports observers would say it is really not matter of "if," but "when." Many will watch such premier athletes hoping that another dethrones them. The unknown outcome drives this interest.

The Olympics have been creating special experiences for decades, long before the term "experiential marketing" was ever formalized. The Winter Olympics of the mid-2000s feature seven sports and 84 events, versus one sport and one event for most other competitions. The Summer Olympics have 28 sports and over 300 events. Yet the various events are but one dimension of the Olympic Games experience. Part of the success in any sport is orchestrating the timing, including populating interludes between action with other activities, such as fan giveaways, announcements, statistics updates, and information about other events and/or teams. The Olympics are a highly choreographed entertainment event in which world-class athleticism is the principle focus, but numerous parallel storylines are occurring as well. From the opening "Parade of Nations" to the closing festivities in which three flags are raised—the Greek flag in the center (recognizing the historical birthplace of the Olympics); the host country flag on the left pole—and the flag of the host country for the next Olympics on the right pole; the Games evoke a celebration of the human spirit, exemplified by athletic competition and a general spirit of cooperation. The events are not just everyday events. They are time-honored spectacles in which we know that the athletes within are the world's best, supported by each host country's efforts to ensure a spectacular overall atmosphere, from venues to service to culture.[14] The Olympics are enormously complex undertakings and not everything goes well. But the overriding sense of honor, hope, and goodwill helps overcome most of the difficulties that can arise.

Olympic Myths and Heroes

Global sports events now take the form of recurring spectacular commercial media festivals. Consumer cultural events take place in which sports stars, and those elevated to an iconic global celebrity status, represent local and/or national communities. The celebrities serve as role models, as objects of adulation and identification, but also increasingly as exemplars of consumer lifestyles to which spectators and television viewers alike are enticed to aspire. [15]

History teaches innumerable lessons, many of which are memorable because of the actions of people who rose to the occasion. Heroes stand out because their accomplishments and achievements were exceptional and often recognized as virtually impossible to duplicate. This infuses legions of athletes and fans with the energy to pursue their own ambitions, whether it is imitating what we have seen or using the effort as a springboard for improving many aspects of our lives. As fans, we gain a feeling of added confidence after our favorite team or athlete has won. When a loss occurs, while discouraging, we also feel frustrated and search for ways to improve.

Interestingly, the many inter-related, unpredictable storylines among athletes and events at each Olympics are a major catalyst propelling fan interest and are not the result of an IOC or corporate sponsor's script. While that goes without saying, the serendipitous nature of every Olympiad is part of the appeal and must always be at

31

the forefront of any sponsor's interest. In other words, companies are investing in a wholly unpredictable, unscripted set of athletic performances within a structured format. The sponsors merely benefit from these serendipitous events. This amalgam of different activities, emotions, people, and images is an integral part of the Olympic brand, creating arguably the strongest and best-known brand in the world today.

The Olympics continued to grow throughout the twentieth century, with the 1936 Berlin Olympics featuring nearly 4,000 athletes from 49 nations, more than 300 of whom were women, competing in 129 events. The 1972 Munich Olympics saw the number of female athletes break 1,000, out of a total of 7,134 athletes from 121 countries competing in 195 events. The 2008 Olympic Games in Beijing are planning to have 302 events in 28 sports with over 11,000 male and female athletes.[16] If the 2000 Sydney and 2004 Athens Olympics are any indication, then the number of female athletes will be close to 4,400, or 40%. The variety of sports and the diverse mix of athletes make the Olympic Games a unique competitive event in the world, capturing a growing base of fans. The size of both the Summer and Winter Olympics now provides sports fans with hundreds of competitions in which a myriad of factors can affect the outcome, from weather, to sickness, to technique, to fans, to the media, to experience, and more. The unpredictability of each event, despite what may appear to be clear favorites, makes the appeal of the Olympics even stronger. After all, if we knew how an event was going to turn out, then it would obviously reduce or even eliminate its appeal. We watch because we want to see what will *really* happen, versus what we *think* will happen.

Television has been a key driver of fan interest in the Olympics over the years as well, providing literally billions of fans around the world with access to sport at its best. Interest is further stimulated by the athlete profiles that country-specific television networks often develop to keep the attention of their home television viewing audience and, hopefully, tell compelling human-interest stories. Even though the ancient Greeks lacked the conveniences afforded by television, crowds of up to 40,000 people regularly attended the ancient Olympics Games[17] suggesting that sports fans are not a modern invention and that the spectacle of sport has been attractive for thousands of years (despite many parallels between the ancient and modern Olympics, one should not automatically conclude that the ancient Greeks exhibited many of the more passionate, and sometimes questionable, behaviors that often characterize today's sports fans). Aside from being fans of sport, part of their interest was because the ancient Games were a religious festival and athletic success was considered a tribute to the gods. Another part of the average Greek's interest was rivalry with other Greek city-states. An athlete's victory brought honor to his hometown and conferred heroic status on him, just as defeat brought shame, and when combined with the religious aspects of the Olympics (the ancient Greeks believed that the gods favored the victors), a powerful attraction to the thrill of competition was created.

Famous athletes have a unique appeal that often transcends reason. For example, why do many sports fans support athletes of dubious social character? Partly because their questionable non-sport behavior is not seen as a threat to their athletic success. People support those who have accomplished significant athletic feats, even if they are less-than-ideal role models, although our worship typically ends when it is discovered that an athlete's success was achieved by cheating. Perhaps reflecting situational values, while we might forgive marital infidelity, competitor mud-slinging, or even violence from our favorite athletes (many societies today find the transgressions of the famous humorous and entertaining, whether it is film stars, rock stars, or athletes), we find it far harder to forgive sports stars when they cheat in preparation for and/or during competition. Competitive malfeasance means that the victory was not achieved honestly, and that the violator is not playing by the rules that the other competitors, indeed the rest of society, play by. In many Western societies, people encourage individual expression and inventiveness, as long as they do not unfairly bias the spirit of competition. Fans celebrate individual achievement, but only if it is attained legitimately. The socially negative consequences of cheating are not exclusive to sports. The corporate accounting scandals of the early 2000s reminded us that while some in society may disagree with corporations earning substantial profits, this may be forgiven if the profit is earned responsibly, using commonly accepted business approaches. But when financial performances are fabricated and executives receive excessive compensation while falsely propping up their own companies, then we rightfully question the integrity of the individuals involved, the company, and even the system overall. Society does not celebrate the achievements of those who violate the rules. Furthermore, those found guilty often face financial penalties, prison time, extended community service, and lifelong disgrace. Witness the sudden and startling fall of former NFL quarterback Michael Vick in 2007 for illegal dogfighting and associated gambling activities. He went from being an All-Pro, top quarterback in professional football with a 10-year, $130-million-dollar contract to a felon, destroying his remaining football career and reputation.[18] We want our heroes and their performances to be genuine, born of honest effort and sincere intentions. While we will forgive some character flaws, we will shun them the moment they are found to have flagrantly violated our sense of right and wrong.

Every Olympics has had its heroes from whom many fans and observers draw inspiration. Olympic heroes succeed in capturing our imagination through their athletic prowess, determination, and personality. They often represent both our individual and collective ideals, serving as our alterego in sport and giving us a sense of what is possible. We admire their many talents and cheer for them as they compete, more loudly when they win. We feel their anguish and console ourselves in the face of their defeat, knowing (or certainly hoping) that they will return again one day to capture the victory that eluded them, while reassuring ourselves that not all is lost, despite our hero's failure, because we were fortunate witnesses to stunning performances featuring many gifted competitors.

From the ancient to the modern Olympics, athletes have been coveted by teams and rewarded for their achievements. There were fans of the ancient Greek athletes, just as there are fans of today's stars. Each Olympics attracted large numbers of people who attended to watch the competitions, attend speeches and recitals, partake in religious celebrations, and, in an early indication of today's commercialism, sell food and crafts to visitors. The ancient Greeks celebrated the human body, seeing it as a source of inspiration and beauty, and they were immortalized in art and sculpture. Additionally, a physically fit athlete saw his body as a form of intimidation over his competitors, with highly trained and sculpted muscles a sign of ability and prowess. Athletes undertook strict training and nutrition regimens under the watchful eye of trainers—practices that obviously continue today. The ancient Greeks were often soldiers, sometimes military heroes, as well as freeborn Greeks from humble backgrounds, as illustrated in Exhibit 2-1.

Exhibit 2-1
Greek Olympic Athlete

Glaucus, the son of Demylus, was a farmer. The ploughshare one day fell out of the plough, and he fitted it into its place, using his hand as a hammer; Demylus happened to be a spectator of his son's performance, and thereupon brought him to Olympia to box. There, Glaucus, inexperienced in boxing, was wounded... and he was thought to be fainting from the number of his wounds. Then they say that his father called out to him, "Son, the plough touch." So he dealt his opponent a more violent blow which brought him the victory. (Pausanias, Description of Greece, 6.10.1).[19]

Their accomplishments were considered honorable and an acknowledgment of extraordinary achievement reflecting well on the city-state they represented. Pindar, the Greek poet, wrote many odes celebrating and chronicling athletic achievements and Olympians, including this:

> In athletic games the victor wins the glory his heart desires
> as crown after crown is placed on his head,
> when he wins with his hands or swift feet.
> There is a divine presence in a judgment of human strength.
> Only two things, along with prosperity, advance life's sweetest prize:
> if a man has success and then gets a good name.
> Don't expect to become Zeus. You have everything
> if a share of these two blessings comes your way.[20]
> Isthmian Odes 5.8-15

The performances of the ancient Greeks were as noteworthy for their time as any today. From pure athletic achievement to unusual training

35

habits to lapses of common sense, the ancient Greeks exhibited many of the idiosyncratic tendencies found in the modern era, reinforcing the notion that there is no single, prototypical set of qualities, aside from exceptional physical and mental toughness, as illustrated in Exhibit 2-2.

Exhibit 2-2
Selection of Famous Greek Olympic Athletes

Chionis of Sparta was a remarkable athlete, competing as a runner and jumper. As a sprinter, he ran in an event known as the *stade*, a 192-meter race, and another event called the *diaulos*, a 2-lap event that equated to 384 meters. Chionis also competed in the equivalent of the long and triple jumps, where some scholars claim he jumped 23 feet and 52 feet respectively (the exact measurements are not known and the claims are still openly debated today). Chionis's athletic achievements are even more impressive due to their longevity. Both jumping marks would have earned him a gold medal in the 1896 Olympics and a place among the top eight finishers in each Olympics until the 1952 Helsinki Games, and would be excellent marks in many university competitions around the world today. Certainly, if Olympic success were measured by duration, Chionis stands the test of time and offers a true challenge to today's athletes, whose records rarely last more than a few years. He garnered a well-deserved reputation for extraordinary athleticism, evidenced by the length of his jumps and the duration of the marks, particularly in comparison to today's athletes. At a time when top athletes were often seen as nearly immortal, Chionis of Sparta captured the essence of hero worship.[21]

Melankomas of Caria was the greatest boxer of his day. His skills were legendary. He won in the 207th Olympic Games in 49 AD using an unconventional style one would find inconceivable in today's brutal boxing matches because his best skill was avoiding the hits and punches of his opponents and,

---

even more oddly, never taking a swing in return. He believed that hurting an opponent was a sign of weakness and was not competitively sporting. Instead, he would keep moving, eventually beating his opponents because they would give up due to exhaustion, frustration, or both. He had a reputation for extraordinary physical fitness, resulting from a relentless dedication to training, included reputedly keeping his arms raised for two days straight to condition them for the rigors of his unique boxing style. He died at a young age, but had successfully earned a reputation for his unmatched, albeit unique, boxing ability. Melankomas's style would suffer heavy criticism in today's boxing world, yet like many leading athletes, he was an innovator and his success vaulted him to legendary status for 2,000 years—certainly not a bad legacy.[22]

Milo of Kroton won six Olympic wrestling titles in the Olympic Games of 540, 532, 528, 524, 520, and 516 BC. He was known for his enormous strength, which legend suggests he gained by lifting a calf everyday. Milo also had a voracious appetite, evidenced by his rumored devouring of a bull after he carried it around the Olympic stadium. His life ended less glamorously when he chanced upon wedges in a partially cut tree. While attempting to remove the wedges, his hands were caught in the tree, trapping Milo, who was subsequently eaten by wolves later that night. Athletes are sometimes stereotyped as lacking proper mental faculties, and Milo of Kroton may indeed be the first example of brawn over brain. Yet there is little question Milo was one of the toughest and longest-lasting Olympic champions, competing successfully for 24 years. Winning one gold medal is hard enough, and doing so for six Olympiads in a row suggests that Milo was an impressive, and fit, competitor, embodying the competitive toughness and prolonged accomplishment in the most stressful of contests that symbolize and characterize Olympic competitions to this day. His stature grew as he continued to win, serving as a beacon of athletic virtue, partly because of his longevity.[23]

Leonidas of Rhodes was the most famous of the ancient Olympic athletes. A runner, Leonidas won 12 Olympic events over four Olympics (164, 160, 156, and 152 BC). He remains one of the most decorated athletes to ever compete in the Olympics. His victories were particularly noteworthy given the challenges runners face in sustaining competitive success over many years—simply, it is quite hard to be the best in every race and every Olympics over 12 years. His physical conditioning was undoubtedly outstanding for his time and explains his winning streak over four Olympiads. As a model for today's athletes, Leonidas of Rhodes demonstrates that true greatness is achieved when one can sustain extraordinarily high levels of performance over many years, and not just one race or one success, as admirable as one victory is.[24]

These athletes of the ancient Olympics are just a sample of the many famous, incomparable, and heroic souls who earned favor from their city-states, politicians, and citizens. Their athletic feats were astounding for their time and would have been credible performances in the early Olympiads of the modern era. They received riches, fame, and recognition analogous to the sponsorships, product endorsement deals, and cash bonuses received by the very best of today's athletes. Their accomplishments facilitated their notoriety, adding to the reputation of the Olympics being a unique event likely to produce extraordinary athletic feats. Knowing their background and legendary status gives further dimension, weight, and credibility to the Olympic Games, reinforcing the preeminent position as a pillar of sportsmanship that the Olympic games has become. Had there been corporate sponsors in the ancient Greek world, these athletes and more would undoubtedly have been the Tiger Woods of their day because their athletic achievements were exemplary, elevating them to a higher societal status, just as we have done with top athletes today.

The modern era boasts a long list of Olympic heroes as well—athletes whose accomplishments were extraordinary even if expected. Many went on to greatness in other pursuits, from business to professional sports to broadcasting to politics, which suggests that achievement in one field can affect success in another, although one should not infer direct causation. A few are highlighted in Exhibit 2-3:[25]

Exhibit 2-3
Selection of Famous Modern Olympic Athletes

Jesse Owens is perhaps one of the best-known icons of the modern Olympic era. Winning four gold medals in the 1936 Berlin Olympics in the 100 m, 200 m, broad jump, and 4 x 100 relay, he was the first American track athlete to win four gold medals at one Olympics. His achievements were all the more impressive given the political tension of the times—the Games were held in Hitler's Nazi Germany. Hitler had hoped that the Berlin Olympics would demonstrate the superiority of Aryan people. Instead, Jesse Owens's victories even had German fans cheering him on. Owens eventually went on to a successful speaking career, and also represented the United States Olympic Committee. He was awarded the Medal of Freedom in 1976, the highest honor a civilian can receive in the United States. Owens was posthumously awarded the Congressional Gold Medal in 1990. To this day, he serves as a visible symbol of the power of determination and one's ability to overcome the most daunting odds.[26]

Bob Mathias won the gold medal in the decathlon in the 1948 Olympics in London—winning at age 17, the youngest winner in track and field in Olympic history at that time—and the 1952 Olympics in Helsinki. He was an exceptionally talented athlete as suggested by the decathlon, which is a varied test of skill, strength, speed, and stamina. He also attended Stanford University, leading the football team to a 1952 Rose Bowl appearance, making him the first person to compete in both the Rose Bowl and then the Olympics in the same year. He "retired" from Olympic competition at age 22, with "nine victories in nine competitions, four United States championships, three world records, and two Olympic gold

---

medals." [27] His sports achievements from age 17 to 22, coupled with his scholarly abilities at Stanford, demonstrated Mathias's ability to succeed in multiple domains. Mathias went on to serve four terms in the U.S. House of Representatives. Subsequently, he served as the director of the U.S. Olympic Training Center. Several years later he was appointed executive director of the National Fitness Foundation. Mathias is an inspiration to those who set out to achieve success in multiple disciplines simultaneously. Mathias once famously observed, "Years ago, in the days of the Greeks, wars were postponed to make room for the Olympic Games. In modern times, the Games have been postponed twice—to make room for wars." [28]

Jean-Claude Killy was one of the great skiers of his generation, winning three gold medals in the 1968 Olympics in the slalom, giant slalom, and downhill in Grenoble, France. His victory in the slalom came after he was apparently beaten by his rival, Karl Schranz, who had been allowed to redo his run because he claimed to have seen someone appear on the course during his initial run, causing him to stop. While he beat Killy's time in the redo, Schranz was subsequently disqualified by a Jury of Appeal, awarding the victory to Killy. Killy went on to serve as co-president for the 1992 Albertville Olympics in France, and serves as an active member of the International Olympic Committee. He succeeded well after his athletic career ended because his personal appeal transcended his obvious athletic accomplishments.[29]

Nadia Comaneci competed for Romania in gymnastics in the 1976 Montreal Olympics at age 14, winning three gold medals, one silver medal, and one bronze medal. Perhaps more impressively, she was the first gymnast to earn a perfect score of 10, a feat she repeated seven times at the 1976 Games. Her accomplishments turned her into an overnight sensation. She competed in the 1980 Moscow Olympics, winning two gold medals and two silver medals. Nadia escaped from

Romania in 1989 shortly before the revolution that brought the collapse of the government. She eventually married American gymnast Bart Conner and the two of them have a thriving group of gymnastics-related companies, from academies to magazines. She is also a frequent motivational speaker and was recognized as one of the 100 Most Important Women of the 20th Century by ABC News and Ladies Home Journal. As the first gymnast to earn perfect scores in Olympic competition, Nadia served as a riveting source of inspiration for gymnasts everywhere, who saw her performances as virtually other-worldly.[30]

Sebastian Coe won the gold medal in the 1500 m in both the 1980 Moscow and 1984 Los Angeles Olympics, the only male to win the 1500 m twice. The picture of Coe as he crossed the finish line in the 1980 1500 m is one of the most famous in the history of the Olympics, showing him with his eyes wide open looking skyward, his mouth agape, and his arms outstretched in a look that combines exhilaration, determination, surprise, and relief. In 1979, prior to his first Olympic success, he set three world records in the 800 m, 1500 m, and mile, establishing himself as one of the great middle-distance runners of all time. In the years 1979, 1981, 1982, and 1986 he was ranked number one in the world in the 800 m. Surprisingly, he was not selected to be part of the 1988 British Olympic team even though he continued to compete successfully in many meets internationally, and he ultimately retired from the sport in 1990. Coe went on to be a UK Member of Parliament from 1992 to 1997. He was head of the successful London bid committee for the 2012 Olympics, and then moved into the role of Chairman of the London OCOG (Organizing Committee for the Olympic Games). Coe is a hero not just to his fans in the United Kingdom, but also to competitive runners everywhere because of his world records, his unique Olympic success at the 1500 m, and his post-athletic career as a successful and respected politician. He has been mentioned as a possible future president of the IOC. Coe is also active in charity, working with and supporting the Helen Rollason Heal Cancer Charity. Finally, he is a worldwide ambassador for Nike and he also owns a chain of health clubs.[31]

The Dream Team is a name synonymous with U.S. basketball. It was the first team comprised of NBA All-Stars and its combination of talent proved dominant in the 1992 Barcelona Olympics, winning the gold medal and each game of the Olympics by an average of 44 points. The players were a who's who of the very best at the time: the biggest names were Magic Johnson, Larry Bird, and Michael Jordan. In addition, the team included Jordan's Chicago Bulls teammate Scottie Pippen, Clyde Drexler, Patrick Ewing, David Robinson, Charles Barkley, the Utah Jazz duo of Karl Malone and John Stockton, Chris Mullin, and Christian Laettner. Their combined success helped accelerate the popularity of basketball around the world as fans everywhere watched their games knowing that the Dream Team was an utterly unique collection of stars unlikely to be seen again. The Dream Team players continued to excel when they returned to the NBA, setting records, attracting legions of fans, and serving as colorful role models for the rapidly growing NBA. Since then, each of the Dream Team players have gone on to success in business, sports, and/or broadcasting.[32]

Katarina Witt won two gold medals in figure skating, one at the 1984 Sarajevo Olympics and one at the 1988 Calgary Olympics, becoming the first skater to win back-to-back gold medals since Sonja Henie in 1932 and 1936. Following her Olympic career, she skated for the "Stars on Ice" show and started a production company called "With Witt" that produced skating shows "Divas on Ice" and "Enjoy the Stars." She won an Emmy award for her performance in "Carmen on Ice" and was nominated for another Emmy in the production "The Ice Princess." She has her own television show, "Stars auf Eis," in which celebrities learn to skate on her show, providing for some humorous situations for those less skilled than she (which is most everyone). She has also endorsed a wide variety of products, including Diet Coke, Swatch, and Mercedes-Benz.[33]

Mark Spitz was one of the most celebrated athletes of the 1970s due to his amazing seven-gold-medal-winning performance in swimming at the 1972 Olympics in Munich, where he also won a silver and a bronze. Plus, he had won two gold medals at the 1968 Mexico City Olympics. He went on to a very successful real estate career. As a professional speaker, Spitz commands approximately $20,000 per speech. During his swimming career he endorsed and/or was sponsored by John Hancock, Xerox, Kodak, Bausch & Lomb, GM, General Mills, and Swatch, and he is currently sponsored by godaddy.com, Nicklaus Academies, Medco, and Laureus.[34]

Scott Hamilton won the gold medal in figure skating in the 1984 Olympic Games in Sarajevo, and he has also won 70 other titles, awards, and honors. He earns between $35,000 and $45,000 per speech. In the late 1980s he developed the successful, award-winning production "Stars on Ice," which travels around North America performing 40 shows per year featuring the world's top skaters, from Olympic medal winners to national champions to world medalists. The tour is sponsored by Smuckers, a well-known consumer company making branded jams and jellies, and it is produced by IMG, one of the largest and best-known sports and entertainment firms in the world. Scott also wrote a best-selling book, *Landing It: My Life On and Off the Ice (Pinnacle 2000)*; enjoyed a career as a successful broadcast analyst with CBS, NBC, and Fox; and appeared in the 2007 movie *Blades of Glory* starring Will Ferrell. Scott is a cancer survivor, and he was treated for a benign brain tumor in 2004. He is actively involved with St. Jude Children's Research Hospital in Memphis, Tennessee, and CARES (Cancer Alliance for Research, Education and Survivorship).[35]

As marketers, we must pay attention to the traditions and achievements of organizations with which we wish to associate if we are to meaningfully understand how our own company "fits" alongside them. The Olympic Games have a rich, storied reputation based on athletic competition at its highest level, not as a one-time event, but literally for thousands of years. Over the millennia, athletes have become heroes and icons, inspiring generations of fans and future athletes to work hard in pursuit of their dreams. Each succeeding generation of athletes strives for Olympic glory because they know competing in the Olympics can have a halo-effect that lasts far longer than the actual athletic events themselves. The athletes have the responsibility to shoulder the weight of thousands of years of history. While that may sound intimidating, and perhaps even beyond the immediate consideration of athletes at the moment of their contest, the long-term implication is that Olympic athletes are carrying on a tradition that has deep meaning across cultures, offering inspiration to millions of people around the world. Ultimately, the athletes are aware of this at a deeper level. And each Olympic stakeholder, from corporate sponsors to suppliers to host cities to media to fans, has expectations that the Olympics (and, indirectly, the IOC) will uphold the formidable reputation that has been built over the millennia.

The temptation for marketers is to take a shortcut, investing in marketing activities that yield short-term financial gain. The risk from such short-sighted reasoning, as compelling as the immediate business rationale may appear to be, is that marketers undermine their company's long-term credibility if the associations and reputations from such an activity appear to be nothing more than opportunistic, versus strategic. Many will read this and scoff, arguing that business boils down to revenues and profits, but that misses a central part of the reason many customers buy products in the first place. Beyond satisfying a basic need, customers buy products because those items tend to reflect their own self-image and their view of the world. You and I will rarely buy products from a company whose practices, values, and products we don't trust or see as aligned with our own interests. In a business-to-business (B2B) context, we won't buy from other companies we don't trust or find reputable no matter how attractive the initial financial projections are, which means we have to know something about how that business operates and has operated in years past. What is their overall reputation? How have they worked with us and treated us? How have they worked with other companies? What do their customers/suppliers and industry competitors say about them? In the context of the Olympic Games, marketers would not (or should not) invest their marketing dollars to build awareness if the Games did not have the rich traditions from thousands of athletes in hundreds of events all competing for the glory of not just being Olympic champion, but also associating with Olympic virtue. This reasoning is not to suggest that financial benefits ought not to be factored, because clearly businesses must make money to survive. But those companies that invest in the TOP program are spending enormous sums for an event with a two-week duration. Those sums would not be spent if there were not significant, obvious benefits beyond pure profit. Part of those benefits are derived from the 2,700 years of Olympic tradition.

CHAPTER 3

The Ever-Changing Olympics

Rise of Athletes as Stars: Before, During, and Post-Olympic Success

Up to this point a basic historical backdrop has been introduced to help explain the popularity and mystique of the Olympics for fans, athletes, and, ultimately, Olympic sponsors. Several examples of representative athletes from both the ancient and modern eras were discussed in Chapter 2 to provide perspective on the connection between athletic achievement and hero worship. With over 2,700 years of Olympic history, the list of iconic athletes is long. Hundreds of thousands of athletes have competed, building and reinforcing the rich and varied traditions that comprise the Olympic ideal, so highlighting the very few always risks excluding other deserving performers. In the modern Olympic era, athletes have undergone a transformation from top athlete into star, a change made easier by the massive growth and popularity of twenty-first-century media and instantaneous communications. With the Olympic Games as a confirmed brand platform, the best athletes can create lifetime opportunities.

Before Olympic Success

Athletes do not have to wait until after the Olympics to gain financial success. Many do so well before an Olympic victory, gaining sponsorship support when their skills and achievements bring them to national and international attention. Qatar is alleged to have paid the Bulgarian weightlifting federation $1 million in 1999 for eight top weightlifters. Hossein Rezazadeh, a top Iranian weightlifter, was offered $20,000 per month, an exclusive estate, and an additional bonus of $10 million if he were to change nationalities and compete for Turkey's Olympic team during the 2004 Olympic Games in Athens. He turned this generous offer down and still went on to win the gold medal, national pride outweighing financial gain.[1]

Should they succeed in winning a medal at the Olympic Games, their home countries often offer financial rewards. Table 3-1 provides reported data on the differing rewards paid to medal-winning athletes:

Table 3-1
Amounts Athletes Receive for Winning a Medal

	Gold	Silver	Bronze
United States[2]	US$25,000	US$15,000	US$10,000
Canada[3]	US$20,000	US$15,000	US$10,000
Russia[4]	US$50,000 (some individual gold medal winners received $100,000 in the 2000 Olympic Games in Sydney)	Not known	Not known
Ukraine[5]	Similar to Russia and/or free housing	Not known	Not known
Romania[6]	US$157,394	Not known	Not known
Singapore[7]	S$1 million (individuals) S$1.5 million (team event) S$2 million (team sport)	S$500,000 S$750,000 S$1 million	S$250,000 S$375,000 S$500,000
Japan[8]	US$46,000	US$27,000	US$18,000
China[9]	US$24,000	Not known	Not known
Australia[10]	AUS$15,000	AUS$7,500	AUS$5,000
Lithuania[11]	US$100,000	Not known	Not known

The figures in this table vary further with some countries, depending on the sport. Japan, for example, will pay $37,750 for a gold medal in canoeing, and $236,000 for a gold medal in table tennis. Russia will pay boxers and wrestlers approximately $100,000 for gold, whereas athletes in other sports will receive $50,000 for winning plus an additional US$50,000 if they break a world record.[12]

Does this harm the Olympic image of competitive purity? Conceivably, yes. But as discussed in the opening pages of this book, the ancient Greek athletes were not amateurs and were compensated for their performances. Furthermore, for many countries winning an Olympic medal is rare and the winning athlete inspires national pride and increases recognition, even if it is for only a short period of time. There is a magnetic, captivating attraction to a medal-winning athlete that bestows a measure of glory on the country itself, just as corporate sponsorship of the Games and athletes benefits companies.

During Olympic Success

While Olympic athletes and their achievements are a source of pride and are celebrated by their home countries, the leap from athlete to marketable star who generates millions of dollars in financial support and a windfall for themselves and their sponsors has become most pronounced in the past 15–20 years. The implications of this are profound because athletes now have an additional motivation to compete in the Olympics and, hopefully, win a gold medal—the potential for lucrative financial gain. However, winning a gold medal is neither a guarantee of long-term financial security nor a guarantee of professional success. Furthermore, a few athletes have achieved fame and commercial success without winning a gold medal. A key to marketable success inevitably includes a backstory that reveals more of the personal sacrifice and challenge an athlete has endured to reach their ambitious Olympic goals. If today's formal business sponsorships and sophisticated marketing techniques were available to the ancient Greeks, one can easily imagine Milo of Kroton (recall that he was alleged to have eaten a bull) being a spot-on spokesperson for a favorite Greek restaurant, or perhaps as an example for a public service announcement about the dangers of being alone in the woods (his unfortunate demise when eaten by wolves). Melankomas of Caria might well have been a sponsor of Greek fitness clubs and aerobic training (if such commercial enterprises had existed).

The Olympic athletes of the modern era enjoy a wide array of support choices from sponsors, donors, product companies, and more. This is not unusual in today's sports world where even athletes who don't win championships make substantial endorsement income. Olympic athletes are different, however, because the title "Olympian" carries a special stature, and gold-medal winners have an even more exclusive claim to fame. Such notoriety does not guarantee a future filled with life-long riches and sponsorship deals. But during their Olympic years, top athletes can certainly enjoy life at the top of their sport as a star. Many societies around the world today celebrate celebrity status, whether it is musicians, politicians, movies stars, or athletes. Having star-quality branded athletes competing in the Olympics brings additional attention to the Games, both in terms of viewers and general word of mouth, or buzz. Sports fans love the stars because these top performers give them somebody to either cheer for enthusiastically or root against with equal passion. Just as with product brands, a branded athlete acts as a filter for attention, separating themselves from those lesser known. Of course, when those Olympic surprises occur (as discussed in Chapter 8), we are not only amazed, but we are also now interested in learning more about the new athlete. Plus, this surprising competitor vaults from obscurity to stardom in the process.

Companies that sponsor relatively unknown athletes early in their careers can find themselves in the fortunate position of vastly increased exposure from the media if the athlete succeeds. This can put the athlete in a position of power, even if only temporarily, since their increased notoriety gives them added leverage to renegotiate with the companies sponsoring them to increase their earning power based on their added value. Corporate sponsors must then decide whether to continue the sponsorship and, if so, how much it is worth. These are not easy questions since the athlete's success may well be fleeting, yet dropping the sponsorship risks losing the increased interest from the public from which the company would benefit.

A key challenge for companies is determining how long the athlete will be at the peak of their abilities and success. Injury can end an athlete's career well before a long-term relationship can be fostered. So why do companies take the risk to sponsor Olympic stars and pay often substantial sums, knowing there is a very real chance they may not win gold, may get injured, or may even find themselves in ethical trouble (such as performance-enhancing drug use) before the financial investment pays off? Companies sponsor athletes for many of the same reasons they sponsor events—they hope the positive qualities of that athlete will be associated with the company. The logic suggests further that fans of an athlete may become fans of the company sponsoring the athlete. A great deal of marketing work goes into making this association happen, and it usually takes a few years.

But just as an Olympic sponsorship can pay dividends over the long run, so too can sponsoring an individual athlete. Michael Greiss of Germany and Michael Phelps of the United States are excellent current examples, as shown in Exhibit 3-1.

Exhibit 3-1
Athlete Sponsorships During Olympic Success

Michael Greiss won three gold medals at the 2006 Winter Olympics in Turin in biathlon (the sport combines cross-country skiing with rifle shooting) in the individual, mass start, and relay events. He was named German sportsman of the year. He went on to win gold in the 2007 and 2008 World Championships in the mass start and mixed relay events, respectively. While biathlon is not as widely covered as other Olympic sports, his success attracted numerous corporate sponsors, including adidas, Powerbar, Excel, DKB Bank, and Erdinger, a maker of non-alcoholic isotonic drinks.[13]

Michael Phelps is an immensely successful Olympic swimmer who continues to compete successfully (when he competes in Beijing 2008 he will have just turned 23) and has leveraged his success at the 2004 Olympics Games in Athens to maximize his exposure and sponsorship value. His primary sponsor, Speedo, guaranteed him $1 million if he won seven gold medals at the 2004 Olympics Games in Athens. He came up just short, winning six gold medals and two bronze medals in Athens, an impressive performance by any standard, tying him with gymnast Aleksander Dityatin (1980 Moscow Olympics) as the only athletes to win eight medals at a single Olympics. His stated ambition was to win all eight gold medals in Athens, and while he did not achieve this, his performance was legendary, attracting fans who wanted to see whether he could accomplish his goals. The last swimmer to be as dominant was Mark Spitz in 1972, who won seven gold medals. According to his own website, www.michaelphelps.com, he is a 23-time world record holder and 17-time world champion (along with numerous

---

other records). At the World Championships in Australia in the summer of 2007, he won seven gold medals and broke five world records. If he is fortunate enough to win four more gold medals in Beijing, then he will have the most gold medals of any Olympic athlete ever. He is a formidable, intimidating competitor, but he is known as a good sport as well, as exemplified in the Athens Olympics when he swam in the qualifying rounds of the four-man medley relay, but then gave up his spot in the final to fellow American Ian Crocker. Crocker and his teammates went on to win the gold medal and set a world record. Aside from Speedo, he is also sponsored by Visa, Omega, Powerbar, and Matsunichi. He has appeared in TV shows and, in a nod to social responsibility, founded a youth swim program called "Swim with the Stars," and is deeply involved with Boys & Girls Clubs of America.[14]

Post-Olympic Success

Champion athletes have the same appealing qualities that attract companies to the Olympics (prestige, achievement, honor, and competitiveness) and this halo can carry with them once they retire, as we have seen in Exhibit 2-3. Once their competitive years are behind them, they can and often do go on to earn significant incomes from motivational speaking, starting their own companies, serving their countries as politicians or in other similar leadership roles, and as recurrent spokespersons and sport experts with each subsequent Olympic Games. Companies continue to seek out former Olympic athletes to sponsor or to get involved in their business. Nike is well known for attracting world-class athletes into its management ranks following their careers. Of course, Nike works with the athletes during the peak of their careers as well on new product design, marketing campaigns, and corporate goodwill, as do many of the other leading athletic companies in the world. The International Olympic Committee (IOC) website is an invaluable resource for Olympic fans who want to learn more about their favorite star athletes. More than 100,000 have competed in the modern Olympics, so most are not stars. But many have gone on to highly successful post-Olympic careers.

New Sports and Events

The IOC has reinvented the Olympic Games, adapting the event to meet the changing sports interests around the world. Many new sports in the Olympics gained attention due to mass media and popular culture, both of which exhibit a hunger for identifying new trends, including extreme sports. The mix of sports is important to the success of the Olympic program, directly affecting fan and, consequently, corporate sponsorship interest. New sports attract new fan demographics and psychographics, which, for established sponsors such as the TOP partners, may increase their awareness, reach, and even sales around the world. Corporate sponsors also gain potential target (or niche) audience opportunities, which can be useful for testing new products and new grassroots marketing campaigns with a smaller market. New sports offerings can also enable a company to link newer products or a different product line altogether to the expanded fan base. Along with customer growth potential come new partnership opportunities, as there may be companies with expertise in attracting a niche audience that could be useful to a large corporate sponsor. The sponsor gains more direct and credible exposure with the partner's customers, and the partner gains from the corporate sponsor's larger overall customer base. Finally, the new sports can offer a company access to future events related to the new sport, not just in the host city market, but anywhere in the world where the sport is played.

The IOC regularly seeks a balance between men's and women's sports to increase the appeal around the world. Once a sport has established a base internationally, with credible athletes and championships recognized by one of the 28 recognized international federations (IFs), a large fan base, athletes, and a history of growing performance and interest overall, it may ultimately find its way into the Olympics. According to the July 7, 2007, edition of the Olympic Charter, the IOC reviews the entire program after each Olympiad. The review includes discussion of sports to add or remove. The total number of sports cannot exceed 28 in any Olympiad (seven sports in the Winter Olympics), so the addition of a sport may also constitute removal of another if the maximum has been reached. As relatively simple as the decision process sounds, the decision itself is governed by a set of IOC bye-laws, involves weighing complex data, and requires the exercising of judgment about the current level of success for a sport, which is not always crystal clear. Nevertheless, a majority vote will approve a program change for the next Olympics.[15]

As new sports are added, the chances of sponsors reaching new audiences increase. Plus, the Olympics maintain a sense of vitality and freshness while adding to the historical traditions of attracting the very best athletes. Table 3-2 outlines the new sports added since 1984:

Table 3-2
New Sports 1984–2008[16]

Olympiad	New Sports Added
1984 Winter Olympics in Sarajevo	Women's 20 km race-Nordic skiing
1988 Winter Olympics in Calgary	Super giant slalom in alpine skiing
	Nordic combined
	Curling (demonstration sport)
	Short-track speed skating (demonstration discipline)
	Freestyle skiing (demonstration discipline)
1992 Winter Olympics in Albertville	Short-track speed skating
	Freestyle skiing with moguls
1992 Olympics in Barcelona	Baseball
	Badminton
	Women's judo
1996 Olympics in Atlanta	Beach volleyball
	Mountain biking
	Lightweight rowing
	Women's football
	Professionals were admitted to the cycling events
	Softball (women's-only sport)
1998 Winter Olympics in Nagano	Curling
	Snowboard giant slalom
	Snowboard half-pipe
	Ice hockey for women
2000 Olympics in Sydney	Triathlon

Table 3-2 continued

	Taekwondo
	Modern pentathlon for women
	Weightlifting for women
2002 Winter Olympics in	Women's two-person bobsleigh
Salt Lake City	Men's and women's skeletons (last held in 1948)
2004 Olympics in Athens	Women's wrestling
2006 Winter Olympics in Turin	Team-pursuit speed skating
	Snowboard cross
2008 Olympics in Beijing	Open-water swimming
	Women's steeplechase

CHAPTER 4

The Sports and Politics Cocktail—Drinking from the Olympic Fire Hose

Religion, Politics, Nationalism, and Sports

The ancient Olympics were religious festivals to honor the Greek gods, particularly Zeus. The Games were both a cause for celebration and conflict. The Games brought together citizens from Greece's many city-states to celebrate and discuss political issues of the day and military victories. Yet the ancient Olympics were a source of internal conflict and competition. The right to host the Olympics was considered a sacred and prestigious responsibility that brought economic wealth and political power, so disagreements arose occasionally between rival city-states, including soldiers from other city-states taking control of the selected Olympic venue. The Olympic truce was created eventually to protect athletes, citizens, visitors, and dignitaries attending the Games from local conflicts. If the truce was violated, then the offenders were punished, as Thucydides, a fifth-century BC historian, describes in this account:

In 420 BC the Spartans engaged in a military maneuver in the territory of Elis during the Truce, using 1,000 hoplites [armed soldiers]. *As a result, and according to law, the Spartans were fined 200 drachmai per hoplite, a total of 200,000 drachmai. The Spartans refused to pay the penalty, claiming that their maneuver had been completed before the Olympic Truce was officially announced. As a result, the Spartans' participation in the Olympic Games that year was prohibited.*[1]

The truce has influence today with the modern belief that, irrespective of conflict, the Olympics must be held and that all sides must cease hostilities during the Games. Of course, as we know, warring nations do not stop their battles. Indeed, the opposite has occurred—World Wars I and II stopped the Olympics. But the truce is a powerful symbol and a key source of inspiration representing Olympic values.

In the earliest days, the Olympics were decidedly local and were certainly not the international event with which we are familiar today, yet politics and nationalism played a central role in the ancient Olympic Games. The early Olympics were a closed affair allowing only Greek male citizens to compete. Foreigners, women, children, and slaves were barred from participating, or even watching. However, aristocratic women were allowed to own chariot teams that could compete in the Olympics as long as they did not drive the chariot themselves. While women did not compete directly in the ancient Olympics, an alternative event for women in honor of Zeus's wife Hera was staged periodically that featured foot races.

Poets were commissioned to write special words of commemoration for the winning athletes, not unlike today's filmmakers turning Olympic success into a full-length movie about the athlete's life story. Pindar wrote the following piece in honor of Hiero's horse-race triumph at the Olympic Games of 476 BC:

Water is preeminent and gold, like fire burning in the night, outshines all possessions that magnify men's pride. But if, my soul, you yearn to celebrate great games, look no further for another star shinning through the deserted ether brighter than the sun, or for a contest, mightier than Olympia where the song has taken its coronal design of glory, plaited in the minds of poets as they come, calling on Zeus' name to the rich radio hall of Hiero.[2]

As we know today, the Olympics as an event are known worldwide by virtually every country and every person. The breadth and depth of awareness of the Olympics is unlike any other commercial phenomenon today. Many of the athletes are known by their fellow citizens, and those who climb to the top of their respective sport's world rankings in the years prior to the Olympics garner additional attention and notoriety. Veterans grow used to the spotlight and many become personalities, with known personality quirks and recognized mannerisms. But when the Olympics are on the horizon, the societal pressures grow, as do the individual ambitions of the athletes. There is something powerful and unique about the Olympics that is unlike any other sports event. Part of it is due to scarcity—with the Games held only every four years (recall that the Summer and Winter Games are each held every four years and were originally held in the same year. Since 1993, they have been separated by a two-year interval). Part of it is due to the centuries-old reputation as the preeminent competition for the world's best. Part of it is due to mass awareness—unlike the ancient Olympics, the modern Games are truly global in stature. Each of these is a contributing factor in the appeal of today's Olympics and the combination creates a powerful, awe-inspiring event with unrivaled magnetic attraction.

To the victors, whether that is a host city or an athlete, comes the potential for substantial pride, riches, and recognition. Even to athletes who do not win come the respect and honor of having competed against the very best in the world's most visible sports event. But the challenges presented are centuries, even millennia old: achieving success through genuine, hard work and honest effort. The pressures on today's Olympians are intense, but so were those faced by the ancient Greek athletes. However, the glare of the media spotlight and the proverbial fishbowl in which each athlete and Olympic host city lives, coupled with instant global communication, creates a wholly more challenging dynamic—staying true to core principles and values, irrespective of the pressure and scrutiny that is part of living under the Olympic microscope.

Olympic Bidding

Every two years different cities around the world put themselves through a rigorous gauntlet of planning activities that use thousands of people and countless hours, and invest millions of dollars in developing their Olympic bid. Only one city wins. The process is heavily politicized, subjected to relentless media scrutiny, and invariably involves far more costs than expected, both in the bidding process and in the operating and capital budget areas for the winning city. Preparing an Olympic host city bid is not for the fainthearted. However, the process was not always this intimidating. The early Winter Olympic Games host cities were selected rather informally, based on having an established ski resort of some renown and the desire to boost visitor traffic. Today the effort is grand in scale and ambition, with cities envisioning a winning bid to inspire urban renewal, raise tourism numbers, foster national pride, and offer the world a more updated, modern image.

Cities that wished to bid earlier in the 2000s had to pay a $100,000 application fee, which simply gave them the right to bid. The 2012 Candidature Procedure and Questionnaire (for cities bidding to host the 2012 Summer Olympics, which were eventually won by London) was 260 pages long, complete with instructions, Olympic vocabulary usage, a detailed host city profile, and 17 themes (topics) that the bidding city had to address in its bid package. This ranged from environmental and meteorological reports to security plans to a business plan for the Olympic Village (and more, of course). The replies were obviously longer than 260 pages and would undoubtedly require not just existing city and organizing committee resources, but extensive volunteer assistance as well as professional outside services (market research, consulting, accounting, legal) to provide expert input. From the initial pool of bids, the International Olympic Committee (IOC) selected a smaller group of the top candidates. To continue, those cities had to pay an additional $500,000 for the next stage. The right to represent the United States during the final bid presentations and selections process for the 2012 Games was narrowed down to two cities, New York and San Francisco. Both cities were required to guarantee $100 million in support of their bid, and sign indemnification agreements protecting the IOC and United States Olympic Committee from financial losses or exposure. New York forecasted that its final bid process would cost $13 million. New York, along with London, Paris, Madrid, and Moscow were selected as the final candidates for the July 2005 host city election, held in Singapore, where London was elected as the 2012 host city.[3]

The obstacles to success both in bidding and hosting are formidable, but the potential rewards are enormous politically, economically, socially, and technologically.

Potential Impact

The Olympic Games have a known beneficial impact over political and commercial institutions. For host cites and, by extension, their home countries, this positive impact is seen in tourism increases in the sheer numbers of visitors and the economic impact of their additional spending. These changes are sought by host nations for many reasons, but certainly Olympic prestige can serve to lift the image of a country and bring it to the attention of the rest of the world. Host cities and nations invest heavily in infrastructure improvements in the years leading up to their specific Olympiad. Each city has growth and modernization plans, but the Olympics accelerate the implementation of these plans because cities are inspired and motivated to be part of the magic image that surrounds the Olympic Movement. Investments in everything from roads to utilities to hotels take on new urgency when a city wins the right to host the Olympics, putting in motion a dynamic economic cycle that creates jobs, rallies citizens, and focuses world attention on the host city thereby generating economic growth well before the Games are held. The investments have grown dramatically as the Olympics have grown in prestige and importance over the decades. Tables 4-1 and 4-2 summarize the growth of both the Summer and Winter Olympics since the modern era began in 1896:

Table 4-1
Summer Olympics[4]

Year	City	Number of athletes	Number of nations	Number of events
1896	Athens	241	14	43
1900	Paris	997	24	95
1904	St. Louis	651	12	91
1906*	Athens	847	20	74
1908	London	2,008	22	110
1912	Stockholm	2,407	28	102
1916	Not held (war)			
1920	Antwerp	2,626	29	154
1924	Paris	3,089	44	126
1928	Amsterdam	2,883	46	109
1932	Los Angeles	1,332	37	117
1936	Berlin	3,963	49	129
1940	Not held (war)			
1944	Not held (war)			

Table 4-1 continued

1948	London	4,104	59	136
1952	Helsinki	4,955	69	149
1956	Melbourne	3,314	72	145
1960	Rome	5,338	83	150
1964	Tokyo	5,151	93	163
1968	Mexico City	5,516	112	172
1972	Munich	7,134	121	195
1976	Montreal	6,084	92	198
1980	Moscow	5,179	80	203
1984	Los Angeles	6,829	140	221
1988	Seoul	8,391	159	237
1992	Barcelona	9,356	169	257
1996	Atlanta	10,318	197	271
2000	Sydney	10,651	199	300
2004	Athens	10,625	201	301
2008**	Beijing	10,800	205	302

* *The 1906 Games were called* The Intercalated Games, *designed as international Olympic contests to be held in between the quadrennial Olympic Games. The Intercalated Games were to be permanently housed in Athens. They were dropped after 1906 because the two-year time frame from regular Olympics was considered too tight, among other reasons.*
** *Estimated*

Table 4-2
Winter Olympics[5]

Year	City	Number of athletes	Number of nations	Number of events
1924	Chamonix	258	16	16
1928	St. Moritz	464	25	14
1932	Lake Placid	252	17	14
1936	Garmisch-Partenkirchen	646	28	17
1940	Not held (war)			
1944	Not held (war)			
1948	St. Moritz	669	28	22
1952	Oslo	694	30	22

Table 4-2 continued

1956	Cortina d'Ampezzo	821	32	24
1960	Squaw Valley	665	30	27
1964	Innsbruck	1,091	36	34
1968	Grenoble	1,158	37	35
1972	Sapporo	1,006	35	35
1976	Innsbruck	1,123	37	37
1980	Lake Placid	1,072	37	38
1984	Sarajevo	1,272	49	39
1988	Calgary	1,423	57	46
1992	Albertville	1,801	64	57
1994	Lillehammer	1,737	67	61
1998	Nagano	2,176	72	68
2002	Salt Lake City	2,399	77	78
2006	Turin	2,508	80	84

The Olympic Games are indeed unique in a city's life and, consequently, for a corporate sponsor as well. No other sports event catalyzes as diverse a range of related development projects as the Olympics. From local urban renewal projects to global marketing campaigns, the Olympics provide an energy boost for host cities that is often sustained for years after the Games. As the Olympics have grown in size, scope, and popularity, so too have the costs to host cities. For corporate sponsors, an important factor to consider is the underlying strength of the sports entity being sponsored. Despite the many known complexities that come with hosting an Olympics, there is little doubt that each Olympiad is a massive undertaking unto its own, not unlike the launch of a new company, the opening of a new market, or the completion of a major public works project. But the complexity implies a certain amount of experienced sophistication— the Olympics are not unprofessional, hackneyed events, so there is some comfort for sponsors knowing that the money they are investing is part of a respected event with unrivaled historic traditions, international recognition and respect, and a powerful, uplifting message that unites nations.

New York City Deputy Mayor Dan Doctoroff offered this observation in 2004 as Athens was finalizing its preparations for that summer's Olympic Games and as New York was preparing its bid to host the 2012 Olympics (a bid won by London in 2005):

The Olympic Games are unique in a city's life. I think when you do look back on the Athens experience 5, 10 or 20 years from now, the single greatest benefit of the Olympic Games will be that they acted as a catalyst for the achievement of truly historic changes in the city. Those changes would not have occurred anywhere near the timeframe that they did if it had not been for the Olympics.[6]

The decision to invest in the Olympics Games requires planners to evaluate the costs, risks, and benefits. Each of these evaluation areas impose structured thinking onto the planning process and help decision makers debate and assess both the big-picture rationale as well as understand the information they will need to effectively tackle the details required for proper planning and implementation.

Costs

There are three primary categories of costs for which each host city must prepare prior to the opening of the Olympics:

1. **Venues**

   Each Olympics is a complicated undertaking, similar to building a small city, but without the luxury of time. Facilities include: all athletic and competition venues; the Olympic Village where athletes, coaches, and related staff are housed; and purpose-built commercial establishments for participants, visitors, and fans.

2. **Infrastructure**

   Host cities have established utilities and transportation designed to support the needs of their local population plus normal numbers of annual visitors. The Olympics significantly impact the demand for infrastructure since tens of thousands of athletes and visitors descend upon the host city for the Games. New roads, expanded utility networks and related power-grid expansion, improvement of existing city facilities, technological upgrades, local hospital/healthcare facility expansion and/or improvements, additional hotel and meetings space, environmental improvements, and new/expanded rail and light rail tracks and related stations, are among many infrastructure-related areas that must be addressed by host cities.

3. Organizational

There are IOC, NOC, OCOG, and host city groups each invested in organizations that ultimately support, run, and promote the Olympics. The organizational activities include: security; community volunteers; events management (athletic and non-athletic); safety/healthcare; transportation services; and travel/leisure/tourism.

These three areas are instrumental to a host city's bid and, upon winning, vital to the eventual success of the Olympics. Table 4-3 shows the Vancouver Organizing Committee's (VANOC) budget that was used in their presentation during the Olympic bidding process:

Table 4-3

Vancouver Organizing Committee 2010 Budget[7]

Revenues	C$ (000)[a]	Expenditures	C$ (000)
IOC Television Contribution	539,681	**Operating Expenditures**	
TOP Sponsorship	131,411	Sports Venues	163,111
Local Sponsorship	396,000	Olympic Village	20,644
Official Suppliers	57,999	Print Media Center	10,250
Ticket Sales	218,223	International Broadcast Center	121,509
Licensing Merchandise	35,001	Games Workforce	231,272
Coin Program	2,771	Technology	208,687
Lotteries	—	Telecommunications	62,022
Donations	20,000	Internet	5,600
Disposal of Assets	10,001	Ceremonies and Culture	84,646
National Government Subsidy	20,000	Medical Services	5,031
Regional Government Subsidy	20,000	Catering	16,568
Other	56,251	Transport	86,789
Total	**1,507,336**	Security	2,199

Table 4-3 continued

		Paralympic Games	42,695
		Advertising and Promotion	51,813
		Administration	123,760
		Pre-Olympic Event & Coordination	18,123
		Other	100,035
		Royalty Payments to IOC	152,580
		Total	**1,507,336**
		Direct Capital Expenditures[b]	
		Roads and Railways	599,850
		Sports Venues	361,843
		Olympic Village	265,300
		Media Center	14,999
		Other	67,658
		Total	**1,309,649**

[a] *All amounts shown in 2002 Canadian dollars.*
[b] *Direct capital expenditures were paid entirely by the federal government, the provincial government, or non-VANOC private entities. Direct capital expenditures did not include the Canada Line transit system. Additional non-capital government costs such as security were not included in the VANOC official budget.*

While it is widely recognized that hosting an Olympics is expensive, it is surprising how little actual information exists about the precise, final costs to host cities, beyond general budget figures. In fact, historical tracking of host city costs is problematic, as no official reports have been produced. A 1993 research report by Dr. Frank Zarnowski in the *International Journal of Olympic History* uncovered select financial data from several of the Olympiads for the first 100 years of the modern era, but the numbers were inconsistent, partly owing to poor budget tracking and record keeping. Sometimes the costs included operating budgets only, other historical cost estimates included infrastructure improvements, and some were a combination of both. In a few Olympic years, no firm numbers exist at all. According to records, the cost of the 1896 Athens Olympics was estimated at $448,000, and the 1936 Olympics in Berlin cost roughly $30 million (in 1936 dollars).[8]

Tables 4-4 and 4-5 present different cost analyses of select Olympiads. Table 4-4 highlights finances for select Summer Olympics between Tokyo in 1964 and Barcelona in 1992 and Table 4-5 offers approximate costs from 1992 forward. The numbers do vary from Olympics to Olympics, but the important point implied by both tables is that Olympiads are not simple, low-cost undertakings. The variation owes more to the unique characteristics of each city than to a uniform escalation of Games costs. Ferran Brunet, author of the report behind Table 4-4, explained the distinction between expenditures and investments in the analysis:

> There was considerable sensitivity to questions of "cost," the necessary resources, and the "financing" of a social event of the importance of the Olympic Games. Thus a distinction was made between organizational expenditures (those for aspects not usable after the event) and project expenditures (those usable after the event). The expenditures in projects were made up of direct investments (or those necessary for the development of the event), indirect investments, and investments induced by the event. The organizational expenditures were the true "cost," the net cost, of which nothing would remain afterwards. For this reason effort was made to minimize them. On the other hand, the investment expenditures are the legacy, what remains. For this reason the effort was made to maximize them.[9]

Table 4-4

Investment Related to the Olympic Games[10]

US$	Tokyo 1964		Montreal 1976		LA 1984		Seoul 1988		Barcelona 1992	
	000s	%	000s	%	000s	%	000s	%	000s	%
Operational expenditures	169,510	1	411,857	13	450,394	86.2	478,204	15.2	1,361,156	14.5
Direct investments	282,605	1.7	2,413,006	76	72,042	13.8	989,649	31.4	1,099,699	11.7
Total Direct Expenditure	452,116	2.7	2,824,863	89	522,436	100	1,467,853	46.5	2,460,855	26.2
Indirect expenditures Indirect investments	6,373,372	97.3	350,012	11.1			1,687,423	53.5	6,915,274	73.8
Total Olympic Investments	6,825,488	100	3,174,875	100	522,486	100	3,155,276	100	9,376,129	100

Brunet's analysis provides an insightful look at the range of costs (expenditures and investments) of host cities. Since host city financials related to the Olympics are challenging to consistently gather, it is not always possible to compare across several Olympiads. Note that the Games cost estimate in Table 4-5 for Barcelona is $10.7 billion, comprised of the $9.3 billion infrastructure (or 'legacy' investments, as Brunet described them) plus $1.4 billion for the Olympic Organizing Committee.

Table 4-5
General Cost of Recent Olympic Games[11]

City (Year)	Bid Cost	Games Cost	Results
Barcelona (1992)[12]	$10 million	$10.7 billion	*See endnotes*
Albertville (1992)	$2–3 million	$2 billion	$57 million loss
Lillehammer (1994)	$3 million	$1.6 billion	$40–50 million profit
Atlanta (1996)	$7 million	$1.7 billion	Broke even
Nagano (1998)	$11 million	$14 billion	$28 million profit for OC ($11 billion debt to various gov't. groups)
Sydney (2000)*	$12.6 million	$3.24 billion	Broke even
Salt Lake (2002)	$7.0 million	$1.3 billion	$100 million profit

* *The dollar values for Sydney are approximations, converting Australian dollars to US dollars at a $0.50 rate.*

Figures 4-1 and 4-2 describe the surpluses and deficits, including and excluding capital costs, based on IOC reports and research done by Holger Preuss for his book *The Economics of Staging the Olympics: A Comparison of the Games 1972–2008*, revealing more about the operational effectiveness of each Olympics. [13]

Figure 4-1

Officially Reported Surplus/Deficit of the Organizing Committee

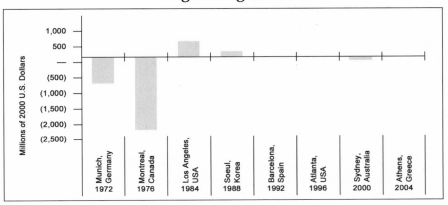

Figure 4-2

Operating Surplus of the Organizing Committee exclude Capital Costs

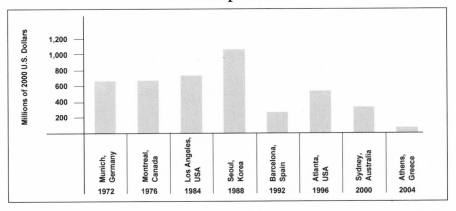

Brunet's definition of expenditures and investments as shown in Table 4-4 provides a useful explanation for understanding how to categorize Olympic investments that may be helpful to sponsors as they consider the range of activities in which they deploy resources. Clearly, as the subsequent charts and tables illustrate, capital costs have an enormous impact on the financial efficacy of the Games, so they cannot be ignored for the sake of a more attractive financial picture.

The Tokyo Games were considered among the very best Olympiads ever held. Japan saw the Olympics as an opportunity to show a "new" Japan with a nearly flawless orchestration of the Games and among the most impressive venues and athlete facilities of any Olympiad up to that time. The 1976 Montreal Olympics resulted in a $1 billion debt, although these numbers have since been disputed, suggesting that the Montreal Olympics were not the financial disaster originally thought and that the debt, if any, was substantially smaller. The original estimate for the main stadium was $74 million, whereas the final costs were closer to $950 million. Much of the cost overruns at the time were attributed to local governments borrowing money for other projects, yet attaching the money to the overall cost of the Olympics. Richard Pound, former vice president of marketing and communications for the IOC, a Canadian-trained lawyer, and a former Olympic swimmer, stated that the key problem with the Montreal Olympics was that the operating and infrastructure budgets were never separated. Had they been, then the Olympics would have turned a $135 million profit on an operating basis. Nevertheless, the concern about cost overruns factored heavily in the Los Angeles Olympic Organizing Committee's planning for the 1984 Games.[14] The 1984 Olympics in Los Angeles were a bargain compared to Tokyo, due partly to the leadership of Peter Ueberroth, organizer of the Los Angeles Olympics, who was determined to keep costs down and turn a profit while also maintaining the prestige and integrity of the Olympic idea. His efforts led to a nearly $223 million profit, the first Olympics to turn a profit in years. A key to the success of the Los Angeles Olympics was the widespread use of existing facilities—very few new venues were constructed, saving a significant amount of money.[15] The 1988 Winter Olympics in Calgary cost an estimated $636 million, with the government contributing nearly half of this amount. The 1992 Barcelona Olympics' total costs factored in both the new venues and numerous civic and publics works projects that were timed to be completed when the Olympics began.[16] The 1996 Olympics in Atlanta were funded without government support, with capital supplied primarily from sponsorships, ticket sales, and advertising. There was an unfortunate side effect, however. Many observers thought the Atlanta Games were overly commercial, detracting from the prestige of the Olympic Movement and from the performance of the athletes.[17] It was the first Olympics in which the IOC president at that time, Juan Antonio Samaranch, did not say that it was the best Olympics ever, which was his usual closing remark. Instead, he said "Well done, Atlanta. The Games were most exceptional." [18] The slight was intentional, signaling disapproval of the overly commercial nature of those Olympics, coupled with significant safety, transportation, and logistics issues that plagued the Games. The 1998 Nagano Olympics were quite expensive due to a myriad of related-infrastructure projects (including a new bullet train line and new highways).[19] The operating budget for the 2000 Sydney Olympics was committed to infrastructure improvements like roads and railways.[20] The wide variation is explained partially by projects attributed directly to Olympics-specific preparation versus projects that were planned or underway anyway that were included in final budget tallies. The 2006 Turin Olympics cost between $3 billion and $3.6 billion.[21]

China certainly sees its 2008 Games similar to how Japan saw its 1964 Games, hoping to show the world that the country's recent prosperity can produce the most impressive Olympics ever. A great deal of national pride is at stake. The Beijing Games have an operating budget of just under $2.4 billion,[22] but as in other host cities, the Olympics are serving as a catalyst to complete numerous other infrastructure projects, with estimates ranging from $23 billion to as much as $40 billion.[23] The range and scale of Beijing's preparation for the 2008 Olympics is impressive. Thirty-one major venues will be built from scratch or completely renovated, in addition to a complete overhaul of the city's major transportation systems, including new roads, new airport terminal buildings and runways, new subway lines, and new public buses and taxis services. The new competition venues include the 91,000-seat Beijing National Stadium in which the opening and closing ceremonies will occur and where most of the track and field and football events will take place; the new Beijing National Aquatics Centre for the water sports-related events; the Beijing National Indoor Stadium for artistic gymnastics; and the Shunyi Olympic Rowing—Canoeing Park where the rowing and kayaking-related competitions will occur. As with the ambition of other host cities, Beijing's many sports venues have been designed to be iconic. The Beijing National Stadium is also called the "Bird's Nest" stadium for the novel external steel architecture that resembles the complex interweaving of a bird's nest. The Beijing National Aquatics Centre is called the "Water Cube" because the exterior looks more like enormous water bubbles than a conventional building. Overall, the Chinese are putting a great deal of effort into these Olympics in the hope that the envisioned success showcases a positive side of China and its rapid emergence onto the world stage. The bid budget for the 2010 Winter Olympics in Vancouver was $844 million, although final costs will not be known for years. [24]

London's forecasted costs have ranged from an original estimate of $6 billion closer to $18 billion at the time of writing. However, members of London's legislative assembly suggest the final costs will be closer to $29 billion. The reasons for the growing expense are similar to those of most of the host cities: low initial budget estimates based on costs at the time of the bid; additional infrastructure challenges and / or needs that arise post-bid; and general price inflation associated with the expectations for luxurious spending for any Olympiad. In addition, the requirements from the IOC inevitably shift throughout the bid and post-bid process, causing significant changes in the original parameters of each Olympics (this is a familiar occurrence to those involved in most business development activities on behalf of their companies. In addition, the requirements from the IOC inevitably shift throughout the bid and post-bid process, causing significant changes in the original parameters of each Olympics (this is a familiar occurrence to those involved in most business development activities on behalf of their companies... In high-tech enterprise software projects, for example, "scope-creep"—where the requirements of a project change from the original design, is a common occurrence. Similar project expansion occurs in consulting projects as well. Part of the reason is that the participants involved simply cannot know all the influencing factors in advance and, consequently, learn more as work on the project deepens).

Host city costs are only part of the Olympics story. While the Summer Olympics have a longer legacy and larger numbers (sports, events, viewers, athletes, revenues), the Winter Olympics have grown rapidly (see Chapter 2) and are just as complex an undertaking. The motivations for host cities include recognition that the Olympics are far more than a sports event. "The public expects us to deliver more than just a sporting event. Vancouver residents expect the Olympics to be a catalyst for improving their lives," explained David Cobb, senior vice president of marketing and communications, Vancouver Olympic Committee (VANOC).[25]

Risks and Benefits

On an event-specific basis, the Olympics are a challenging financial proposition for host cities and nations due to the absolute costs involved. But from a broader perspective that encompasses macro-economic factors as represented by PEST analysis (political, economic, socio-cultural, technological), the rationale for hosting the Olympics uncovers a more positive impact and, conceivably, a more defensible logic that can help companies and cities in their planning. PEST is a common business framework used in marketing and strategy planning to help managers think through the macro-level contextual factors that can affect their approach to a given market. These are external indicators, outside the direct control and purview of the company or organization. To complete the context analysis, firm-specific indicators are needed. Organizational and brand factors complete the framework:

- Political factors relate to tax, employment, political stability, trade, and environmental issues.
- Economic factors include business and market growth rates, interest rates, inflation, and exchange rates.
- Socio-cultural factors describe demographics (such as population growth trends, age, income/wealth...), psychographics (such as attitudes and behaviors), and social fabric variables (interactions between and among people within society).
- Technological factors refer to the technological development of the society (R&D investments, technological change and adoption rates, automation).
- Organizational factors encompass planning, logistics, and manpower needs.
- Brand describes the overall reputation of the organization, whether it is a host city or a corporate sponsor.

Understanding that many resources will be useful and usable after the Olympics, and not only expended during the Games with no

73

longer-term potential, should compel managers to think carefully about the kinds of marketing activities that can have the maximum Olympics-related life span. Marketing investments are not just about spending money to gain awareness and exposure, but also involve programs that demonstrate an understanding of the broader context in which the Olympics are being held, so that companies can offer customers memorable products and services that can exist long after the Games have ended.

POLITICAL

The questions that potential host cities and corporate sponsors need to address include:

1. What is the political climate like for hosting the Olympics? Stable or unstable?
2. What do the changes resulting from the Olympics mean to the local culture?
3. What are the government's trade policies and how will those affect the Olympic Games decision?
4. Does the government's tax policy affect the Olympic investment decision?
5. Is the government's economic policy direct, indirect, or hands-off?

Each of these questions invites more complicated research and fact-finding to assess the attractiveness of supporting the Olympic Games. We will now look at the risks and rewards.

Risks

The Olympics are a powerful, successful, well-known brand and have developed a particularly formidable reputation since television and sponsors became dominant economic forces in the success of the Games. As such, the Olympics are among the most visible, widely known, and broadly communicated events in the world. The good news is that this overall positive brand reputation attracts the very best athletes, companies, and related stakeholders, as well as passionate fans. The challenging news is that the Olympics also serve as an attractive platform for those with political agendas. This has occurred in numerous Olympiads, but among those that stand out are: the 1936 Olympics in Berlin that Hitler hoped would demonstrate the superiority of the Aryan race (fortunately, Hitler was wrong); the horrific 1972 Olympics in Munich when a radical Palestinian group called Black September took the Israeli Olympic team hostage and, in an ensuing rescue attempt, the kidnappers and hostages were all killed; the 1980 Olympics in Moscow and the 1984 Olympics in Los Angeles, when the United States and Soviet Union took turns boycotting the other's respective Olympics; and the Tibetan protesters who, prior to the 2008 Olympics in Beijing, rioted in Lhasa, disrupted part of the Olympic Torch Relay, and threatened additional protests surrounding the Beijing Olympics. While the Chinese government insists the Tibet protests are an internal matter and that politics should not play a part in the Olympics, the Games have been a key political tool in presenting China to the world in a new light. The Tibet protests risk undermining this moment of public glory. However, many countries have used the Olympics as a means for gaining political advantage.

The impact for sponsors is potentially devastating if a political message overwhelms the Olympics since the sponsors' marketing exposure would take on a less visible role compared to the political agenda. The potential problem for sponsors is more than just financial—it is image-related, and since each of the TOP partners is a well-known global brand, part of their reputation is attached to their actions. If the Olympics become viewed negatively, then that point of view will eventually be linked to the sponsors as well. Protestors can also apply pressure on corporate sponsors, either by directly confronting their commercial support of the Olympics (and implying the sponsors are supporting a tainted Olympic Games), or by appealing directly to consumers around the world to boycott any sponsors who do not adequately explain their position on the particular political issue in questions. Beijing has faced criticism over its policies in Darfur and Tibet in particular, and more generally its human rights record. Steven Spielberg, the renowned Hollywood director, withdrew as artistic advisor in protest of China's involvement in Sudan. Additionally, China's rapid economic growth has fueled concerns about the environmental impact such growth is having in the country and, increasingly, the region. The 2008 Beijing Olympic

Torch Relay sponsors are Coca-Cola, Samsung, and Lenovo. Each of them is a TOP partner and they paid an addition $15 million each to sponsor the relay.[26] With significant protests in Paris, London, and San Francisco, the three sponsors came under increased media scrutiny, with questions raised as to why they should continue to support an event that was being increasingly subjected to violence by protesters. Modern Olympic history has also seen the use of boycotts to make a political point, such as the Olympics in Melbourne in 1956 when two boycotts occurred: Egypt, Iraq, and Lebanon protested at the Israeli invasion of Suez; and the Netherlands, Spain, and Switzerland protested at the Soviet invasion of Hungary. In Montreal in 1976, 22 African nations boycotted due to the New Zealands' national rugby team's tour of South Africa earlier in the year. Led by the United States, over 40 nations boycotted the 1980 Moscow Olympics in protest at the Soviet invasion of Afghanistan. The Soviet Union led a 14-nation boycott of the 1984 Olympics in Los Angeles to retaliate against the United States' 1980 boycott. The 1988 Olympics in Seoul were boycotted by North Korea because they were still technically at war with South Korea. North Korea was joined by Cuba, Ethiopia, and Nicaragua.[27] Each of these political issues raises important challenges that cities and companies must confront to properly evaluate the attractiveness of the Olympic Games. Corporate sponsors must pay careful attention to the political dynamics. While political concerns are often pushed aside so that focus returns to the Olympics as a sports contest, companies cannot ignore volatile issues since their sponsorship will raise the question whether the company is indirectly supporting the issue in question by staying financially invested in the Games. Contingency planning, in which responses to different problems and crises are developed, is a highly recommended activity.

Benefits

For the host city and nation, the Olympics offer the potential for fostering goodwill and generating a more positive feeling from the rest of the world. The challenge, of course, is being cognizant of, and prepared for, the almost inevitable political agendas and protests that will occur. In recent years China and the Beijing Organizing Committee have understandably expended considerable effort trumpeting their efforts to produce the best Olympics to date. To be fair, every host city and nation conducts similar promotion of their Olympics' efforts, hoping to bring attention to their city, and cast a positive light for the benefit of local citizens and the outside world. A successful Olympic Games burnishes the host city's image, demonstrating indirectly the ability of the government to deliver on a complex, highly visible event. The spotlight is intense because it begins shining years before the actual Games and for months or even years afterward, in addition to the more concentrated attention when the Games are happening. As the outside world pays increasing attention to the host city in the run-up to the Olympics, government leaders choreograph the timing of planning updates, venue construction progress, infrastructure improvements, and economic impact to gain favor from the scrutinizing eye of public opinion. This is also when and where challenges arise since protest groups heighten their own attention on the host city and nation, hoping to receive media attention for their cause while seeking to cast shadows of doubt across the "feel good" reports emanating from the National Organizing Committee (NOC) and local organizing committee.

The host city and nation also seek to inspire their own citizens with regular updates about progress and how the Olympics benefit them and improve their lives. An important objective is rekindling a sense of national pride and patriotism. Citizens of every country hosting an Olympics should be justifiably proud because the Olympics do convey a sense of prestige while commanding the attention of the world. These are, of course, classic marketing appeals designed to attract interest. But employing marketing communication techniques this way should not be interpreted as a license to mislead. Properly conceived and executed, a marketing campaign can and should be based on actual activities and the positive contributions these make.

Another, perhaps more subtle, by-product of hosting the Olympics is that any resulting success can serve to validate government policies. However, one must be cautious in assuming too much regarding direct connections in the public's mind between the government of the host nation and implied approval of their politics. The public is generally quite capable of separating the

Olympic Games from the politics of the host city and nation, recognizing that having an Olympics is not the same as approving that country's way of life or political institutions. Nevertheless, the Olympic Games can provide a needed boost of confidence and support for the host city and nation that can reflect positively, if temporarily, across the associated political institutions.

Similarly, the Olympics can boost the visibility and promote the political agenda of protest groups. While such protests are highly unlikely to change a government or political philosophy (such protests are rare anyway), they can inspire the public around the world to be more engaged with the political issue in question and, given enough word-of-mouth support, can inspire a degree of change in policy. China provides a good example again. Global concern over air pollution has caused the government to initiate a selection of domestic reforms designed to make the capital "greener" during the Olympics, a positive outcome assuming the efforts are part of a long-term plan to more actively support environmental protection. Some factories and government workshops have been relocated outside the city to reduce industrial emissions, for example. Automobiles are being regulated, with access to the capital allowed only on select days of the week based on license plate numbers. These moves are designed to allay criticism and fears about Beijing's severe air pollution in the hopes that it will be alleviated when the Games commence in August 2008, and this can be viewed as a positive result of efforts to persuade government leaders of the importance of genuine, long-term action. There is another incentive as well: IOC President Jacques Rogge has mentioned shifting the competition schedule around to minimize athlete exposure to bad pollution days. A scheduling change during the Olympics would draw unwanted negative attention to Beijing, something that government leaders want to avoid.[28]

Companies have an opportunity to affect the political process by being a constructive part of the planning for the Olympics, and not being perceived as merely a commercial entity seeking the exposure benefit of having their name attached to the Games. Also, companies can contribute by providing needed jobs in the host city, a politically pleasing activity that can create goodwill for the company with the public while also fostering more positive relations with the local government, which could help the future development of their business interests.

ECONOMIC

The Olympic Games are a major catalyst spurring economic activity for the host city, nation, and associated companies. Questions to consider:

1. How will the added economic activity affect interest rates?
2. Is inflation a factor (or how will it affect market perceptions of cost)?
3. How will the Olympics affect the lives of the local community (jobs, prices, business growth, goods availability) in both the short- and long-term?

Risks

Each organizing committee is ultimately responsible for ensuring the economic success of its Olympics. However, the economic risks are not just local. The IOC risks revenue challenges if the Games' and related expectations, are not properly managed. The members of the IOC and Organizing Committees for the Olympic Games (OCOG)s must aspire to the highest levels of integrity and credibility for the sponsors, indeed all stakeholders, to have confidence in each specific Olympiad. Scandals, such as the bribery cases associated with the Sydney and Salt Lake City Olympiads (and allegedly with the 1996 Atlanta Olympics as well), can be potentially devastating since such activities make sponsors nervous, consumer groups upset, and the general public disenchanted. The net effect can be a severe reduction in economic impact from sponsorship and tourism loss should any of those groups believe that the Olympics have lost its integrity. Another risk is over-commercialization, as happened at the 1996 Summer Olympics in Atlanta, offending those who believe the Olympics stand for something far more significant than commercial gain. Another challenge relates to the overall attractiveness of the Olympic model as a platform to celebrate honor, hope, peace, and goodwill. These admirable virtues are also daunting because each succeeding generation of Olympic caretakers (from the IOC to individual organizing committees) has to ensure that the entire Olympic brand remains true to the values it espouses.

Any faltering risks losing key funding sources, including sponsors, without which the Olympics would not be able to support the wide range of nations that compete in every Olympiad. Many teams do not have sufficient individual funding sources and depend on the IOC and its marketing-related revenues to provide the necessary support for their athletes.

Benefits

The host city's local economy will receive a significant short-term increase in economic activity from visitors during the Games since they will tend to spend their money locally in retail, hotel, restaurant, and similar businesses. The increased consumer and tourism spending, in particular, benefits local governments by boosting the host city's income and sales tax bases. Yet consumer-led revenue benefits are only part of the economic story. The earlier discussion of costs and investments highlights the major impact of infrastructure investments (as well as the disruption that related construction can cause). Capital contributions for infrastructure improvements come from each host city's organizing committee, trickled down from the IOC's total revenue pool. These investments yield positive structural improvements in the local community through improved transportation systems, expanded and updated utilities, enhanced local services, and even a more favorable perception of the host city by the world community. Additional external funding, such as cash contributions or in-kind trade, spur the local economy as well. Such benefits were demonstrated in several Olympic host cities, including Tokyo, Barcelona, Sydney, Salt Lake City, and Turin, in particular. Favorable perceptions, while intangible, can have lasting, or certainly longer-term, economic impact. Salt Lake City enjoyed significant economic increases as a direct result of the boom in tourism, conventions, and hotel occupancy increases. One hotel executive in Salt Lake City commented: "You simply cannot buy this type of publicity. The potential implications to the hotel industry are tremendous."[29]

The Olympics can have a projective impact as well. Vancouver's hosting of the 2010 Winter Olympics is generating substantial new interest in the city. Tourism Vancouver commissioned research that showed that "24% of consumers were more likely to visit Vancouver, 43% of the travel trade was more likely to book business for Vancouver, and 25% of meeting planners were more likely to book meetings in Vancouver."[30]

The combination of these different tangible and intangible factors can lead to positive, long-term benefits, as the Barcelona description in the following box illustrates.

Exhibit 4-1
Barcelona's Transformation[31]

The 1992 Olympic Games in Barcelona generated significant, positive economic benefits for the city, which was literally transformed as a result of the Olympic Games. As shown in Table 4-4 "Investment Related to the Olympic Games," the total Olympic investment supporting Barcelona was nearly US$9.4 billion. Urban planning projects invested in revitalizing an old industrial area that had been built in the nineteenth century near the old city. This area was transformed into the Olympic Village, but it was designed with the intent to blend with the existing city so that following the Olympics it would become a fully integrated neighborhood, with the living spaces rented and sold on the open market, and not an unusable white elephant. Railroad tracks that originally lay between the city and the beaches were rerouted elsewhere, including underground, so that there was access to the beaches and the sea front. The beaches were also cleaned up. A new underground highway was built to divert traffic away from key city areas, connected to a ring road that moved traffic around the perimeter of the city. Old parks were renovated and new ones built. Private investment saw hotel space expand by 38%, enabling the potential of more than 420,000 tourist visits during the Olympics.

Construction for the 1992 Barcelona Olympic Games[32]

Investment between 1986 and 1993	Accumulated values in 1995 Pesetas	Distribution
Road construction	343,804,115,503	35.9%
Construction at Poble Nou Olympic area	212,681,960,000	22.2%
Construction at other Olympic areas of Barcelona	117,973,650,000	12.3%

Montjuic area	58,138,020,000	6.1%
Vall d'Hebron area	29,425,740,000	3.1%
Diagonal area	30,409,980,000	3.2%
Other projects in Barcelona	182,449,775,658	19.1%
New Western urban axis	7,979,130,000	0.8%
New Eastern urban axis	16,395,880,000	1.7%
Remodeling of Old Port	6,890,000,000	0.7%
Service galleries	10,071,325,658	1.1%
Other facilities (cultural, sanitary, and other)	21,229,090,000	2.2%
Improvement of hotel facilities	119,884,350,000	12.5%
Projects in Olympic sub-sites	69,916,420,000	7.3%
Other sports infrastructure projects	29,804,169,039	3.1%
Total	956,630,090,000	100%

Barcelona has since witnessed enormous growth in several economic and business sectors. The city has become one of the top destinations in Europe. The number of overnight hotel stays nearly tripled, from 3.8 million in 1990 to over 10 million in 2004. The average length of stay increased from 2.8 days to 3.6 from 1990 to 2004. The number of tourists visiting grew from 1.7 million in 1990 to over 4.5 million in 2004 as well. Infrastructure improvements that had been planned but not enacted previously were accelerated as a result of the inspiration provided by wining the Olympic bid.

The economic benefits for sponsors when planned thoroughly and implemented successfully can be significant, as illustrated in the selection of TOP partner case briefs in **Section IV: Winning Marketing Gold**. It is incumbent that sponsors inject a sense of realism in their planning objectives for the Olympics, lest they set themselves up for disappointment during the Games and from a post-Olympics marketing audit that shows little for the investments made. The sponsorship planning process must include recognition of the likely or assumed commitment to the sponsorship in terms of time, resource investment, and purpose. Knowing the potential length of time will enable the marketing team to plan a sequence of brand-building initiatives that evolve as the company's familiarity with the sponsorship grows and the results come in. Common benefits arising from clear objectives include: market-share goals, revenue and profit targets, awareness levels, brand-value increases, reputation improvements, and product-units-sold increases. As we will see in detail later, Visa began its Olympics sponsorship in the 1980s with the basic objective to increase awareness. With over 20 years of subsequent Olympic sponsorship experience, the company's objectives changed and grew more sophisticated, designed around a multiplatform marketing approach designed to accomplish specific objectives. However, pushing for overly ambitious objectives and pouring substantial additional resources into a concentrated effort for a short period of time is unlikely to produce results consistent with expectations, and a more long-term, evolutionary point of view, particularly with a globally known brand like the Olympics, can offer substantial benefits.

SOCIO-CULTURAL
The Olympics are a force for good in a broader, more global context. The impact at the local level is important as well:

1. Will the Olympics and our involvement with them foster positive goodwill among the local populace?
2. How will the social dynamic of the community be impacted?
3. What are the attitudes about foreign visitors, organizations, products, and media?
4. Does religion play a role locally and, if so, how might it be impacted and also affect the success of the Olympic investment?
5. Are citizens actively engaged in the local community?
6. Is there support for environmental causes and, if so, how might that affect the Olympics?
7. Are leisure and sports actively supported?

Risks
The selling of the Olympics to the local population requires sensitivity to the realities of daily life. Disruptions related to construction and

added international attention risk alienating the local population and, thereby, undermining their support. Demands placed on local citizens to put their best foot forward may ring hollow, prompting people to withdraw and eye the Olympics with suspicion, dreading the future influx of visitors whom locals may see as outsiders who can change the local way of life. Host city officials must find ways to overcome these risks through thoughtful, ongoing community meetings and communications.

Benefits

Citizens of host cities and nations have historically rallied to support their country's efforts to host the Olympic Games. There are exceptions, such as when citizens of Denver, Colorado rejected their city's winning bid to host the 1976 Winter Olympics for cost and environmental reasons. Innsbruck stepped in and agreed to host the Games despite having done so in 1964 as well. For Innsbruck's citizens, the gesture reflected positively on them, generating international goodwill. In general, cities and countries bid for the Olympics because the overarching benefits and positive image gains serve to boost civic and national pride, helping people believe that they are special.

A properly conceived and executed corporate sponsorship campaign can improve the company's standing as a responsible corporate citizen, an issue that is increasingly important today as consumers seek more evidence that the companies whose products they buy offer something more that benefits society.

TECHNOLOGICAL

The Olympics are a complex logistical and technical event requiring state-of-the-art infrastructure to facilitate proper delivery of essential services (electricity, for example) and support the demands of sophisticated reporting and communications needs. Consider:

1. Are technological services accessible?
2. Are communications channels scalable and open?
3. Are newer technologies, including mobile and digital media, widely supported?
4. Are there any barriers to the use of technology?

Risks and Benefits

The risks here are less obvious, but can relate to the general quality and state of the host city's technical infrastructure for supporting the increased demands that will be placed on a wide range of utilities and services on which local citizens survive. Host city officials often use the Olympics as a catalyst for investing in wide-ranging infrastructure upgrades, including technological ones. For the 2008 Olympics in Beijing, government officials are intent on changing world perceptions that, despite rapid economic progress, China is technologically outdated and lacking innovation. The government is spending over $150 million on 450 technology projects specifically linked to the Beijing Olympics. In addition, companies are providing another $200 million in support of these projects to ensure that the Olympics are seen as the most technologically advanced. Clearly, the hope is that the Olympics introduce to the world a picture of China that is more advanced and sophisticated than conventional Western stereotypes promote.

Corporate sponsors stand to benefit by investing in technology infrastructure (new products, communication sites, local hardware and utility usage and investment, computer-related services) that not only supports the local government's upgrading and modernization of its services, but also provides invaluable relationships and partnerships with companies that could provide sustained, long-term business opportunities.

ORGANIZATIONAL

Host cities and companies will face increased demand for their myriad products and services, not just during the Olympic contests, but also well before and after the Games. As demand changes, organizations must be prepared to deliver on expectations.

1. Do we have the competence, skills, and expertise to plan and implement our Olympic efforts? If not, what do we need to succeed and are those resources easily available and affordable?
2. Who are the key groups we need to coordinate with?
3. Are the various organizations in approximate alignment (Olympics, city, companies, other) on what needs to be done and how to do it?

4. Are there philosophical differences that must be addressed?
5. Do we share a common vision for what needs to be done?
6. Is our infrastructure capable of handling the increased demand?

Risks

Given the inherent complexity of running an Olympic Games, the chance of organizational snafus occurring is reasonably high. Most organizational problems are localized, however, to manageable issues that are rarely the subject of media reports. But there is also the possiblity of something larger and more significant occurring that can disrupt the Olympics. In 1964, at the Innsbruck Winter Olympics, weather conditions had not yielded a consistent snowpack. The Austrian Army was recruited to carve 20,000 ice bricks out of neighboring mountains, then carry them to the competition area for building the bobsled and luge track. The Army also carried 40,000 cubic meters of additional snow from other mountains to the main ski areas. Both of these were monumental organizational challenges that were vital to ensuring a successful Olympics. The 1980 Winter Olympics in Lake Placid faced different organizational challenges that detracted greatly from the enjoyment of the Games for the fans—poorly coordinated ticketing and transportation left spectators stranded, unable to get to the Games. Consequently, many of the events were not full. The 1992 Winter Olympics in Albertville were held in eight different towns, reducing the shared feeling that the Olympics tries to instill in fans and athletes. Only 18 of the 57 total events were actually held in Albertville, creating an organizational challenge for participants and fans.

The 1996 Summer Olympics in Atlanta illustrated organizational challenges related to security when a bomb exploded in Centennial Olympic Park, resulting in the death of two people and injury to eleven others. Atlanta also confronted organizational challenges with respect to sponsorship transparency when it was learned that the City of Atlanta had negotiated separate commercial sponsorship deals with companies other than the IOC's TOP partners, giving these non-TOP companies direct visibility in and around the Olympic venues, despite the practice being against Olympic rules (not to mention generally accepted rules of good faith). This was also a surprise to the Atlanta Organizing Committee, which succeeded in stopping some of the unsanctioned activity, along with the IOC. The challenge in this situation was not just about the overbearing commercial activity, but that the companies approved by the City of Atlanta were effectively making money at an event with which they had no prior role or involvement, whereas one of the reasons the TOP partners are so important to every Olympics is because their financial support funds a substantial portion of the Games and they work for years to create a sizable infrastructure that supports both their own efforts and that of the host city on behalf of the Olympics. Organizational issues related to planning and construction have dogged past Olympic Games, notably in Montreal with the construction overrun and organizational issues related to the lack of separation between the operating and infrastructure efforts. The 2004 Olympics in Athens, while successful, were under pressure in the months and days leading up to the opening ceremony, as many of the venues had not been completed. By the time the Olympics started, the venues had been successfully completed, although some design shortcuts were taken to ensure the facilities would be ready in time. The Games were successful. However, one can imagine the contingency plans and organizational stresses prior to the Games that undoubtedly put many people under significant pressure in case some of the facilities were not ready. While it is normal for organizations to plan for the worst, the added pressure prior to the world's biggest sports event creates its own unique challenges that can affect the spirit and enthusiasm of the Games. In October 2007, tickets for the 2008 Beijing Olympics went on sale via the Internet and telephone. Nine thousand tickets were sold in two hours, but then the system collapsed due to the high demand levels. Consumer response was rapid and overwhelming, with the ticketing website receiving eight million hits and the telephone lines bombarded with two million calls seeking help. The problem was eventually resolved.

Beyond these event-specific illustrations are organizational issues related to the Olympics construction and preparation activities that precede the Games for several years. Organizational challenges here include disruption to the host city's way of life from infrastructure construction that alters traffic patterns, changes commute times, and impacts the real and perceived quality of life for its citizens. The host city organizing committee, in coordination with city officials, must work together from the very beginning (even at the earliest bid stage before a city even wins) and subsequently throughout. This effort should include regular, public, transparent town-hall meetings with citizens that enable them to air their views on the impact that Olympic-related projects are having on their lives. Concurrently, the various Olympic bodies must actively communicate the benefits and upcoming activities related to the preparation for the Games. These are just a few illustrations of the organizational challenges that have occurred. Obviously, one can envision a variety of setbacks that can trip up virtually any activity at the Olympics. As each of these issues highlights, organizational coordination and response is a critical component of Olympic planning. For sponsors, organizational planning is vital as well, since their own operating, infrastructure, and marketing activities require similarly complex organizational plans.[33]

Benefits

The 1984 Los Angeles Olympics were considered among the best-run, best-coordinated Games in history. From transportation to venue access to ticketing to customer service, the Los Angeles Olympics garnered widespread praise and recognition, serving as a model for future Olympiads. The positive results were contrary to the pre-Olympics concerns about Los Angeles's notorious traffic problems, air pollution, a lack of new facilities, and unappealing urban sprawl undermining financial, fan, and athlete success. The Los Angeles Games faced further complication from the Soviet-led, 14-nation boycott and the resulting negative PR, and the Montreal Olympics from eight years before that fomented global concern about the long-term financial viability of the Olympic Movement overall. The Los Angeles Olympic Committee, under the leadership of Peter Ueberroth, actively coordinated with volunteers, city and state officials and agencies, the IOC, corporate sponsors, and a myriad of support organizations (from utilities to healthcare to transportation services) to orchestrate a relatively smooth Olympic Games. The net result had both quantitative and qualitative contributions. Quantitatively, the Los Angeles Olympics were a financial success, producing a $220+ million profit. Qualitatively, Los Angeles received favorable media coverage and the vast army of volunteers and paid-service providers reinvigorated an Olympic Movement that had diminished somewhat following the Montreal financial problems and the more recent Olympic boycotts.[34]

BRAND

Reputation is everything. Whether personally or professionally, in business or nonprofit or government work, one's reputation determines success because expectations are developed based on this. Among the questions to consider are:

1. What is our current reputation?
2. How will the Olympics affect our reputation?
3. What are the ingredients/touchpoints that create the brand reputation we have?
4. Are we well-known, or do we have to educate the market about who we are?
5. Are the people who represent us good brand ambassadors?
6. How will the Olympics affect our brand value?

Risks

The Olympics are a chance to present a fresh face to the world. The reputation of every host city and country is at stake. When problems occur, the impact can be immediate (the scandals in Sydney and Salt Lake City demonstrate this), although lasting damage is rare. But sometimes host cities can suffer undue harm to their reputation, even if the Games succeed (and most Olympics are perceived as successful when seen through the lens of goodwill and international cooperation), such as the aftermath of Montreal's cost overruns and budget mismanagement. Other times, attempts to use the Games as a vehicle to demonstrate Olympic values are viewed as contradictory to actual behavior and, therefore, used for political purposes (such as the boycotts of Moscow in 1980 and Los Angeles in 1984). With "brand" an all-encompassing term describing any entity as seen through the eyes of its stakeholders, there are numerous touchpoints that can directly and indirectly affect a host city's brand. Managing these different touchpoints is a fundamental challenge for Olympic Organizing Committees as well as marketers.

Benefits

The Olympics offer the opportunity for organizations to thoroughly map their various touchpoints and determine how those touchpoints affect people's perceptions. Touchpoints literally include any item or service with which people are in contact. Each of these touchpoints is a point of contact that can shape a person's beliefs and confidence in the organization. Planners who wish to improve the image of their brand will focus on two key areas: tangible and intangible assets.

Tangible

As implied, tangible assets are physical elements of your brand. Products, packaging, advertising, store or destination environments (furniture, fixtures, physical design, layout), and people. Relevance and resonance are two key evaluative dimensions of tangible asset success. Asking "are the products *relevant* to my customer's needs and, if so, do they *resonate* with them?" is vital to creating a positive brand experience. "Relevant" products simply mean that the offering fills a specific need, and "resonance" means that the specific product fits a person's unique situation, perhaps connecting with them emotionally and with their lifestyle.

Intangible

Intangibles are: services, atmosphere, ambience, and attitude. Intangibles can inspire or inflame a person's passions and emotions. Taking great care of customers, while a known sentiment today, is not consistently understood or practiced around the world. This is complicated by cultural differences that can create conflict with the overall perception of the brand. But understanding intangibles and, more importantly, how to imbue everyone in the organization with delivering extraordinarily well on intangibles presents every organization with a unique and significant opportunity.

The combination of tangible and intangible touchpoints contributes directly toward creating a customer's overall experience. For companies and host cities, having a clear, detailed understanding of their tangible and intangible touchpoints can help identify strengths as well as areas that require additional attention. A useful tool is a brand touchpoints map as shown in Figure 4-3, which is a visual device created by an organization's managers to aid in seeing the complete range of factors that can affect market perceptions. By drawing these out as a chart, managers can also identify those factors whose impact may affect another area of the organization and, consequently, shape consumer beliefs and experiences. The end result is a snapshot of the many individual contributors to an organization's overall brand reputation and the connections among different factors:

Figure 4-3
Brand Touchpoints Map

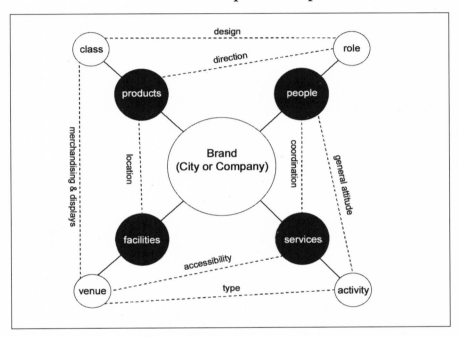

Figure 4-3 is a stylized, simplified illustration of a touchpoints map. Every circle represents a touchpoint that does, or can, affect market perception and interaction with an organization. The central circle is the primary branded entity, whether that is a nation, city, company, or even a product. The dark circles are major thematic groups in the organization (most organizations will have more than the four shown here). The smaller white circles are specific activities or offerings captured and produced by that theme area. Each darker theme area will have more smaller white circles connected to it than the few shown here. The dotted lines represent relationships between themes and specific offerings, along with single-word descriptors highlighting the nature of the relationship. Of course, an actual organization would have many more themes, offerings, and dotted-line connections than shown here, but this was kept simple for illustrative purposes. Your diagram does not have to follow this specific design scheme. In fact, the key to successfully using this tool is *not* to copy the diagram in this book. Instead, each organization must create a map based on its unique circumstances, offerings, and expertise, developing categories and subcategories accordingly. This tool can be particularly useful when a scoring/evaluation system is applied to each touchpoint. For example, using a 1–5 scale (1=poor, 5=excellent), organization management can ask two questions about each touchpoint, then score using the scale:

1. How important is this touchpoint to our customer?
2. How would our customers rate our ability to deliver successfully on this touchpoint?

Let's say that the small white circle labeled "venue" is scored 5 and 2 for the two questions. This tells management that "venue" is very important to customers, but that the organization's actual venues are not seen positively. This creates a gap that management must then determine whether to fix or not, with the attendant repercussions on the brand openly discussed. Working through this exercise requires more than one person with a sheet of paper and pencil basing it on their own opinion. It requires a group of organization leaders openly debating the touchpoints, identifying as many as possible, well before organizing them into themes and, ultimately, creating the diagram and subsequent evaluation. This will take several hours, or in some cases, days. But the result will be a more thorough understanding of the organization and its touchpoints, developed by a team working collaboratively that identified the main areas where the organization needs to invest the most resources to ensure it is ready for success on the Olympic stage (or any situation, for that matter).

CHAPTER 5

Section I: Sponsorship Preparation Questions

This section on 100 Years of Olympic Marketing provided a basic overview of over 2,700 years of historical precedent that have helped shape the image and reputation of the modern Olympics we enjoy today. Part of my research on successful organizations, whether events or companies, suggests that the best-performing succeed because they pay attention to the traditions that give any organization its personality and *raison d'être*. Understanding both past and current contexts of the Olympics gives us insight into the factors that have elevated the Games to their unique status as a transcendent event. Such an examination is useful if one wishes to understand whether an entity has true credibility and authenticity, or is merely a superficial construction designed for expedient commercial purposes. Assuming reputation is important, as it is with the Olympics, then knowing the background gives us richer insights and a clearer picture of the personality characteristics with which we wish to associate our company. As a marketer weighing and evaluating the attractiveness of sponsoring the Olympics (and/or other sports events), the following questions will help guide the initial evaluation. They are organized into four themes.

The first section, **Dream/Objective**, sounds insubstantial and idealistic. Instead, this theme helps describe and capture the positive and appealing aspects of an event by providing insights into the event's origins. The Dream of an event's founders is no different than that of any start-up business. The founders often find gaps in the market to fulfill, and/or they simply have a passion to do something that already exists but with a different approach. The spark is often the founders' Dream or, more prosaically, the Objective, which ignites and then guides the planning and actions that follow. There are several explanations for the founding of the ancient Olympics. One suggests that the Games were founded in recognition of Zeus's defeat of his father Cronus in a wrestling match after which he became ruler of the world. As the legend goes, to mark his achievement, Zeus founded the Olympics, perhaps to provide a single event devoted to competitive success. Another story says that the Olympics evolved into one event after generations of athletes and warriors from various city-states had been competing regularly in chariot and foot races as a component of regular religious celebrations. Yet another story says that the ancient Olympics began in 776 BC when a cook named Koroibos of Elis competed and won in the 600-foot stadion race.[1] These are hardly definitive, scientifically proven theories, and those with a skeptical or even cynical view would consider these explanations dubious. But the specific circumstances surrounding the founding of the first Olympic Games in 776 BC are less important than the broader nature of sports and competition that defined Greek life. Contests between city-states were common, from discus throwing to the aforementioned foot and chariot races, and a great deal of honor and prestige was attached to these competitions. As a marketer, knowing the origins of an event can be useful in understanding the linkage between a proposed event and the company or products they wish to promote. There may even be parallels between the marketer's company and that of the event, particularly in terms of philosophy.

The **Values** theme simply describes the core values by which the event and its organizers/founders live. Values are important when genuinely conceived because they have meaning and resonance among people and organizations. We know the values, or can assume we know, the values, of people and organizations with which we have familiarity. Familiarity can be further split into respect or distrust. Those we respect often serve as models of the values to which we subscribe (generosity, selflessness, etc.), whereas those we distrust can have negative values (greed, selfishness, etc.) that are quite recognizable even if we find them reprehensible. Marketers must pay attention to the values of the organizations they work with for the simple reason that someone else (a potential customer, for example) is likely doing so anyway and will gladly point out when sponsor and event do not match (imagine, hypothetically, a tobacco company sponsoring the Olympics and the fallout for both organizations if this hellish mismatch were to occur).

The **Creating Value** theme concerns how the event creates and adds value to its various stakeholders, from competitors to suppliers to customers to fans, and more. Part of the appeal of the Olympic Games is that they promote peace, goodwill, and sportsmanship. While those may not be directly tied to profit and loss, it is clear that the absence of these characteristics would undermine the appeal of the Games. For business people and marketers, creating value can also describe how the event ultimately creates a profitable financial result. But value is also created by gifted athletes and compelling contests from which memorable results emerge and last for years. In the modern era, the achievements of Jesse Owens at the 1936 Olympic Games in Berlin have transcended everyday records to become legendary in nature. As we think back on the ancient Greek Olympics, we can picture those events, conjuring colorful images of what it must have been like, which feeds into our positive feeling about the Games even today, creating indelible impressions. Marketers seeking event sponsorship opportunities need to pay attention to how the event creates value if the marketer wants to effectively associate their company with the event.

The **Personality** theme is the one we most commonly, and unconsciously, experience. As fans, we can describe an event's personality almost like we can describe another person or an animal. The Ironman Triathlon's personality is "tough" and "extreme." World Cup skiing is "fast" and "aggressive." These are, of course, simple illustrations. But understanding an event's personality has ramifications for a marketer's business. Try to picture Apple (innovative, bold, non-traditional) sponsoring a Scottish Games caber-tossing event (unchanging, conservative, traditional)—the connection would not make sense, other than as a lark or novelty. Personality should be an influential factor when considering sponsorship investments. But personality may not always be a deciding factor, as the dozens of sponsors of EPL, NBA, NFL, F1, and other major sports events show. The lack of a clear personality match does not mean the sponsorship should be avoided. Instead, marketers need to decide if the event reaches the right audience and represents the overall values their company espouses. As a marketer concerned with proper positioning and alignment between their company and related marketing investments, having a clear sense of the personality fit between the two organizations is a useful, although not rigid, guide to ensuring that the marketplace views the marketing effort as consistent with its perceptions of both organizations. We will learn more about sponsorship criteria as the book progresses.

Given the intangible nature of concepts such as founding principles and guiding philosophy, the audit questions in this section are more qualitative in nature, designed to help you think through the attractiveness of the event overall from a conceptual point of view. Understanding the particular context of an event, its founding, and its development can provide marketers with a clearer sense of the event's fit with their own company. There may not always be clear answers, but that does not remove the obligation from marketers to reflect seriously on the overall meaning and relevance of the event, as this will help focus the ultimate marketing and sponsorship approach taken.

Dream/Objective

1. How or why was the event started?
   a. Who were the founders?
   b. What inspired the original event?
   c. What types of athletes competed?
2. What is the guiding philosophy of the event?
   a. What is the event's ultimate ambition (i.e., biggest, best)?
   b. What does it stand for (i.e., sportsmanship, teamwork)?
3. What are the objectives of the event?
   a. What communities does it attract (i.e., local, regional, national, global)?
   b. What are its general aims (i.e., raise money, increase awareness, attract volunteers)?
   c. Is it for-profit or not-for-profit? How does this affect your decision?
   d. Does it benefit a cause (i.e., disease, social/political, or economic problems)?
4. What are the event's social connotations?
   a. How is it perceived (i.e., positive, controversial, innovative)?
   b. Does the event enjoy status appeal?

Values

1. What values best represent this event (e.g., virtue, purity, honor, integrity)?
   a. Who associated with this event, past or present, embodies these values (e.g., athletes, fans, community leaders)?
2. Are the event's values widely known?
   a. Who communicates the values?
   b. How are the values communicated?
3. Are the values an authentic, genuine reflection of the event's leaders and their behaviors?
   a. What are the backgrounds of the current and historical leaders and organizers of the event?
   b. Do the leaders live the values themselves in their other work?
4. Does the event consistently uphold its values through its practices (communication, partnership with suppliers/sponsors, reputation in the market)?
   a. Are the event's communications consistent with the event's image and history?
   b. Do the various stakeholders associated with the event uphold the same values? If not, are there any stakeholders whose association might be negative or controversial?

Creating Value

1. How does the event create value (financial, community support, benefit a cause, market exposure, sport reputation enhancement)?
   a. What are its revenue sources?
   b. What are the specific ways the event actually benefits its stated cause (i.e., how are the proceeds spent, is there transparency in the use of proceeds, does the event attract media attention that in turn attracts donors)?
2. Who have been the past winners and/or notable competitors?
   a. Are these athletes well known?
   b. What are their reputations?
   c. Have any of the previous competitors achieved distinction outside this event?

3. Does the event have ongoing awareness? If so, what type?
   a. Does the event enjoy top-of-mind awareness recall (the first event that comes to mind when a person is asked) or dominant awareness recall (the only event recalled)?
   b. Is the awareness recognition-based (meaning that a person has to be prompted before the event comes to mind)?
4. Is this awareness positive or negative?
   a. If positive, are the associations with this event likely to directly or indirectly benefit your company?
   b. If negative, are the associations likely to harm your company's reputation (i.e., scandals, controversies)?

Personality

1. What are the most common associations with this event historically?
2. How would you describe the event's personality (friendly, intense, elitist, accessible, competitive, casual, quirky, predictable)?
3. Do the event's stakeholders (athletes, sponsors, suppliers, fans) share similar personality characteristics?

II

When Things Go Well...

CHAPTER 6

The Global Stage

The 2004 Athens Olympics attracted 3.9 billion unduplicated viewers (unduplicated refers to viewers who watched the Olympics at least once) with a cumulative total of 34.4 billion viewer hours (determined by multiplying the total number of viewers by the duration of the program),[1] and the 2008 Beijing Olympics are projected to attract over 4 billion viewers and generate viewing hours in excess of 36 billion. For a concentrated two-week period, those numbers are nothing short of huge and they are a key reason companies find the Olympics an especially attractive marketing opportunity. The Olympic Games generate numerous real-life stories about the athletes and their efforts that add color and depth to the event, beyond the sports themselves. Much like the stories of the ancient Greek competitors such as Chionis of Sparta and Milo of Kroton, the modern athletes are celebrated for years following their Olympic performances. Their stories serve as a point of comparison with the athletes of the current Olympiad and, prior to the final competition, the surrounding buzz and speculation over who will win this time creates a global chorus of interest. This naturally evolving word-of-mouth from blogs, dedicated sports websites, video sites, and similar digital media takes the choreographed, professionally developed media profiles of athletes and adds a raw, more honest voice, creating an informal filter of public opinion that adds further credibility to the Olympics because these "conversations" are perceived as more honest and real. Specific numbers of this "underground" viral effect are imprecise at best, but tens of millions, if not billions, of additional discussions and postings undoubtedly add to the cacophony. Add to this the many other story lines about the host cities, the people, and cultural insights, and hard news on the business of the Olympics itself, and one can understand the appeal of this athletic celebration with its vast, complex array of parallel stories. For corporate sponsors, this combination of professionally orchestrated and grassroots enthusiasm is seductive, providing a rich stage on which a viable marketing effort can be implemented.

Olympic Broadcasts

The impact of television on spreading the popularity of the Olympics cannot be overstated. TV has enabled more people around the world to be connected to the Olympics than ever, even though the Games are thousands of miles away for most fans. People everywhere can share in a collective viewing of the various events at the Games that the advent of strong national broadcast networks has enabled. Smart marketing includes reaching customers where they are in a way that is both consistent with their expectations and relevant to their needs.

However, television did not create the global fan base for the Olympic Games; as you have no doubt discerned thus far, this book has shown that the appeal of the Olympics is neither an invention of the modern era nor due exclusively to the advent of television. The Olympics have achieved their unique appeal from 2,700 years of experience and tradition-building (aside from a few centuries, like the Dark Ages when apparently very little occurred; the Middle Ages when The Plague killed close to 75 million people and 60% of Europe; followed by the Renaissance—although one should not infer any cause and effect here. The horrific suffering, leading to death within seven days, that characterized victims of The Plague was not a source of creative inspiration leading to the Renaissance. In fact, the challenges from The Plague would have provided a great reason to skip the Olympics for a while). So aside from this extended hiatus, the Olympics have been a well-known event for quite a long time, well before the aid of modern broadcasting. This is a profound lesson for companies that has been a consistent finding in my research over the past several years—the great brands and successful companies have not been products of overnight success from well-financed advertising campaigns, despite conventional thinking to the contrary. Successful brands, reputations, and companies are institution-building efforts that each succeeding generation of leaders oversee for a limited time. If the people leading these institutions manage them well, then they have done so by paying close attention to the traditions that have shaped their organization's reputation, including successes and failures, while simultaneously planning new directions that reflect the past and the ambitions for the future. Most traditions are known inside a given institution to those who work there, handed down by their predecessors, versus being the result of some clever marketing campaign. Arguably, the often inaccessible nature of the Olympics throughout its history has added to its appeal as citizens everywhere learned of the exploits of their favorite athletes through traditional word of mouth and, in the early years of the modern era, print media, particularly since very few people in the ancient era actually attended these events, as was true in the early Olympiads of the modern era. Of course, television has made the Olympics more accessible for obvious reasons. More fans around the world follow the Olympics than ever before because of broadcast coverage, providing an attractive audience for advertisers. The International Olympic Committee (IOC) knows this, of course, and has been able to generate higher broadcast revenues from higher fee premiums with each succeeding Olympics because of the significant, positive reputation and ongoing goodwill associated with the Olympic ideal. Figures 6-1 and 6-2 illustrate the dramatic broadcast revenue growth of the various Olympiads since 1980.[2]

Figure 6-1
Summer Olympic Games Broadcast Revenues

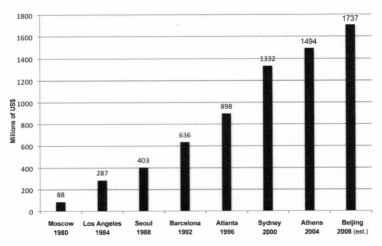

Figure 6-2:
Winter Olympic Games Broadcast Revenues

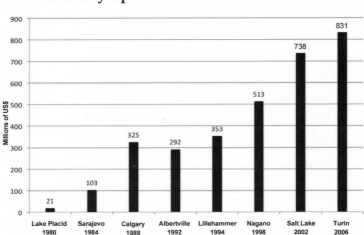

The broadcast revenue growth is impressive and, as we will see, coincides with the increasing sophistication of the Olympic Games as a viable marketing platform for companies. The revenue increases reflect not just the sheer appeal of the growing global stage that the Olympics command in a commercial sense, but also the credibility born of thousands of years of reputation-building that reminds fans of the utterly unique values and aspirations closely associated with the Games. When such a reputation is developed over centuries, the associated integrity is almost beyond compare, conferring the mythical, gold-plated status we now associate with almost anything related to the Olympics. The power of this appeal is not lost on the world's countries and companies, hence the continued increases and sophistication of host city bids, rising Olympic sponsorship fees, and the vigilant protection the IOC exerts over the Olympics and Olympic-related trademarks and intellectual property. Because of the quality associated with the Olympics and the large global audience, companies clamor for the right to reach this attractive and influential group of viewers. National broadcasters around the world, particularly those in the United States (whose broadcast networks invest the largest amounts for both rights and ensuing coverage logistics), know that this vast audience offers tremendous commercial appeal to advertisers. Thus, they bid aggressively large sums for the right to broadcast the Olympics, knowing that their own fortunes as a broadcaster are tied directly to their ability to create compelling content that offers extensive coverage of the various events, athlete profiles, and stories of Olympic success and failure, while also capturing the intangible appeal of the Olympic traditions.

The number of countries broadcasting the Olympic Games and the Winter Olympic Games has grown exponentially in the modern era, coinciding with the technological change and adoption of television around the world. Table 6-1 shows the increase in countries broadcasting the Olympics in the modern era:

Table 6-1
Worldwide Broadcast Coverage of the Olympics[3]

Olympic Games		Winter Olympic Games	
Olympic Games	Number of countries and territories broadcasting	Winter Olympic Games	Number of countries and territories broadcasting
1936 Berlin	1	1956 Cortina	22
1948 London	1	1960 Squaw Valley	27
1952 Helsinki	2	1964 Innsbruck	30
1956 Melbourne	1	1968 Grenoble	32
1960 Rome	21	1972 Sapporo	41
1964 Tokyo	40	1976 Innsbruck	38
1968 Mexico City	n/a	1980 Lake Placid	40
1972 Munich	98	1984 Sarajevo	100
1976 Montreal	124	1988 Calgary	64
1980 Moscow	111	1992 Albertville	86
1984 Los Angeles	156	1994 Lillehammer	120
1988 Seoul	160	1998 Nagano	160
1992 Barcelona	193	2002 Salt Lake City	160
1996 Atlanta	214	2006 Turin	200
2000 Sydney	220		
2004 Athens	220		
2008 Beijing	220 (est.)		

The absolute number of countries has grown through 2000 and the broadcast rights fees have increased as well. Furthermore, the broadcast revenues have grown even though in recent years the number of countries broadcasting has remained steady for both the Olympic Games and Winter Olympic Games. Table 6-2 shows the growth in total revenues from broadcast rights fees and Table 6-3 shows broadcast fees paid by region.

Table 6-2
Olympic Games Broadcast Total Revenue History[4]

Olympic Games		Olympic Winter Games	
Olympic Games	Broadcast revenue in US$	Winter Olympic Games	Broadcast revenue in US$
1960 Rome	1.2 mil	1960 Squaw Valley	50,000
1964 Tokyo	1.6 mil	1964 Innsbruck	937,000
1968 Mexico City	9.8 mil	1968 Grenoble	2.6 mil
1972 Munich	17.8 mil	1972 Sapporo	8.5 mil
1976 Montreal	34.9 mil	1976 Innsbruck	11.6 mil
1980 Moscow	88 mil	1980 Lake Placid	20.7 mil
1984 Los Angeles	286.9 mil	1984 Sarajevo	102.7 mil
1988 Seoul	402.6 mil	1988 Calgary	324.9 mil
1992 Barcelona	636.1 mil	1992 Albertville	291.9 mil
1996 Atlanta	898.3 mil	1994 Lillehammer	352.9 mil
2000 Sydney	1,331.6 mil	1998 Nagano	513.5 mil
2004 Athens	1,494 mil	2002 Salt Lake City	738 mil
2008 Beijing	1,737 mil (est.)	2006 Turin	831 mil
		2010 Vancouver	1,127 mil (est.)

Table 6-3
Olympic Games Broadcast Revenue History Breakdown By Region[5]

~ AMERICAS ~

United States

Olympic Games			Winter Olympic Games		
Host City	Broad-caster	Rights Fees in US$	Host City	Broad-caster	Rights Fees in US$
1976 Montreal	ABC	25 mil	1976 Innsbruck	ABC	10 mil
1980 Moscow	NBC	72.3 mil	1980 Lake Placid	ABC	15.5 mil
1984 Los Angeles	ABC	225.6 mil	1984 Sarajevo	ABC	91.55 mil
1988 Seoul	NBC	300 mil	1988 Calgary	ABC	309 mil
1992 Barcelona	NBC	401 mil	1992 Albertville	CBS	243 mil
1996 Atlanta	NBC	705 mil	1994 Lillehammer	CBS	295 mil
2000 Sydney	NBC	793.5 mil	1998 Nagano	CBS	375 mil
2004 Athens	NBC	793.5 mil	2002 Salt Lake City	NBC	545 mil
2008 Beijing	NBC	893 mil	2006 Turin	NBC	613.4 mil

Canada

Olympic Games			Winter Olympic Games		
Host City	Broad-caster	Rights Fees in US$	Host City	Broad-caster	Rights Fees in US$
N/A			1984 Sarajevo	CBC/CTV	1.8 mil
N/A			1988 Calgary	CBC/CTV	3.4 mil
1992 Barcelona	CTV	16.5 mil	1992 Albertville	CBC	10.1 mil
1996 Atlanta	CBC	20.75 mil	1994 Lillehammer	CBC	12 mil
2000 Sydney	CBC	28 mil	1998 Nagano	CBC	16 mil
2004 Athens	CBC	37 mil	2002 Salt Lake City	CBC	22 mil
2008 Beijing	CBC	45 mil	2006 Turin	CBC	28 mil

Central/South America

Olympic Games			Winter Olympic Games		
Host City	Broad-caster	Rights Fees in US$	Host City	Broad-caster	Rights Fees in US$
N/A			1980 Lake Placid	Televisa	100,000
N/A			1984 Sarajevo	Televisa	250,000
N/A			1988 Calgary	Selected countries	310,000
1992 Barcelona	OTI	3.55 mil	1992 Albertville	Selected countries	459,000
1996 Atlanta	OTI	5.5 mil	1994 Lillehammer	Selected countries	501,000
2000 Sydney	OTI	12.0 mil	1998 Nagano	OTI	985,000
2004 Athens	OTI	18.0 mil	2002 Salt Lake City	OTI	1.25 mil
2008 Beijing	OTI	28 mil	2006 Turin	OTI	1.75 mil

Caribbean

Olympic Games			Winter Olympic Games		
Host City	Broad-caster	Rights Fees in US$	Host City	Broad-caster	Rights Fees in US$
N/A			1984 Sarajevo	Bermuda	6,750
N/A			1988 Calgary	No broadcast	
N/A			1992 Albertville	Trinidad and Tobago	5,000
1996 Atlanta	CBU	190,000	1994 Lillehammer	Selected countries	13,500
2000 Sydney	CBU	250,000	1998 Nagano	Jamaica CVM	12,000
2004 Athens	CBU	350,000	2002 Salt Lake City	Jamaica CVM	15,000
2008 Beijing	CBU	500,000	2006 Turin	No broadcast	

Puerto Rico

Olympic Games			Winter Olympic Games		
Host City	Broad-caster	Rights Fees in US$	Host City	Broad-caster	Rights Fees in US$
2000 Sydney	Teleonce	1 mil	N/A		
2004 Athens	Telemundo	1.25 mil	N/A		
2008 Beijing	Telemundo	1.58 mil	N/A		

~ ASIA ~

Asia

Olympic Games			Winter Olympic Games		
Host City	Broad-caster	Rights Fees in US$	Host City	Broad-caster	Rights Fees in US$
N/A			1984 Sarajevo	HK-TVB	20,000
N/A			1988 Calgary	ABU	278,000
1992 Barcelona	ABU	2.2 mil	1992 Albertville	ABU	471,000
1996 Atlanta	ABU	5.0 mil	1994 Lillehammer	ABU	515,000
2000 Sydney	ABU	12.0 mil	1998 Nagano	ABU	540,000
2004 Athens	ABU	15.1 mil	2002 Salt Lake City	ABU	150,000
2008 Beijing	ABU	7.5 mil	2006 Turin	ABU	600,000

Japan

Olympic Games			Winter Olympic Games		
Host City	Broad-caster	Rights Fees in US$	Host City	Broad-caster	Rights Fees in US$
N/A			1980 Lake Placid	NHK	1.05 mil
1984 Los Angeles	Japan Pool	19 mil	1984 Sarajevo	NHK	2.50 mil
1988 Seoul	Japan Pool	50 mil	1988 Calgary	NHK	3.90 mil
1992 Barcelona	Japan Pool	62.5 mil	1992 Albertville	Japan Pool	9 mil
1996 Atlanta	Japan Pool	99.5 mil	1994 Lillehammer	Japan Pool	12.7 mil
2000 Sydney	Japan Pool	135 mil	1998 Nagano	Japan Pool	37.5 mil
2004 Athens	Japan Pool	155 mil	2002 Salt Lake City	Japan Pool	37 mil
2008 Beijing	Japan Pool	180 mil	2006 Turin	Japan Pool	38.5 mil

Arab States

Olympic Games			Winter Olympic Games		
Host City	Broad-caster	Rights Fees in US$	Host City	Broad-caster	Rights Fees in US$
1992 Barcelona	ASBU	550,000	N/A		
1996 Atlanta	ASBU	3.75 mil	N/A		
2000 Sydney	ASBU	4.5 mil	N/A		
2004 Athens	ASBU	5.5 mil	N/A		
2008 Beijing	ASBU	8.5 mil	N/A		

South Korea

Olympic Games			Winter Olympic Games		
Host City	Broad-caster	Rights Fees in US$	Host City	Broad-caster	Rights Fees in US$
1984 Los Angeles	Korea Pool	2 mil	1984 Sarajevo	KBS	180,000
1988 Seoul	KBS	2.85 mil	1988 Calgary	No broadcast	
1992 Barcelona	Korea Pool	7.5 mil	1992 Albertville	No broadcast	
1996 Atlanta	Korea Pool	9.75 mil	1994 Lillehammer	No broadcast	
2000 Sydney	Korea Pool	13.75 mil	1998 Nagano	KBS	50,000
2004 Athens	Korea Pool	15.5 mil	2002 Salt Lake City	Korea Pool	750,000
2008 Beijing	Korea Pool	17.5 mil	2006 Turin	Korea Pool	900,000

~ EUROPE ~

Europe

Olympic Games			Winter Olympic Games		
Host City	Broad-caster	Rights Fees in US$	Host City	Broad-caster	Rights Fees in US$
1960 Rome	EBU	700,000	N/A		
1964 Tokyo	EBU	N/A	1964 Innsbruck	EBU	300,000
1968 Mexico City	EBU	1 mil	1968 Grenoble	EBU	500,000
1972 Munich	EBU	2 mil	1972 Sapporo	EBU	1.40 mil
1976 Montreal	EBU	6.6 mil	1976 Innsbruck	EBU	1.20 mil

1980 Moscow	EBU	7.1 mil	1980 Lake Placid	EBU	3.855 mil
1984 Los Angeles	EBU	22 mil	1984 Sarajevo	EBU	5.6 mil
1988 Seoul	EBU	30.2 mil	1988 Calgary	EBU	6.9 mil
1992 Barcelona	EBU	94.5 mil	1992 Albertville	EBU	20.3 mil
1996 Atlanta	EBU	247.5 mil	1994 Lillehammer	EBU	26.3 mil
2000 Sydney	EBU	350 mil	1998 Nagano	EBU	72 mil
2004 Athens	EBU	394 mil	2002 Salt Lake City	EBU	120 mil
2008 Beijing	EBU	443.4 mil	2006 Turin	EBU	135mil

~ OCEANIA ~

Australia

Olympic Games			Winter Olympic Games		
Host City	Broad-caster	Rights Fees in US$	Host City	Broad-caster	Rights Fees in US$
N/A			1980 Lake Placid	ATRANSA	60,000
1984 Los Angeles	Channel 10	10.6 mil	1984 Sarajevo	Channel 7	750,000
1988 Seoul	Channel 10	7.4 mil	1988 Calgary	Channel 9	1.14 mil
1992 Barcelona	TV Olympics	34 mil	1992 Albertville	Channel 9	8.5 mil
1996 Atlanta	Channel 7	30 mil	1994 Lillehammer	Channel 9	5 mil
2000 Sydney	Channel 7	45 mil	1998 Nagano	Channel 7	6 mil
2004 Athens	Channel 7	50.5 mil	2002 Salt Lake City	Channel 7	11.75 mil
2008 Beijing	Channel 7	76.5 mil	2006 Turin	Channel 7	12.8 mil

New Zealand

Olympic Games			Winter Olympic Games		
Host City	Broad-caster	Rights Fees in US$	Host City	Broad-caster	Rights Fees in US$
N/A			1984 Sarajevo	BCNZ	25,000
N/A			1988 Calgary	No broadcast	
1992 Barcelona	TVNZ	5.9 mil	1992 Albertville	TVNZ	135,000
1996 Atlanta	TVNZ	5 mil	1994 Lillehammer	TVNZ	500,000
2000 Sydney	TVNZ	10 mil	1998 Nagano	TVNZ	600,000
2004 Athens	TVNZ	3.5 mil	2002 Salt Lake City	TVNZ	600,000
2008 Beijing	TVNZ	4.25 mil	2006 Turin	TVNZ	350,000

The broadcast fees are complex, but the increases over the years are partly explained by the expansion of broadcast options in each country in addition to the premium associated with the Olympic Movement overall. This premium would be less likely if the Games did not yield positive results for corporate sponsors and country hosts alike, suggesting that the Olympics' brand reputation remains healthy despite the challenges from scandals and skyrocketing investments in infrastructure.

With respect to host city infrastructure investment increases, recent Olympiads have shown that bid committees regularly under-forecast the construction and preparation costs, yet this repeated pattern does not seem to affect the perception of the Games overall or the sponsorship investment of companies, at least as far as fans are concerned. The 2000 Sydney Olympics were originally bid to cost AUS$3 billion (about US$2.7 billion, not including an additional US$4 billion budget by the federal and regional governments to improve transportation and related logistics), but the final tally was closer to AUS$6.6 billion (US$5.9 billion).[6] The 2004 Athens Olympics bid was AUS$4.6 billion (US$6 billion), but the final costs were closer to AUS$10 billion (US$13 billion).[7] The 2008 Beijing Olympics were originally bid at US$1.6 billion,[8] an estimate that quickly rose to US$4 billion. Beijing planners indicated that associated infrastructure projects such as roads, water treatment plants, pollution controls, public transportation improvements, and a new airport would bring the costs closer to US$40 billion.[9] The 2012 London Olympics bid committee forecasted a budget of £2.4 billion in 2005 (approximately US$4.6 billion). In 2007, the budget figure had swelled to £9.35 billion (roughly US$18.2 billion), an increase partly attributed to updated information and data on the logistics and development costs for each of the proposed Olympic venue sites.[10] None of these budget overruns are positive, nor should readers construe these comments as an endorsement of under-forecasting, whether deliberate or not. If this book were just about the economics of host city bids, the analysis would have a different tone, especially when one considers the ongoing tax burden such facilities place on citizens just to support maintenance and related expenses in the years following the Olympics. The host city has a responsibility to continue using the Olympic venues for a wide range of cultural activities and mega-events to ensure their economic viability. On the other hand, the host city bids often include costs for permanent infrastructure improvement, from public transportation to roads to new services to utilities, all of which arguably benefit the host city, its citizens, and visitors for years if not generations to come. While the bid budgets are often exceeded, perhaps the social and economic impact includes the creation of goodwill that enhances the reputation and attractiveness of the host city.

Additionally, the sheer number of people accessing the Olympics coverage has grown impressively. The 2000 Sydney Olympics were accessed by 3.6 billion people, for a total of 36.1 billion viewer hours (determined by multiplying the length of the program by the number of viewers), while 3.9 billion did so during the 2004 Athens Olympics, for a total of 34.4 billion viewer hours.[11] This slight decrease in viewer hours is not explained by the IOC's available information, but it may be due partly to the first-time use of streaming technology in Athens, transferring viewers from traditional television broadcasts to newer, non-traditional formats on the Internet and mobile devices. These figures compare to the 450 million viewers who watched the 1972 Munich Olympics, perhaps the first truly live Olympic broadcast, whereas preceding Olympic television coverage was tape-delayed.

Just as the Olympics have grown in broadcast popularity, the IOC's efforts to create successful broadcast partnerships have grown in sophistication. Olympic host broadcast organizations are responsible for covering the entire range of competitive events, redistributing this content out to the Olympic broadcast partners for use in their own country. Each broadcast partner is free to tailor its national broadcast to reflect the interests of its home fans. The broadcast feed hours provided by each host have grown over the years. For example, the 1988 Seoul Olympics broadcast feed hours totaled 2,572 while the broadcast feed hours for the 2004 Athens Olympics grew to 3,800, a 50% increase. The 1992 Albertville Winter Olympic Games had 350 host broadcast feed hours, while the 2006 Turin Winter Olympic Games offered over 1,000 broadcast feed hours.[12]

The number of broadcast feed hours explains only part of the increased popularity and growing audience size for the Olympic Games. Each country's Olympic broadcast partner creates additional content to supplement the host feed content. In Turin, while the host feed hours totaled more than 1,000, the total coverage amounted to 16,000 hours of Olympics-related content when all Olympic broadcast partners' coverage was added together. These additional hours reflect each broadcast partners' efforts to supplement and enhance the core broadcast feed with content specific to each country. For example, broadcast partners may create and show athlete profiles prior to their Olympic event, offering viewers insights about an athlete's background. These profiles cover a range of topics that may include a synopsis of their life story, providing a greater understanding of that athlete and his or her particular circumstances. Carefully crafted athlete histories and profiles can turn an unknown athlete into a celebrity and transform him or her into a fan favorite, depending on the unique aspects of that athlete's life. The profiles can stretch the broadcast length of an event by several minutes. Furthermore, the broadcasters create interesting side-stories, interviewing family members and friends, and/or showing scenes of the athlete's hometown, with the various chapters of an athlete's life revealed as he or she progresses through the Olympics from qualifying to the finals. The U.S. broadcast network NBC paid for the U.S. rights to the 2008 Beijing Olympic Games. NBC has had a website devoted to its Olympics coverage, complete with web profiles of likely U.S. athletes (visit http://www.nbcolympics.com/ for more details).

One can easily foresee these profiles being transformed into full-fledged television vignettes for those athletes who make the final U.S. Olympic team. The NBC website also includes a selection of athlete video profiles from past Olympics. The same is true for the UK's BBC, where athletes from Athens in 2004 and those likely to make the 2008 Beijing Olympics are featured (see http://news.bbc.co.uk/sport2/hi/olympics/default.stm). Broadcaster profiles are told in a story-like fashion, adding interesting context and insights about the athlete's life, enhancing their appeal. The creative dimensions to this effort are important not because they are a license to mislead or misrepresent an athlete (like any successful marketing, the best approach is to be accurate, truthful, and authentic), but because the right selection of imagery and stories about an athlete can create a memorable experience for viewers, turning an athlete from an unknown into a favorite. Olympic advertisers want viewers to watch the additional content because there is a greater chance their own advertisements will be noticed and associated with both the Olympics in general and athletes in particular. The IOC wants each broadcast partner to create the most relevant content that is home viewing audience would find appealing to ensure viewers watch as much of the Olympic broadcast coverage as possible. The better the content, the easier it is for the IOC to retain existing corporate sponsors and broadcast partners while attracting future partners as well.[13]

CHAPTER 7

Olympic Halo Effect:
Long-Term and Short-Term

The Olympic "halo" effect is an important theme throughout this book. To interpret it as merely a way to gain quick exposure underutilizes the sponsorship and, despite strong temptation to ride on the coattails of Olympic-mania for the purpose of increasing sales in the short term, may lead to disappointment for marketers and their companies. There are cheaper ways to gain a brief sales increase. Thus far, this book has argued that the key to success with an Olympic sponsorship is to enter into it with one's eyes wide open, and with a deep respect for history and an equal appreciation for one's own company and its relative fit with the spirit of the Olympic Movement. While your company may have the latest new casket design, that does not mean marketing it during the Olympics would be appropriate or sensible. Assuming this self-analysis confirms that an Olympic sponsorship makes sense, then marketers must determine the most effective and appropriate way to take advantage of it since the halo effect can be powerful yet fleeting if executed poorly. Companies must first focus on their strategic brand objectives with the Olympic sponsorship, so that they can then determine the range of short-term tactics and marketing programs that can be employed for building toward the envisioned future. That may sound counter-intuitive to some. After all, reasonable business minds sometimes argue that to even get to the future requires selling products that produce revenues now, otherwise the company will go out of business before the future ever arrives. The response to this is deceptively simple: without a long-term map for guidance, any initial steps will certainly take you somewhere, but very likely in the wrong direction. Brand value, brand strategy, and anything else are long-term efforts and are unlikely to see any measurable short-term gain, particularly since most of these activities are intangible and require companies to build deep connections with customers, which will not happen over the course of 17 days.

Long-Term

The audit questions at the end of Section I provide a good starting point for sponsors in determining the long-term objectives for their company and the role the sponsorship plays in moving the company closer to succeeding. Recall that the questions provided guidance for evaluating the attractiveness of any sports event, organized around four themes:

- Dream/Objective
- Values
- Creating Value
- Personality

These same questions should be used in reviewing your own company as they will help tighten up your own understanding, plus they will create a common foundation of knowledge for management in its sponsorship decision-making process. The questions are to be answered as a management team and not by any one individual. This allows key decision makers to debate each of these themes and questions and work collaboratively to arrive at a common view of their own firm. Exploring each of these themes will crystallize management's thinking about image issues vital to the long-term success and attractiveness of the company. Long-term brand planning includes focusing on three key areas: positioning, awareness, and market growth objectives.

Positioning

Positioning refers to how customers view a company, its products, and/or services. Substantial thinking and creativity is expended by marketers on influencing their company's position, but it is important to recognize that a company's position is really more a reflection of how customers see the company than an overt advertising message telling the market one's position. The believing is in the seeing or, more specifically, in the doing. How a company handles its customers determines its position in their minds. Positioning can be affected by choosing the right marketing vehicles, such as sports sponsorships. Indeed, sponsorships can help customers view a company differently or simply more carefully, assuming the other themes of Dream, Values, Creating Value, and Personality are consistent with the position communicated.

The Olympics are a prestigious event and the strong halo effect suggests corporate sponsors will have some of this prestige rub off on them, benefitting their position in the market. For example, Visa's brand preference (a measure of loyalty that indicates consumer preference for one brand versus the offerings of competitors) increased to 50% in the United States, rating Visa as the "best overall card." While this is not a specific measure of prestige, the connotation of "best" is clear, affording Visa a measure of prestige in the credit card category.

Visa's image as the "best overall card" did not happen during or immediately after, its first Olympic sponsorship in Calgary in 1988. The Visa case brief in Chapter 12 will discuss Visa's rise in detail, but its improvement has occurred over 20 years, a reasonable indication that Visa took a long-term view of its Olympic sponsorship.

Lenovo became a TOP sponsor in time for the 2006 Turin Winter Olympics and 2008 Beijing Olympics. The timing was crucial for the company because it had just acquired IBM's PC division in 2005, changed its name from Legend to Lenovo, and was intent on positioning itself as a reputable, innovative computer maker globally. The effort is challenging given the compressed two-Olympic, four-year time horizon of its sponsorship. To date, the company is making positive progress toward its goals, gaining in market share, launching award winning computers, and innovating in both computer and non-computer design, as its winning Olympic torch design illustrates. Lenovo's case brief discusses this in detail in Chapter 12.

Awareness

Companies want to increase their awareness because the more they are known the greater the chance of acquiring customers (it is hard to ask for, let alone buy, something one is not aware exists). Awareness is measured several ways, but aided and unaided awareness are most common (also known as aided or unaided recall). Aided awareness is measured by showing survey respondents a product, ad, brand name, or trademark and asking them when they recall last seeing it. Unaided awareness asks respondents to recall any product, ad, brand name, or trademark they recall seeing recently.[1] Prior to the 1994 Winter Olympics in Lillehammer, consumers were asked to name brands associated with the Olympics. Coca-Cola was correctly identified as a TOP sponsor, with 22% unaided awareness (meaning that consumers did not need product or category prompting). Sponsorships have grown in sophistication ever since in an effort to achieve equivalent top-of-mind recall. Visa has enjoyed important gains in awareness, as one might expect. These increases played a key role in driving the company's financial performance improvements during the past 20 years. The company's unaided awareness grew to 72% following the 2000 Olympics in Sydney, for example, although one should not confuse this number with Coca-Cola's because Visa was measuring overall unaided awareness and not any specific association with the Olympics.[2]

In 1996, Samsung senior management set forth a plan to revamp its business and substantially raise its brand value. Samsung has been an Olympic TOP sponsor since 1997 in the wireless communications category. The company's market awareness has increased substantially since then, with a 5% rise in unaided awareness to 16.2% from its sponsorship of the 2000 Sydney Olympics alone. Awareness grew again, from 57% to 62% following the 2004 Athens Olympics. Since 1999, its brand value has grown over five-fold to $16.8 billion.[3] Samsung has agreed to be a TOP sponsor until the 2016 Olympics. While not all of this brand value or awareness increase is directly attributable to the Olympics sponsorship, Samsung management believes its association with the Olympic Movement has been instrumental in reshaping the company's image.[4]

Market Growth

Market growth describes changes (increases or decreases) in business year over year, either in units sold or total dollar volume. Market growth can also be measured by reviewing market share (total company sales as a percentage of the total market).[5]

Visa's market share rose from 33% in 1986 to 54% in 2007, with MasterCard the next closest competitor at 29%, followed by American

Express at 13%.[6] This increase coincides with the company's Olympic sports marketing investments. Total transaction volume grew from $111 billion to $3.48 trillion during this time, and the total number of cards issued grew from 137 million to 1.4 billion.[7]

Samsung's mobile phone market share increased from 5% in 1999 to 13.4% in 2007, and sales increased from 17 million units to 154 million units during that time, surpassing Motorola in the fourth quarter of 2007 to the number two market-share position behind Nokia. Samsung saw telecommunications sales increase 44% following the 2000 Sydney Olympics.[8]

Short-Term

As we will see in Section IV: Winning Marketing Gold, and in the case briefs in particular, sponsors do have short-term objectives. These vary significantly based on each company. But the important point is not to focus on the differences in the short-term tactics they employ. Instead, short-term tactics will depend entirely on a company's business situation. To increase short-term growth means that a company will have to improve the sales and/or profits of its offerings. The Ansoff Matrix[9] shown in Figure 7-1 is a useful device for structuring marketing thinking around product and market growth choices, and the resulting marketing implications. First, we will look at growth choices since part of marketing's job with a sponsorship may be to increase sales

Table 7-1:
Growth Choices

	Current Products	New Products
Current Markets	**A** **Grow in current markets** Increase market share Increase products usage	**B** **Product development** Add product feature New generation products
New Markets	**C** **Market development** Expand geographically Identify new segments	**D** **Diversification** Related Unrelated

Quadrant A

Selecting this quadrant means planning focuses on increasing sales with current products in current markets. There are two ways to accomplish this:

1. Increase market share: to do this requires taking share and customers away from competitors.

    Implications for sports sponsorships
    Company management must have a clear understanding of their strengths and competitor vulnerabilities if competitors' customers are to be convinced to switch.

2. Increase product usage: this means existing customers must buy more of the company's products.

    Implications for sports sponsorships
    Company management must have detailed customer profiles and needs if they are to persuade their own customers to buy more.

Quadrant B

Choosing this quadrant focuses the company on selling new or improved products to current markets. There are two ways to do this:

1. Add product features: R&D attention must focus on improving existing products to appeal to existing customers to increase their purchases.

2. New-generation products: R&D's emphasis is developing wholly new products based on their understanding of existing customers and then hoping the new products are appealing, convincing customers to either supplement their current product purchases or replace them with the new product.

    Implications for sports sponsorships
    In both cases, company management must commit to a more complex and expensive product strategy since money will be spent on explaining the new product features and/or the new

products to existing and/or competitors' customers (to increase share) while also implementing the other facets of the sports sponsorship plan.

Quadrant C

This quadrant directs company management attention on finding new markets for current products. This is accomplished two ways:

1. Expand geographically: management must select new locations (regions, countries), preferably where the customers are similar to existing customers in existing markets.

    Implications for sports sponsorships
    New geographies create new logistical and operational challenges, including possible language and culture differences. Management must be prepared to handle demand and communications issues as interest grows.

2. Identify new segments: new segments can be in existing or new geographies, requiring more extensive knowledge of different customer groups and their associated characteristics. Ideally, preference should be given to those segments with some overlap with existing segments to minimize investment.

    Implications for sports sponsorships
    New segments can be in existing or new geographies. If the segment(s) are in existing geographies, then management must focus on making the products relevant to the new segments. If the segments are in new geographies, then management has to emphasize product relevance in the cultural and language context.

Quadrant D

Selecting this quadrant means developing entirely new products for entirely new markets. There are two ways to achieve this:

1. Related: this means the company pursues new products sold to new markets, but within the same industry.

Implications for sports sponsorships
In this case, companies must be careful not to dilute or erode their current brand position or detract from the sports sponsorship effort. This is akin to launching a new company, albeit in a familiar industry, so it is a major effort unto itself, let alone the existing effort to execute on the sports sponsorship properly. It is unlikely a company would do this as a linked growth strategy to the sports sponsorship since they are fundamentally two separate business efforts.

2. Unrelated: this is pure pioneering work in both new products and new markets.

Implications for sports sponsorships
This is the highest-risk growth choice of all and, as such, requires extraordinary dedication and resources (financial, people, energy, time) in order to succeed. Given the existing demands on supporting the sports sponsorship, this choice has little or no benefit for the sponsorship and would not make sense unless the company has enormous resources.

The quadrant D choices are the least attractive since growth objectives cannot be clearly tied to the sponsorship. Marketers will want to concentrate on quadrants A, B, or C as they leverage existing knowledge and experience, and can conceivably be linked to the sponsorship.

Now that marketers have made a growth choice, attention must be turned to the marketing implications (Figure 7-2), including what marketing mix components should be employed to maximize the growth opportunity in each quadrant.

Quadrant A

To convince existing customers to buy more or steal customers from competitors, marketing has two tactics at its disposal:

1. Heavy marketing and sales: "heavy" means spending more money and/or increasing the frequency and/or diversity of marketing and selling activities. For existing customers, the

Figure 7-2
Marketing Implications[10]

	Current Products	New Products
Current Markets	**A** **Grow in current markets** Heavy marketing and sales Price penetration	**B** **Product development** R&D investment Heavy marketing and sales Market research Price skimming or penetration Channel development
New Markets	**C** **Market development** Heavy marketing and sales Market research Channel development	**D** **Diversification** Heavy R&D investment Heavy marketing and sales Heavy market research Price skimming or penetration Intensive channel development

marketing message and sales education effort must explain clearly why they should buy more products and what the benefits are. When trying to take customers from competitors, the communications effort will need to persuade customers why your product is different, how that difference is relevant, and why they should care.

2. Price penetration: increasing share and/or taking competitors' customers can sometimes be a function of price—charge less for the same or equivalent products and more customers will be attracted. The downside is handling complaints from existing customers who paid a higher price previously (as Apple faced when it reduced the price of its iPhone by $200 just two months after its introduction).

Implications for sports sponsorships
Spending more on marketing and sales, or price penetration, is primarily a promotion-focused strategy designed to sharply increase sales over the short term. This is the same as discounting—either the discount is applied directly to the product, or the added marketing expense is ultimately deducted from revenues—and both lead to reduced margins. Reduced price

and margins may be counter-intuitive or even contradictory, particularly if the sports event is the Olympics with its premier position in the market and the company's long-term brand strategy is to enhance its profile and reputation.

Quadrant B

Convincing existing or competitor customers to purchase the new or improved products requires marketing to develop a multi-part plan:

1. R&D investment: in many companies, such as consumer products firms, marketing may have responsibility for product-line development, which means planning each product, extension, and level. Product development expenditures (sourcing, molds, samples, prototypes) are allocated to associated departments, including marketing.

2. Heavy marketing and sales: since this is either an entirely new product launch or an update to a known product, marketing communications programs that explain the products to the market are required. The new product, in particular, will need to be properly positioned, even though the audience consists of customers from an existing market.

3. Market research: investment in customer data acquisition (updating profile data, trends...) will help marketing understand how to position the products.

4. Price skimming or penetration: unlike price penetration discussed above, price skimming targets a very select customer subset, often early adopters, who will pay more for the new product. The term refers to skimming the best customers off the top, knowing that they will pay more and that the rest of the customers will not. The benefit is higher margins and the development of a more exclusive image. The disadvantage is unit sales and revenues may be lower, as will market share.

5. Channel development: marketing must place the products into the existing company distribution channels, which means

convincing channels to accept this new product in addition to existing products, and/or identify new channels that also reach the existing customers but are uniquely qualified with this particular type of product or new feature.

Implications for sports sponsorships

The marketing challenge is increasing with the addition of new products and/or features since resources and organizational coordination must also successfully manage the products in addition to the core sponsorship activities. The company is already spending effort creating a marketing communications plan to implement the sponsorship investment, so the new products' communications plans have to be carefully incorporated if additional sponsorship leverage is to succeed.

Quadrant C

Selling existing products to new markets through geographic expansion or to new customer groups means marketing has to introduce the company and/or its products since the target audiences may well be unfamiliar with them. Areas of marketing communications focus should be:

1. Heavy marketing and sales: new audiences require clear communication just as new products do. Marketing's planning efforts will have to carefully tailor campaigns to each new market, and will require additional coordination with new partners and agencies. Field sales will need to learn about the customer profiles in order to develop a workable sales plan, which means training investments will be required.

2. Market research: similar to the market research needs for the quadrant B choice, marketers need to gather useful information and insights about their new target customers if marketing and selling campaigns are to be properly developed.

3. Channel development: new markets may have different distribution channels, so regional management and field sales will need to learn about the differences. The possibility of working

with local partners emerges here, which is helpful, but can add expense.

Implications for sports sponsorships

Marketing to new customers is a different, but equally tough, challenge. The company may be able to leverage previous investments in marketing communications, but it would be well advised to ensure proper translation into terms relevant to new markets. This, too, requires additional marketing spending and resource effort, which must be coordinated with the overall sports sponsorship plan.

Quadrant D

Selling new products into new markets requires an even more comprehensive, expensive, and resource-intensive effort than quadrant C's. This is analogous to Coca-Cola trying to sell surgical tools to doctors under a new brand name (they aren't). Hypothetically, while research might have suggested this as a good growth opportunity, it would be hard to imagine how this could be linked with their Olympic Games sponsorship.

In **Section IV: Winning Marketing Gold**, company briefs are presented that describe the actual Olympic sponsorship activities of four TOP sponsors. Their short- and long-term objectives are discussed, giving detailed insights into the unique approaches each company takes with its Olympic sponsorship.

CHAPTER 8

David vs. Goliath—
Those Delightful Surprises

The Olympic spirit is often best seen during surprising moments. Throughout the history of the Games, athletes or teams have come through with completely unexpected performances that defeat the favorites, earning them a permanent place in the memories of fans and athletes. Surprises are not always victories either. An athlete can rise up from obscurity and capture the imagination of the public, if only for a short while. Each Olympic competition is an unknown, even if recognized favorites are competing. There are no guarantees that the presumptive favorite will strike gold. This hint of uncertainty is a fundamental interest driver in most sports, but it takes on special meaning in the Olympics because of the relative infrequency of the Games as compared to the championships of other sports, and the exalted status accorded Olympic athletes. The term "Olympian" conjures images of grand performances, even if the athlete does not win. It is used in society to describe particularly impressive or heroic accomplishments in many professions. An Olympian is someone who has reached the highest level of his or her sport and is competing in the most revered sporting event in the world. The Olympics are replete with true stories of surprising accomplishment, which put us in a state of disbelief. Each Olympiad produces its share of amazing stories, some of which are not always about an unexpected victory but about the character and personality of particularly captivating athletes. A few are highlighted here to illustrate the ability of these athletes to inspire and provide added vitality to the Olympic legend.

Vera Caslavska—1968 Olympics in Mexico City
When surprises occur, the world takes notice, as do companies, because the accomplishment is out of the ordinary. There are many

examples of athletes whose Olympic success occurred over multiple Olympiads and in the intervening international competitions between Games. That is not surprising. Al Oerter won gold in the discus over four consecutive Olympics from 1956 in Melbourne to 1968 in Mexico City. People would have been surprised had he not won. But a Czechoslovakian gymnast named Vera Caslavska was the notable winner in Mexico City in 1968. She had won three gold medals and a silver medal at the 1964 Olympic Games in Tokyo and was expected to repeat her success in Mexico City. But in the weeks leading up to the Olympics, the Soviet Union invaded Czechoslovakia and she fled into hiding in the mountains to avoid arrest, where she maintained her fitness by practicing in the trees and fields. She was eventually granted permission to compete in Mexico City, but no one knew what toll her experience might have taken on her abilities. She won four gold medals and two silver medals, an amazing accomplishment considering her very recent adverse circumstances.[1]

Miracle on Ice—1980 Olympics in Lake Placid

The Soviet Union dominated ice hockey in 1980. Its team had well-known government support, superb coaching and training facilities, and played consistently well internationally. In the year prior to the Olympics, the Soviet team played several exhibition matches against teams from the NHL, ending with a 5-3-1 record. For NHL fans, their professional hockey players were considered the best in the world, so being on the losing end of the win-loss record against their arch rival (this was during the Cold War, when passions and suspicions between the United States and the Soviet Union were at an all-time high) was difficult to endure. As with prior Olympics, the United States fielded a team of talented young amateurs, some from the college-level. But the team was seeded seventh out of 12 and was clearly not considered a favorite to win any medal, let alone gold.[2]

The U.S. team surprised many sports fans by tying with Sweden, considered a superior team, 2–2. The U.S. team then defeated the Czechoslovakian team 7–3, a dramatic and impressive win over a team many believed to be as formidable as the one from the Soviet Union. After another three wins the U.S. team qualified for the medal round of play. The Soviet team crushed most of its competitors en route to the medal round, including a 16–0 blow out of the Japanese team. The Soviets were heavy favorites to win their sixth gold medal, out of the seven previous Olympics.

The U.S. and Soviet teams met in the penultimate game, with the winner moving on to the gold medal game. The game went back and forth and eventually the U.S. team took the lead, 4–3, with about eight minutes to play. As the game wound down to its final seconds and the clearly pro-American crowd cheered wildly, an American TV broadcast announcer named Al Michaels, sounding as astonished as everybody else, described the last few seconds of the game and shouted what are now immortal words, "...Eleven seconds, you've got ten seconds, the countdown going on right now! Morrow, up to Silk...five seconds left in the game...**Do you believe in miracles? Yes! Unbelievable!**"[3]

The U.S. team went on to win the gold medal by defeating Finland 4–2 in the championship. But for U.S. sports fans, the game against the Soviet Union was the sports event of the year. It was a culminating event that translated into a wave of national pride that lasted long after the Olympics ended and serves as a vibrant reminder of why the Olympics are so widely loved.

Eddie the Eagle—1988 Winter Olympics at Calgary

Michael "Eddie the Eagle" Edwards competed for the United Kingdom in ski jumping at the 1988 Calgary Olympics. He had no outside financial support, self-funding his training and Olympic journey. His surprising fame was not due to winning the gold medal. Edwards was notable because he finished last (55th and 58th in the two ski jump events) and, in the process, won the hearts of fans (Edwards contends that he did not finish last in one of his events because he beat a French ski jumper who had broken his leg the day before. As Edwards said jokingly, "I'm going to take it because he's French"). Part of his charm was his relaxed attitude, everyday appearance, and humor. As he recounted in a 2007 interview about how he was able to qualify for the Olympics, [4]

> *At the time there was a rule that a country could send one representative to each sport in the Olympics. I loved skiing and as a kid I wanted to be a stuntman, so I decided to put them together. Nobody else applied. I mean, I wasn't completely incompetent: I'd done*

a 77 m jump, which wasn't big by Olympic standards, and I held the record for stunt jumping [10 cars and six buses]. I realised two years before the Olympics that I might be able to get to Calgary because no one else was going to apply and so started training. I got a lot of advice from Austrian and French ski-jumping coaches, but because I can't speak French or German, a lot of it went over my head.[5]

His poor eyesight required Edwards to wear thick glasses during his jumps, which often fogged up. His equipment was decidedly average compared to that of his competitors and it was rumored that he had to wear five to six pairs of socks to keep his boots fitting snuggly. Despite his lack of a typical athlete's support or equipment, Edwards was the United Kingdom's best ski jumper and held the British record, although it must be stated he was also their only ski jumper at the time and the first to have competed in the Olympics. This list of rather unremarkable qualities still enabled him to compete and win the hearts of fans around the world. Whenever he jumped at Calgary, fans chanted his name, cheering his jumps enthusiastically. Eddie the Eagle was even referenced by the president of the Calgary Olympics in his closing remarks when he said that some athletes soared like an eagle. Following the Calgary Olympics, Edwards enjoyed several years of celebrity, "I did things I thought I'd never get chance to do. I sung a few records, opened nightclubs... I did loads of TV and radio work all over the world—travelling by private jet and helicopter from one job to the next. It was great. And the attention from these beautiful women who two weeks before Calgary wouldn't have even noticed me. It was amazing."[6]

Edwards earned a law degree in the 1990s, but has since settled into a comfortable life working in construction in the United Kingdom and giving motivational speeches.[7]

Jamaican Bobsled Team—1988 Winter Olympics at Calgary

The 1988 Winter Olympics in Calgary saw Jamaica enter the four-man bobsled event for the first time. Their entry was unusual to say the least, given the lack of snow in their country. To finance their Olympic training and travel, they sold reggae records, t-shirts, and sweatshirts. Their Olympic debut was marred by crashes and technical glitches, but they became media and fan favorites in Calgary and their efforts inspired a 1993 movie called *Cool Runnings* starring John Candy. They tried again in Albertville in 1992 where they finished 14th, ahead of teams from Italy, France, Russia, and the United States, surprising fans around the world. They entered a two-man event as well, finishing 10th, ahead of the Swedish national champions. In 2000, the team won the gold medal at the World Push Championships in Monte Carlo. They are aiming next for the 2010 Winter Olympics in Vancouver after unsuccessful efforts in 2002 in Salt Lake City and 2006 in Turin, due partly to poor funding. Despite not winning an Olympic medal as a team, former Jamaican team members have gone on to success. Lascelles Brown, who was the brakeman on the Jamaican team, moved to Canada to train. He became a Canadian citizen one month before the Turin Olympics and went on to win the silver medal in the two-man event (along with non-former Jamaican Pierre Lueders). The Brazilian team claims an indirect connection to the Jamaican team in that the founder and president of the Brazilian ice sports federation, Eric Maleson, states that he was inspired to start the Brazilian team after seeing *Cool Runnings*.[8]

The 1994 Russian Winter Olympics Team

The end of the Soviet Union came in August 1991 following a failed coup attempt by a group of former KGB and military leaders. Boris Yeltsin climbed onto a tank outside the Russian White House, urging people to oppose the coup. By December 1991, Yeltsin and Mikhail Gorbachev (the former Soviet leader) had worked out a transfer of power, and by January 1992, the Soviet Union was no more and suddenly 15 former Soviet republics were now independent states. As the former republics went their separate ways, so did their athletes. When the 1994 Winter Olympics came along, there was uncertainty about how the Russian team would perform. The Russian team surprised everybody by winning 23 medals, 11 of which were gold— the most of any country, marking a successful and remarkable performance by a country still in the early stages of its new political direction.[9]

There are hundreds of surprising tales such as these that remind us why the Olympic brand is so powerful. This element of surprise, uncertainty, and unpredictability defines most sports. Companies weighing sponsorship decisions need to understand that the event they are considering offers no guarantees that the fans will like it or that the athletes will perform amazing feats. The unpredictable nature is part of the appeal for fans and athletes, and it adds to the media spectacle surrounding a sports event. For companies, the surprises in sports are a central, although not always clearly articulated, factor in the sponsorship investment decision. Companies want fans around the world having those proverbial water-cooler conversations at work as they talk about sports from the previous day, and with such a variety of sports during the Olympics, the chances of multiple surprises adding to the global conversational buzz is an irresistible attraction.

CHAPTER 9

Section II: Sponsorship Preparation Questions

In this section we discussed the significant visibility the Olympics have and bring to corporate sponsors. Given the size of the global stage, sports sponsorship marketers must approach their planning and preparation differently than a conventional marketing campaign. While the duration of the Games is a little more than two weeks, the sheer enormity of the spectacle and the variety of events creates the potential for unprecedented exposure. Questions to address:

Global Stage (these questions apply to both TV and in-venue considerations)

1. What do we want the world to know about us?
   a. Focus on two to three key "must haves" and resist the temptation to add more.
2. What do we want the world to see?
   a. What are the signage limitations in our sponsorship agreement?
   b. What is our plan for signage?
   c. What is the enduring image we want people to remember?
3. How do we leverage media relationships?
   a. Who do we know at the major broadcasters and can they help us?
   b. What media kits do we need to provide? What should the content be?
4. Are there conflicting or competing sponsorship agreements that may hinder or inhibit the visibility of our brand (such as official Olympic apparel vs. the athlete's individual apparel sponsorship)?

    a.   How do we address any potential conflicts?

    b.   What do we tell our athletes? The IOC?

5.   Are there any partnerships we want to highlight during the Games, either via marketing communications or through providing equipment and supplies?

    a.   What is the best way to promote this partnership without diluting our brand?

6.   What is the perception of the sports event?

Halo Effect
Long-Term

1.   What is the market position we want to own and how will this sports event help us get there?

    a.   What do we consider a reasonable long-term time horizon?

    b.   What checkpoints do we need to determine if we are staying on track?

2.   What are our awareness objectives, both qualitatively and quantitatively?

3.   What are our long-term market growth objectives?

    a.   Market share?

    b.   Revenue?

    c.   Profits?

    d.   Number of customers?

    e.   Customer loyalty measures?

Short-Term

1.   What are the product tactics we want to implement?

    a.   Existing or new products? Both?

    b.   New features?

2.   What are the short-term market growth objectives?

    a.   Increase customer usage?

    b.   Steal customers from competitors?

    c.   Identify new segments?

Dealing with Positive Surprises

1. Do you have a plan for supporting serendipitous events that may benefit your company (e.g., an athlete you sponsor wins gold, defeating the heavily favored winner)?
   a. How will you handle increased demand?
   b. Who is accountable for taking proper advantage of good news situations?
   c. Are roles clearly understood?
   d. Which people are assigned responsibility for keeping the attention focused on the opportunity?
2. Can you leverage the situation to benefit your company, even though you are not affiliated with the athlete or team in the surprising situation?
   a. If so, can you do so genuinely, or will it risk turning off customers?
   b. Who else needs to, or should, be involved?
3. How would you prevent this from turning negative?
   a. Do you have a plan for avoiding over-commercialization?
4. What will you do to celebrate this success with:
   a. Employees?
   b. Customers?
   c. Stakeholders?
   d. The market?

III

When Things Go Wrong...

CHAPTER 10

Marketing Challenges

The Olympics have had their share of challenges, scandals, and switched loyalties throughout history, whether it was because of politics, cheating, financial bribery, or even an ill-considered effort to better one's lot in life.

Astylos of Crotona earned fame as a sprinter, competing and winning in the *stade* and *diaulos* in the 73rd, 74th, and 75th Olympiads in 488, 484 and 480 BC, making him famous as it matched the running success of Chionis of Sparta. Besting Chionis, Astylos also competed and won an event called the *hoplites*, in which competitors race wearing a suit of armor. Astylos was particularly noteworthy because he first competed for Crotona but then switched to Syracuse in an attempt to gain support from Syracuse leader, Hieron, a tyrant. His switch of loyalties was not a well-received move, angering the people from Crotona who subsequently destroyed his house and statue to demonstrate their anger and disapproval. In 388 BC, Eupolus of Thessaly bribed three boxers to throw their fights against him and he was subsequently fined and required to build six bronze statues of Zeus. City-states were known for their efforts to recruit top athletes from rivals by paying substantial sums, asking them to lie about their home. The ancient equivalent of boycotts occurred when athletes' city-states refused to participate due to ongoing tensions with sister territories.[1]

Much later, Rome's Emperor Nero (37–68 AD) saw himself as artistic and cultured. Finding many of the athletic aspects of the Olympics crude, he eliminated most sports, replacing them with arts contests featuring poetry, singing, and music. As mentioned in Chapter 1, he chose to compete in a chariot race in 67 AD in which he fell off and lost. However, the judges, sensing catastrophic personal harm, declared him the winner anyway, in addition to winner of every other contest in which he participated. His chariot fall was an embarrassment, however, and it served to begin undermining the credibility of the Olympics.[2]

We have seen the direct impact when winners cheat in their efforts to win gold, whether through drugs or other devious means. In 1904, the American Olympic marathon runner Fred Lorz rode in a car for 11 miles on his way to winning the gold. There is an odd admiration one has for such an obvious violation of sportsmanship as we marvel that he had the audacity to pull such a brazenly offensive maneuver. Yet that admiration is muted by the klaxon call of deception and trickery his victory revealed. As it turns out, Lorz's victory was short-lived when it was discovered by officials how he won, and he was subsequently banished from all future competitions. However, he was reinstated within a year after a convincing appeal whereby Lorz persuaded officials that he rode in the car because he suffered severe stomach cramps during the race and he did not mean to intentionally defraud—instead he finished as "a joke."[3] His sense of humor was undoubtedly lost on his fellow competitors and suggested a mild hostility toward the image of Olympic virtue. However, Lorz went on to legitimately win the Boston Marathon in 1905,[4] so he apparently had real athletic talent to go with his talent for comedy. One can only imagine the headlines if such a stunt were pulled by an Olympic athlete today—"Marathoner Wins in Less Than 45 Minutes–And Doesn't Break a Sweat," or "Steroids Not Involved in Gold Medal Marathoner's Victory," or "6 Billion People Changed Channel Just Before Marathoner Climbed Into Car En-Route to Victory."

Controversy surrounded Nancy Kerrigan and Tonya Harding, two competitors in the 1994 U.S. Olympic trials in figure skating. Kerrigan was clubbed in the legs after skating practice by an assailant who was linked a few days later to Tonya Harding's ex-husband. Harding was not implicated at the time (just prior to the Olympics), denying any involvement although she did say she had learned after the attack that people close to her were involved, including her ex-husband. With no specific findings of wrongdoing, Harding was allowed to skate in the Lillehammer Olympics, where she finished eighth and Kerrigan earned the silver medal. Because of the attack on Kerrigan, Olympic TV ratings increased dramatically, and the women's short program became the sixth highest-rated show in U.S. television history. However, this should not be construed as approval for athletes maiming each other prior to the Olympics to boost their sponsor's financial interests. But it does underscore the unpredictable nature of Olympic competition and how fan interest can be generated by unfortunate circumstances.[5] Less than a month after the Olympics ended, Harding admitted guilt in hindering the investigation, and in June that same year she was stripped of her 1994 National Title and banned for life from the sport. The controversy was one of the most visible at the 1994 Olympics and heightened viewer interest in the Games.

The 2002 Winter Olympics in Salt Lake City saw a pairs figure-skating competition marred by controversy. Judges awarded the gold medal to the Russian pairs team that skated a technically difficult but flawed final routine. The Canadian pairs team skated a flawless final routine, which most analysts and observers said was the better routine. But when the final scores for technical merit and artistic impression were given out, the Russian team edged out the Canadians, causing a raucous chorus of boos from fans and obvious dismay from expert analysts commenting on live TV. After the competition, the French judge confessed to having been pressured by the French skating president to score the Russian team higher, then recanted her confession shortly thereafter. However, her controversial remarks sparked a scandal that led to her three-year suspension from the sport and that of the president of the French skating association, who subsequently resigned his position in 2004.[6] As a consequence of the judging scandal, the International Skating Union (ISU) changed the scoring system in 2004. The former system, used for 100 years, scored skating based on a 6.0 scale (6.0 being the top mark). A panel of nine judges from different countries would each render their own individual score, which was displayed for all to see, including the judge's country of origin, along with the total skating score. The new system gives the judges anonymity. The new system is fairer for the athletes, but it is more confusing for the fans, a potentially unfortunate but necessary by-product of good intentions since the old system allowed fans to cheer and jeer the individual judges' scores, thereby

143

involving the fans more directly in figure skating. Skating analysts are confident that fans will get used to the new system. More importantly, the new scoring system's anonymity will reduce the chances of judges being pressured or bribed.[7]

Performance-enhancing drugs have become the more common route for athletes seeking an unfair advantage, despite the serious consequences if discovered. Witness Ben Johnson, the Canadian sprinter who was stripped of his gold medal in the 100 meters from the Seoul Olympics when he tested positive for banned substances. More recently, Marion Jones, the American sprinter who won five medals at the 2000 Sydney Olympics (three gold and two bronze), admitted in 2007 to using performance-enhancing drugs. Her confession came after years of denial that she had ever cheated in her track career, despite ongoing suspicion from international sport governing bodies and fellow athletes. Subsequent to her admission she returned her Olympic medals even before the International Olympic Committee (IOC) officially disqualified her Sydney performances and issued its formal demand that she return her medals, and she faces an ignominious future at best beginning with a six-month jail sentence in 2008. Authenticity is indeed a vital part of the Olympic appeal.

When athletes are found to have cheated, their integrity is damaged, the credibility of their sport is diminished, and both the athlete's and sport's long-term brand reputation is harmed, often severely and sometimes irreparably. The controversies surrounding professional cycling and exemplified by certain riders in the Tour de France (although not limited to that event) have tarnished cycling's reputation and cast a negative pall over the sport and its more honest participants. The same is true for Major League Baseball in the United States, where a months-long investigation produced a report published in December 2007 revealing that more than 80 active players were using or had used performance-enhancing substances, including steroids. This may prove to be the most damaging situation professional baseball has faced since the 1919 "Black Sox" scandal, when the favored Chicago White Sox intentionally lost the World Series to the underdog Cincinnati Reds, providing the Chicago players involved in the "fix" with a financial payout. Such antics cause fans to become skeptical, the commercial appeal declines, and the sport sees its overall reputation diminish as a result. The central appeal of sport as a genuine, authentic, and unscripted event is lost, reducing the competition to a mere staged performance.

Today, with hundreds of millions of dollars of sponsorship money at stake, the fallout from an unexpected, negative surprise can be felt quickly and can engulf many stakeholders concurrently. In 1998, a major bribery scandal surrounding the Salt Lake City Olympics threatened to irreparably harm the Olympic Movement. The Salt Lake City Organizing Committee was accused of bribing IOC officials with substantial gifts and money to influence the host city selection process. Subsequently, four IOC members and two Salt Lake City Organizing Committee officials were forced to resign. Corporate sponsors at the time, including Coca-Cola, John Hancock, UPS, Kodak, IBM, and Visa considered removing their support. Such a move would imperil the Olympic Games since several hundred million dollars of Games funding is supplied from corporate sponsorships. In 1999, the Australian Olympic Committee announced that $1.2 million had been paid to 11 African nations in 1993, just a few weeks prior to the 2000 Olympic site selection vote. Both events rocked the IOC and the Olympic Movement. As David d'Alessandro, CEO of John Hancock at the time, said,

> *The IOC's sponsorships have become radioactive. All corporate Geiger counters are going off the chart. They've got to find a way to make sponsorships safe again…If they fail to do that and something else comes up, the rings won't be tarnished, they'll be broken.*[8]

Lance Helgeson, senior editor of the IEG Sponsorship Report, echoed similar sentiments, "Make no mistake about it, the scandal and the flap surrounding it are not helping the Olympic brand."[9] Yet many sponsors focused on the historical legacy of the Olympics and the values represented by the Games. The scandal was seen as frustrating and disappointing, but it was viewed in the context of a short-term problem within an event that has thousands of years of positive contribution. Burke Stinson, a spokesman for AT&T, an Olympic sponsor at that time, said, "We've chosen to take the long view. It's an awkward time for the Games, and by inference the sponsors, but it's a time for sponsors to close ranks, not kick someone when they're down."[10] Ben Deutsch, spokesman for Coca-Cola, agreed,

[Coca-Cola]...isn't going to discard that relationship. This is a serious issue and a cause of great concern for us. But we've expressed our concerns to the organizing committees and the IOC, and we've been assured that they will take swift steps to bring the situation to a positive closure.[11]

The IOC either reprimanded or forced officials to resign, depending on their level of involvement. New ethics guidelines were adopted that prevent IOC members from visiting bid cities and accepting gifts over $150 in value. Juan Samaranch, president of the IOC at the time, was given a vote of confidence in 1999 by the IOC, clearing him of any wrongdoing. His tenure began in 1980 and he is widely credited for the growth of the Olympics and the dramatic increase in corporate sponsorships (he has also been criticized for overly-commercializing the modern Olympics). But when his term expired in 2001, he chose not to seek another term.[12]

Two factors have been identified as primary drivers that ultimately led to the corruption and bribery scandal. First, as the 1980s began, Olympic revenues grew dramatically, in part due to Juan Samaranch's efforts to reach out to corporate and commercial interests seeking their support of the Olympics. Second, the IOC was historically comprised of a wealthy club of lifelong members. In the 1980s, this began to change as the IOC sought a broader range of interests in its membership, many of whom did not have the same wealth as the original members. As broadcast interests grew around the world, so too did the revenues from broadcast partners. Some IOC members sought ways to increase their wealth. As the money flows increased further, the economic attractiveness to host cities grew. The stage had effectively been set for backroom deals between bid cities and select IOC members that ultimately led to the Salt Lake City scandal.[13]

Other types of less scandalous controversies impact perceptions of the Olympics as well. Michelle Kwan is one of the most successful figure skaters in United States history to not win gold medal, winning nine United States Championships, five World Championships, and two Olympic medals: a silver at the 1998 Nagano Olympics and a bronze at the 2002 Salt Lake City Olympics. In January 2006, *SportsBusiness Daily* conducted a poll of 200 sports executives and the results said she was the most marketable winter sports athlete. She had and still has a reputation for being an ideal athlete due to her clean image, enthusiastic personality, and famous smile. Michelle had an injury-plagued year in 2005, prior to the 2006 Turin Olympics, and was unable to compete in the United States Figure Skating Championships. Normally, this would prevent her, or any athlete, from making the Olympic team, but Michelle applied for a special waiver because of her medical situation. The United States Ladies Figure Skating Association approved the waiver as long as she could demonstrate to a special figure skating panel that she was physically capable of competing, which she successfully did. The skating panel's approval was both unorthodox and highly controversial. However, just prior to the start of the Olympics she withdrew due to yet another injury suffered during practice.[14] The accompanying media coverage was extensive, particularly in the United States. Part of the challenge was the impact on two of her key sponsors, Coca-Cola and Visa, both of which had created television commercials with her as a spotlighted athlete. Her withdrawal caused Coca-Cola to drop the TV commercial featuring her. Visa continued because there were several other athletes featured along with her in the advertisements, so Visa was less dependent on her image in that campaign.[15]

In the 2004 Athens Olympics, Brazilian marathoner Vanderlei de Lima, who was leading the race with four miles to go, was tackled by a spectator, surprising and shocking everyone watching. The incident slowed de Lima considerably, and he ended up winning the bronze. Fans who had been watching the event unfold on large screen monitors in the stadium were understandably horrified, and they cheered enthusiastically when de Lima entered the stadium in a show of affection and support. At the closing ceremony, de Lima was awarded the Pierre de Coubertin medal, the highest honor given to athletes who exemplify the Olympic spirit. As the IOC said at the time, "We decided to do this in recognition of de Lima's exceptional demonstration of fair play and Olympic values during this evening's marathon."[16]

David Masse, a media veteran of prior Olympic broadcasts, was asked why this particular event was repeatedly shown. Masse said, "Athletic accomplishments or a Michael Phelps are incredible but I think the world loves to see someone struggle against something even bigger than the other athletes, so maybe that's what this Brazilian athlete did."[17]

In early 2008, the athletic company Speedo was the center of controversy over the design of its Speedo LZR Racer swimsuit, introduced in February 2008. Over the first few weeks of its competitive use, 22 world records were set, compared to five in the same period prior to the 2004 Olympics in Athens. The world governing body for swimming, FINA (Fédération Internationale de Natation), ruled the suit legal in April 2008, setting controversy in motion. The Italian national team coach, Alberto Castagnetti, said that the Speedo LZR was akin to "technological doping." However, FINA's president, Mustapha Larfaoui, was thrilled swimming records were falling as athletes prepared for the Olympics. His concern was only that the same technology was available to everybody. This may be problematic given that many leading swimmers around the world are sponsored by Speedo rivals and do not have the same access. The final weeks leading up to the Olympics may clear up this situation, but it will certainly be a source of some controversy, irrespective of the outcome.[18]

An unfortunate side effect of many of these controversies is the negative brand associations, from the concept of a "French judge" describing any untrustworthy or corrupt judging practice to Salt Lake City as the "bribery tarnished Olympics," illustrating the hazards a negative brand reputation can have, no matter how unfair or exaggerated the claim may be. The impact on corporate sponsors is likely to be far less direct, but companies must pay attention to controversy related to the sports they sponsor and prepare a crisis communications plan should something overtly negative occur. In the run-up to the Beijing Olympics, the Tibet protests could have a detrimental impact on sponsors if they are deemed to be unresponsive to the controversy or if the situation escalates into increased violence during the Olympic Torch Relay or even during the Games. While the decision may seem deceptively simple to observers (i.e., cease the sponsorship), it involves unwinding extensive contractual relationships, eliminating jobs created to support the sponsorship, and harming relations among the various Olympic stakeholders (sponsors, suppliers, partners, customers, fans, athletes, the IOC), making the decision complex both socially and financially. On the other hand, a politically untenable situation may be so severe that the only sensible solution is stopping all sponsorship support immediately, despite the many ramifications. So far, such a severe outcome has not occurred, undoubtedly a by-product of the power of the Olympic brand to stand for something above typical controversies and, therefore, the public's support for keeping politics out of the Olympics whenever and wherever possible.

CHAPTER 11

Section III: Sponsorship Preparation Questions

The range of negative scenarios is quite broad and your response will depend entirely on the unique dynamics of the situation. The bribery scandals such as those of Sydney and Salt Lake City led to changes in IOC rules regarding member travel to bid cities, encouraged by collective sponsor actions and reactions. But during the unfolding of the revelations of an impending scandal is when companies need to pay particularly close attention to their handling of the crisis. The initial reactions to any crisis are obviously sharper, more intense, and more emotional than later, so the actions taken at the outset will determine whether a company can successfully navigate its way through.

Unexpected, Negative Surprises

1. Do you have a crisis management plan and team?
   a. Who is the main spokesperson?
   b. Are roles clearly understood?
   c. Have firm internal rules been established regarding who can and cannot speak to the media?
   d. Who or what is at risk?
   e. What is the plan for diffusing a crisis?
   f. Which outside groups need to be brought in and/or influenced?
   g. What actions would be taken? (Be as specific as possible.)
2. How do you want the company portrayed?
   a. Is your objective reasonable, practical, and realistic?

3. What is the worst-case impact of a crisis on your company?
    a. How much is at risk?
    b. Can it escalate?
    c. Who would be involved?
    d. What is the spill-over effect?
4. Do you have a plan for helping employees and/or victims deal with the negative surprise?
5. How will you monitor the situation?
6. Barring horrible physical tragedy or calamity, can this be turned into a positive over time?
    a. What is your plan for recovery?
7. What is the event's response to these questions?

IV

Winning Marketing Gold:
Work Like Crazy

CHAPTER 12

Sponsorships

Jerry Maguire, the name of Tom Cruise's character in the eponymous motion picture, shouted the now famous line "Show me the money!" capturing what many believe to be the stark reality of sports marketing today—that it is all about the money. Honor, glory, hard work, achievement, and winning have been replaced by multimillion-dollar product endorsements and corporate sponsorships as the primary goal of today's athletes. Yet as Jerry Maguire also showed, success at sports can and should be about far more than the money. One should not dwell too deeply on the philosophical implications of a Hollywood movie, but in this case, the story provides a useful lesson about determination and values. To be fair, the Olympics have evolved over the decades into a huge economic event for host cities, athletes, and sponsors. GE will generate about $600 million in revenue from sales of its products and services in support of the 2008 Beijing Olympics.[1] Each sponsor plans for the Olympics to improve its financial performance to a certain degree. Yet while the Olympics have certainly grown dramatically in size, scope, and financial power, driven by a more sophisticated funding model with corporate sponsorship at its core, the values associated with the Olympics remain vital to their appeal. The sense of competitive fair play, honor, and integrity are qualities athletes strive for, even if some fall short in the quest for glory. Just as controversy shines the spotlight of scrutiny on bad behavior and practices, it also stirs the calls for keeping the Olympics' centuries-old ideals firmly at the forefront and reminds the world that despite problems, the Olympics are still a force for good. To ensure the broadest possible representation of sports and nations and to keep Olympic values at the forefront of the public's collective imagination requires a professional funding model that can support less-financially stable nations while spreading the message of international goodwill.

Official Olympic Sponsorship

The IOC produces the Olympic Marketing Fact File, which contains a detailed breakdown of funding sources. There are six revenue-generating programs:

1. IOC-managed broadcast partnerships (discussed in Chapter 6)
2. The TOP partners sponsorship program (discussed starting on page 161)
3. IOC official supplier and licensing program (discussed starting on page 160)
4. Domestic sponsorship programs run by OCOGs (Organizing Committees for the Olympic Games) (discussed starting on page 157)
5. Ticketing programs in host country (discussed starting on page 159)
6. Licensing programs in host country (discussed starting on page 160)

Most of the analysis in this book is devoted to the TOP partners program due to the global coverage this program affords participating companies and the multifaceted marketing programs sponsors develop to leverage the investment, providing readers with insight into the inner workings of complex sports sponsorships. The revenue generated by domestic sponsorships is actually larger than that from TOP sponsors, but it involves several times as many companies and is beyond the scope of this analysis, although the lessons from both the TOP and domestic sponsorship programs are similar. A quick look at the revenue provided by the ticketing and licensing areas will be included to provide the complete context for the IOC funding model. Table 12-1 provides a breakdown of Olympic revenue sources since 1993.

Table 12-1
Olympic Marketing Revenue Sources[2]

Source	1993–96	1997–00	2001–04
Broadcast	US$1,251 mil	US$1,845 mil	US$2,232 mil
TOP program	US$279 mil	US$579 mil	US$663 mil
Domestic sponsorship	US$534 mil	US$655 mil	US$796 mil
Ticketing	US$451 mil	US$625 mil	US$411 mil
Licensing	US$115 mil	US$66 mil	US$87 mil
Total	**US$2,630 mil**	**US$3,770 mil**	**US$4,189 mil**

The IOC redistributes the revenue to the related Olympic Movement organizations, comprised of NOCs (National Olympic Committees), IFs (international federations), and the OCOGs. Of the total revenue generated, 8% is kept by the IOC to cover its operating costs and the remaining 92% is allocated to the NOCs/IFs/OCOGs.[3] The OCOGs are responsible for organizing the Games in their city and developing the sponsors from companies in their region. Table 12-2 provides an OCOG revenue breakdown for the Summer Olympics since 1996.

Domestic Sponsorship Revenues

An interesting trend to note from Table 12-2 is the decrease in the number of partners involved with the Summer Olympics since 1996. A possible, though not confirmed, explanation may be because of the widespread criticism of the overly commercial nature of the 1996 Atlanta Olympics—a claim seemingly reinforced by IOC President Juan Samaranch's closing ceremony remarks in which he did not say that the Games were "the best ever," wording that was considered a subtle slight against the Atlanta Games. This may have affected the way Sydney and Athens planned and selected domestic sponsorship partners for their respective Olympiads (although Sydney's efforts generated more dollars than Atlanta, the number of partners declinedby 18. The dollars per domestic sponsor rose, however, with each subsequent Summer Olympiad from US$3.8 million per sponsor in 1996 to nearly US$8 million in 2004).

Table 12-2
OCOG Sponsorship Programs—Summer Olympics
(since 1996)[4]

Olympic Games	Number of Partners*	Revenue and Support
1996 Atlanta	111	US$426 mil
2000 Sydney	93	US$492 mil
2004 Athens	38	US$302 mil

* *Domestic OCOG sponsorship programs usually encompass several tiers of partnership, which may include sponsors, suppliers, and providers. The figures in this column represent the total number of marketing partners from all tiers of the domestic program.*

Table 12-3 is similar to Table 12-2, but the figures are for the Winter Olympics since 1998.

Table 12-3
OCOG Sponsorship Programs—Winter
Olympics (since 1998)[5]

Olympic Games	Number of Partners*	Revenue & Support
1998 Nagano	26	US$163 mil
2002 Salt Lake City	53	US$494 mil
2006 Turin	57	US$348 mil

* *Same description as Summer Olympics in Table 12-2*

Interestingly, the number of Winter Olympics partners increased during this time, perhaps owing to the growth of the Winter Olympics, as discussed in Chapter 2: How the Olympics Make Us Feel. The dollars per domestic sponsor rose from $6.3 million at Nagano in 1998 to $9.3 million per sponsor at Salt Lake City in 2002, then dropped again to $6.1 million per sponsor in Turin in 2006. This is a result that has not been clearly examined, but could be due to challenges associated with each Winter host city's unique geographic limitations and/or the varied economic conditions for Winter Games cities.

Ticketing Revenues
Each OCOG is responsible for its own ticketing program, with guidance and support provided by the IOC. Ticketing revenues have grown significantly, as Tables 12-4 and 12-5 illustrate.

Table 12-4
Summary Olympics Ticketing Revenues (since 1984)[6]

Olympic Games	Tickets available	Tickets sold	% of tickets	Revenue to OCOG
1984 Los Angeles	6.9 mil	5.7 mil	82%	US$156 mil
1988 Seoul	4.4 mil	3.3 mil	75%	US$36 mil
1992 Barcelona	3.9 mil	3.021 mil	77%	US$79 mil
1996 Atlanta	11 mil	8.318 mil	75%	US$425 mil
2000 Sydney	7.6 mil	6.7 mil	88%	US$551 mil
2004 Athens	5.3 mil	3.8 mil	71%	US$228 mil

Table 12-5
Winter Olympics Ticketing Revenues (since 1988)[7]

Olympic Games	Tickets available	Tickets sold	% of tickets	Revenue to OCOG
1988 Calgary	1.9 mil	1.6 mil	84%	US$32 mil
1992 Albertville	1.2 mil	900,000	75%	US$32 mil
1994 Lillehammer	1.3 mil	1.207 mil	92%	US$26 mil
1998 Nagano	1.434 mil	1.275 mil	89%	US$74 mil
2002 Salt Lake City	1.605 mil	1.525 mil	95%	US$183 mil
2006 Turin	1.1 mil	900,000	81%	US$89 mil

Ticketing revenues are a function of Olympic location, proximity of venues, size of venues, transportation, and general destination appeal. Total tickets sold consistently average around 86% of the total available, providing Olympic organizing planners and sponsors with a reasonable indication of the number of visitors and, by extension, the potential economic impact. In turn, this general knowledge can assist sponsors as they finalize their location-specific marketing programs and determine financial allocations.

Licensing Revenues

Similar to ticketing, the OCOGs run their own licensing programs with guidance from the IOC. The philosophy is to support local branded companies, reflecting the domestic cultural and business practices of the host city and nation. Summer Olympics license revenues are shown in Table 12-6 and Winter Olympics license revenues in Table 12-7.

Table 12-6
Summer Olympics License Revenues (since 1988)[8]

Olympic Games	Licenses	Revenue to OCOG
1988 Seoul	62	US$18.8 mil
1992 Barcelona	61	US$17.2 mil
1996 Atlanta	125	US$91 mil
2000 Sydney	100	US$52 mil
2004 Athens	23	US$61.5 mil

The 1996 Atlanta Olympics saw a doubling of the number of licensees and a quadrupling of revenues over the preceding two Olympiads. The licensee numbers dropped significantly by Athens in 2004 (again, perhaps due to the overcommercialization effect from 1996), while the revenues per licensee climbed sharply.

Table 12-7
Winter Olympics License Revenues (since 1994)[9]

Olympic Games	Licenses	Revenue to OCOG
1994 Lillehammer	36	US$24 mil
1998 Nagano	190	US$14 mil
2002 Salt Lake City	70	US$25 mil
2006 Turin	32	US$22 mil

Nagano in 1998 was a busy Olympics with respect to the number of licensees. The dollars per licensee, however, were far lower than in

Lillehammer. Since Nagano, the licensing revenues have returned to their pre-Nagano levels and the number of licensees has returned to its Lillehammer level.

The Olympic revenue programs reviewed in this section provide a financial context for understanding the growth and maturation of the Olympic Movement funding model. As we saw in Table 12-1: Olympic Marketing Revenue Sources, the total revenues from all six programs have increased from $2.6 billion to nearly $4.2 billion since 1993. Domestic sponsorships grew 49% since 1993, a substantial increase. However, the single biggest revenue program change has been the significant growth of the TOP programme, which grew 137% during this time.

TOP Program Sponsorship

For marketers and their companies, success at sports marketing is more than just a chase for financial gold. While the investment for TOP (The Olympic Partners) program sponsors is substantial, many of these companies have been sponsors for several Olympics, generating financial returns and societal goodwill. Table 12-8 lists the twelve companies that comprise the TOP program partners, which is the most exclusive Olympic sponsorship level and the most expensive. Estimates suggest that these companies invest an average of $72 million just for the right to be a TOP sponsor, although several sources claim some sponsors paid as much as $100 million.[10] Another three to four times that amount is then spent by each TOP partner on media, creative, logistics, infrastructure, and similar investments to maximize its Olympic exposure.[11]

As TOP partners, companies have exclusive rights in their category to be the official sponsor for the Winter and Summer Olympics in each four-year period. The program is structured to provide unique benefits to each participating sponsor. These benefits include: [13]

- The rights to use Olympic imagery and identities
- Hospitality events at Olympic Games sites (tents, receptions, et al.)
- Direct marketing (advertising, promotions, broadcast)

Table 12-8
TOP Sponsors 2008 Olympic Games in Beijing[12]

Company	Sponsor start date
Kodak	Supported Olympics since 1896 (became TOP sponsor in 1986, its sponsorship will end following the 2008 Beijing Olympics).
Coca-Cola	Sponsor since 1928 (longest continuous sponsor).
Omega	Olympic relationship, sponsor, and/or official timekeeper since 1932.
McDonald's	Involved with Olympics since 1968; sponsor since 1976.
Panasonic	Started its Olympic involvement in 1984; sponsor since 1987.
Visa	Sponsor since 1986.
Samsung	Sponsor since 1997.
GE	Sponsor since 2003.
Lenovo	Sponsor since 2004 (its sponsorship will end following the 2008 Beijing Olympics).
Manulife	Sponsor since 2004 (Manulife merged with John Hancock Financial Services in 2004. John Hancock first became a U.S. Olympic Committee sponsor in 1993, then a TOP partner in 1994).
Atos Origin	Sponsor since 2002.
Johnson & Johnson	Sponsor since 2005.

- Product promotion opportunities
- Ambush marketing protection
- Regular support acknowledgment via IOC sponsorship PR

As the Olympics have grown, so too have the sponsorship revenues from TOP partners. Despite reported TOP program fee increases, the exclusive nature of the TOP program and the associated range of benefits, the most obvious of which is a vast global audience for seventeen consecutive days for the Olympics itself, continue to make this program attractive. Table 12-9 shows the revenues generated since the IOC introduced the TOP program, as well as the number of partners (corporate sponsors) and National Olympic Committees (NOCs):

Table 12-9
The Olympic Partner Program[14]

Quadrennial	Games	Partners	NOCs	Revenue
1985–1988	Calgary/Seoul	9	159	US$96 mil
1989–1992	Albertville/Barcelona	12	169	US$172 mil
1993–1996	Lillehammer/Atlanta	10	197	US$279 mil
1997–2000	Nagano/Sydney	11	199	US$579 mil
2001–2004	Salt Lake City/Athens	11	202	US$663 mil
2005–2008	Turin/Beijing	12	205	US$866 mil

Quick calculations show that the nine partners in the 1985–88 quadrennial paid approximately $10.7 million each for the right to be a TOP partner, and by the 2005–08 quadrennial the TOP fees were over $72 million each. Factor in three to four times additional investment in infrastructure, media, creative, and support, and the total TOP expenditure is close to $290 million per sponsor. According to the IOC, corporate sponsorships provide over 40% of the total Olympic marketing revenue. The IOC has also indicated that fewer than 30 of the more than 200 countries that participate in the Olympic

Games can afford to come to the Olympics if required to rely on their own funding, indicating the importance of corporate sponsorship support in ensuring both the continuity and broadest possible representation of countries at every Olympics. The revenues received from TOP partners are redistributed by the IOC to the NOCs and OCOGs as shown in Figure 12-1:

Figure 12-1
Redistribution of TOP Revenues[15]

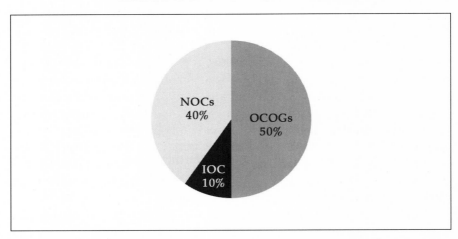

Given the substantial sums involved, a natural question is, "Is it worth it?" The answer depends on your company's objectives, plans, and implementation. It is tempting to calculate the ROI (return on investment) for the TOP investment, arriving at a figure and then deciding if that figure is attractive or not. But the decision to invest in being a TOP partner goes beyond merely measuring the investment return. Marketers must consider how their company fits in with the Olympic ideal. Why, then, do the 12 current TOP partners become sponsors in the first place (one could argue that Omega's long-standing relationship with the Olympics as an official timer involve it more directly in sports)? That is not to suggest that only companies whose products and services are in sports and fitness should be TOP sponsors, because clearly many of the sponsors do not fit this criterion. But part of the answer is simply that the Olympic audience is both large and diverse. Only two sports events command a truly global audience—the World Cup and the Olympics—and, arguably among these, the Olympics have a more universal appeal (despite the larger overall audience for the World Cup with a cumulative audience of over 26 billion,[16] it is not nearly as widely followed in the United States—the world's biggest consumer market—as it is in the rest of the world). Furthermore, recalling the lessons from the opening sections of this book, which discussed the history of the Olympic Games, marketers must pay heed to the traditions and imagery that shape the perceptions of the Olympics in the first place. Companies searching for a good match for their marketing investments may initially be persuaded to force-fit their marketing programs into the massive media effort surrounding the Olympics, thinking that any association with a recognized event would be good for their business. Such sloppy reasoning would be a mistake, and a waste of company resources. To determine whether a fit even exists, marketers must begin by conducting a brand audit of their own company and its traditions just as they review and scrutinize the important characteristics of the Olympics (or any event, for that matter). Many managers see branding as a narrow activity that focuses on creative design, logos, and slogans. But those represent only a small percentage of the overall brand-building effort.

Businesses must make money to survive. To thrive, businesses must build valuable brands. Brands act as a filter that helps consumers and businesses decide which products and companies they want to do business with. A recognized brand can and should be a competitive advantage, assuming your company has performed well over time and is respected. In my work with companies, both as an executive and through my academic research, four dimensions have been identified that help shape and determine a brand's total value. These dimensions will be familiar since some have been studied separately through both business and social-science research. The same themes keep recurring in the stronger companies my students and I study. Their combination encompasses the internal and external dimensions of a brand, a crucial distinction in recognizing the potential power of a well-conceived brand. They are:

Figure 12-2
Dimensions of Brand Value

Dimensions of Brand Value Descriptions
Financial
Businesses are practical organizational constructions, operating much like the human body. Feed it properly, invest in the right strength-building activities, set ambitious goals, and learn from failures as well as successes, and you can create long-term health and success. There are no shortcuts. Marketers must carefully weigh the programs they develop, from products to communications, to determine what is likely to help the business best grow and add real value. Real value is an important concept to understand because it has different meanings depending on the context. In branding, real value includes financially measurable gain. Classic accounting practice teaches us that the leftover assets we can't easily explain on a balance sheet are "goodwill," effectively a crude form of "brand." But business practices have grown in sophistication over the years, just as the components of value have changed over time. David Haigh, CEO of BrandFinance, a global brand consultancy, says that 63% of the value in today's companies is intangible, which is a significant change in corporate value from a few decades ago when 90% of corporate value was tied up in tangible assets (factories, inventory, etc).[17] This suggests that there is something more to business success than selling a product

for a profit. There are many methods for measuring brand value, and none of them are perfect. But they do shed light on the impact brand has on company value.

One of the most popular surveys of brand value is conducted by Interbrand (another brand consultancy). Each year, Interbrand publishes its "Top 100 Global Brands" survey in *BusinessWeek* magazine. These top 100 brands are based on financial value contributed by the brand, not popularity, market share, or awareness. In 2006's survey, Coca-Cola was the world's most valuable brand at just over $65 billion.[18] At the time, Coke's market capitalization was roughly $125 billion. Thus, Coke's brand value was more than 50% of the company's total value. In another survey, conducted by the global brand consultancy BrandFinance,[19] Coke's brand value was cited as just over $43 billion. While the $20+ billion differential between these two brand values may seem significant, this is due to calculation methodology. There is no universal method for determining brand value because the variables differ depending on your definition of brand (Is it a trademark? Is it goodwill? Is it a product? Is it the entire organization?) and whether you combine tangible and intangible assets. If intangibles are included, then value determination can get tricky (how does one value "leadership," or "reputation," for example? We know intrinsically that these are important, but precisely specifying a value involves judgment as well as hard facts). The key takeaway is that the size of brand value in Coke's case should impress you, because it means that a significant portion of Coke's total value is due to air. Not the kind we breathe, but the intangible concept of air, or vapor, or ether, or any other invisible ingredient. In other words, you cannot touch it, yet it has an enormous impact on the wealth of the enterprise. This is a troubling idea to many literalists and CFOs; however, many also recognize that brand is not just important, but vital to the success of the business. So when CFOs ask marketers to be more accountable and measure the performance of their marketing programs, marketers should pay attention.

The Olympic Games certainly have a high level of brand value. The tangible components, such as revenue streams from broadcast rights ($2,232 billion, or 53%), sponsorship (comprised of TOP and Domestic sponsors, total $1, 459 billion, or 35%), ticketing ($411 million, or 10%), and merchandise and licensing ($87 million, or 2%), total $4,189 billion.[20] Yet we know that the Olympics represent more than purely a commercial opportunity. In fact, the commercial success would not have been possible without the 2,700-year reputation of goodwill and competitive virtue that comprise the Olympic ideal. Calculating the intangible brand value of the Olympics presents challenges. But there is little doubt that the intangible value is significant.

Financial brand value is clearly important. But it would not be terribly useful or relevant without the other three components of value.

Trusted Reputation

Brands are a sign of trust. As consumers, we will not buy products from companies we do not trust, and as businesses we will not work with companies we do not trust (unless we are desperate or naive). To earn trust, however, requires that businesses engage in transparent practices that yield quality products. In fact, quality products are the minimum cost of entry into almost any market today because it is hard for any business to last long if its product is below average or of poor quality. Therefore, trust is developed and reinforced when companies surround their products with great service, support, warranties, innovation, compelling communications, and a host of other business benefits. As customers experience companies through their products, reputation, and service, trust is built further. A trusted reputation is never an end-point. There will never come a day when a company's leaders can say, "We have finally arrived and our trusted reputation will last forever." It is an ongoing effort that changes as customers, management, and societal expectations change.

Traditional marketing practices guided marketers to build good products that were reasonably priced, distributed through known channels, and worked when used, with trust strengthening throughout this sequence. If the products did not work as promised, consumers had to purchase another product, often from the same company, because only a limited number of competitors and channels existed. To borrow very loosely from Henry Ford, you can buy any product you want as long as it's ours (because we're all there is). Fast forward to today, with innumerable competitors offering high-quality products, and one can see that brand value is reinforced and enhanced when companies exceed the basics of a reasonably priced quality product by thinking through, planning, and offering an experience-based approach to inspiring customers. This means marketers must control as many of the elements of the customer's experience as they can. Fortunately, today's marketers have more tools at their disposal for developing relationships with customers, from traditional marketing to non-traditional (such as digital media). But the additional tools also mean there are many more variables to consider, so the complexity of building a trusted reputation has grown commensurately. But the benefit is that when trust is developed from multiple touchpoints in the customer's experience (pre-, during, and post-purchase phases), it becomes a more memorable and meaningful form of trust. People recognize when a company is working hard to earn their business and they demonstrate their appreciation through loyalty, enjoying the experience repeatedly. Of course, the onus is on the company to ensure the experience is as valuable every time the customer returns.

The trusted reputation of the Olympics has been achieved as a result of 2,700 years of experience encompassing thousands of athletic competitions and competitors, billions of fans, innumerable athletic achievements, and a set of values and principles that silently guide the entire Olympic Movement. Over time, more countries have been involved and the reputation has grown, although challenges have arisen along the way. Despite the challenges, the Olympic Dream is alive for billions of people around the world across cultures in over 200 countries and territories that share a common set of values and aspire to witness or be a part of sports success on a world stage.

Organizational

Organizational brand value, at its core, is about providing all employees in a company with a crystal-clear sense of the company's direction, as well as an ongoing reminder of the traditions that have made the firm successful over time. When company leadership describes its purpose and direction clearly and concisely, then there is a greater chance employees will view their efforts as connected to something important, as opposed to merely performing job-description tasks to earn a wage. Organizational brand value can be particularly powerful when employees feel that they are directly contributing to a cause that benefits customers and even society, as opposed to enhancing shareholder value, which is a financial abstraction relevant to a select few (typically the CEO, CFO, and shareholders). It is challenging to derive inspiration from an abstract concept such as enhancing shareholder value. However, this is not meant to imply that company leadership ought to tell employees to focus on enhancing brand value, as that would be another relatively meaningless abstraction.

Instead, direction from company leaders ought to reflect the investment made in attracting talent that reinforces competencies and reputations for which the company is known. For example, talented engineers at Apple know they are working for a company driven by a larger purpose—to make, as Steve Jobs has said, insanely great products that improve their customers' lifestyle. When a company develops this sense of purpose (or cause, or mission), then it simply feels different inside, somehow more satisfying. And developing strong organizational brand value can help companies deliver on the promises they make to the market, partly because everyone within the company understands their role more clearly and sees how they fit in.

This concept of organizational brand value is easily seen when watching successful sports teams comprised of a collection of talented people with different skills working collectively to win. There is a magical chemistry from which the players feed, and this goes beyond their individual abilities. The management of Real Madrid, the famous Spanish football club, states that since the club's very early days, over a century ago, the organization has always stood for being "a champion and a gentleman."[21] Real Madrid has enjoyed remarkable success during its 100 years of existence, and part of the reason is that its version of organizational brand value describes an ideal, and not a specific number of league championships. Instead, they state the values for which they stand, and if the organization follows its "champion and gentleman" guideline, then the people they recruit, from players to management, should reflect these qualities and lead the team to a consistently high performance over time, which in fact they have.

Organizational brand value for the Olympics is wrapped around the entire Olympic Movement, from the formal structures represented by the IOC and the various other Olympic committees to the dozens of partnerships with companies and host cities. It is a dispersed and diverse collection of interdependent people working toward a common goal: to bring the joy and spirit of pure athletic competition to the world through the unique event called the Olympic Games. While that may sound a bit highbrow, it is hard to imagine the organizational brand value of the Olympics being anything else. If the Olympics were to be more overtly positioned as a revenue-generating commercial enterprise and the IOC organized like a company, for example, then they would lose much of their magic and appeal. We view the Olympics as above typical societal structures and activities, elevating the Games from the mundane to the extraordinary. We want the IOC to champion the Olympic ideal and stand for the very best in human nature. Put more crudely, the organizational brand value is really a straightforward exercise in not screwing up what thousands of years of tradition have built, and each generation of the Olympic Movement's organizers must ensure integrity remains intact. This may sound simple, but as this book points out, challenges regularly confront the Olympic ideal in the form of scandals, unsportsmanlike conduct, and the pressure toward more commercialization.

Societal Relevance

For companies to be successful, they have to be perceived as offering something of value to society collectively and members within individually. After all, why would we want something we do not see as valuable in some way? Societal value alone is not enough, however. True societal value means that any product or service must be relevant to those who want it. Relevance is not a tricky concept, nor is it loaded with hidden meaning. It simply describes an offering as something you and I want and/or need. This is common sense, or at least it should be. Marketers need to translate this common sense into specific solutions (i.e., products or services) that are appealing, both to individual consumers and other businesses.

As we know, humans are social creatures and we gain our sense of identity from the way we see ourselves and how others see us. As consumers, we tend to buy products and services that are relevant to our interests and reflect our values (in other words, we buy things

171

not just because we think we need, but because they reinforce our identity). Doing so makes us feel good, partly because we see the products we are buying as a reflection of who we are. As the world globalizes and a wide range of challenging issues confront us beyond our individual needs, such as threats to our way of life and/or the stability of the society in which we live, we increasingly evaluate companies based not just on whether their products fit our lifestyle, but also on whether the companies themselves are good corporate citizens and, in some form or fashion, are actively and visibly participating in developing solutions to societal problems. A company may have products we love, such as Starbucks coffee, but many customers would not continue buying Starbucks products if the company stopped selling fair-trade coffee.[22] Boeing's 787 Dreamliner is intended to be a more economical (for airlines) and environmentally friendly aircraft design, with its unique composite materials. The hope is that we, as airline travelers, will see Boeing more favorably and would also seek out routes and airlines featuring the 787. Virgin Airways' efforts to test cleaner-burning, biofueled commercial airliners reflect Richard Branson's efforts to reduce dependency on traditional fuel, although there is some controversy that biofuels may create another problem (accelerated deforestation to grow specific biofuel crops).

Thus, for businesses, societal relevance is defined by the company's efforts to get involved in the communities it serves, or even society at large. This goes beyond donating money. To be viewed through the lens of societal relevance, companies must be actively engaged in society, from charitable organizations to church groups to school programs to sports teams to environmental issues. Such efforts are called corporate social responsibility (CSR), although the term is sometimes seen cynically as companies pretending to be concerned about society as a cover to hide their profit-driven ambitions. CSR has grown because people around the world are learning that many of the business practices of the past 100 years, while yielding growth and higher standards of living for many countries, have also led to significant environmental problems. Company leaders are paying closer attention to the CSR practices of their network of suppliers, distributors, and similar business partners, in addition to their own firm's efforts. Such efforts are becoming a far more important factor in determining successful business performance, well beyond basic financial results.

For the Olympics, societal relevance relates to the inspiration we derive from watching top athletes compete and the corresponding message implied by athletic success: you can achieve anything if you work hard enough. We may never be an Olympic athlete, but we can be world-class in anything we choose to do.

It is against this backdrop of the dimensions of brand value that the decision to invest over $200 million dollars must be weighed and the opportunity costs assessed. Olympic sponsorship requires an enormous financial commitment that can easily be invested in a wide range of marketing activities that benefit the brand without having to concentrate them on a single event such as the Olympics.

To illustrate the folly of incautious sports marketing investments, consider the 2000 Super Bowl game in the United States (the most widely-watched sporting event in the U.S. with between 90 and 130 million fans tuning in each year).[23] The period of the late 1990s leading up to the 2000 Super Bowl are better known as the dot.com era, when it seemed any entrepreneur could make money doing anything and common sense was temporarily suspended. Over a dozen Internet companies spent $40+ million collectively for 30-second television commercials during the 2000 Super Bowl game (the average 30 second Super Bowl TV commercial that year cost $2.2 million). The ads covered a wide range of topics and companies, from Pets.com's infamous sock puppet to E*Trade Financial's bizarre dancing chimpanzee. Most of those companies are no longer in business today (E*Trade is one of the remaining few still around, although at the time of writing E*Trade was facing challenges due to large investments in complex bonds tied to the troubled mortgage market[24]) and many went out of business within a year of airing these ads. One of the firms, OurBeginning.com, which specialized in online wedding-invitation design, spent more than $4 million on their Super Bowl ads,[25] an amount several times larger than its actual revenues. The common rationale? The dot.coms saw the Super Bowl as a rare and unique event that could serve as a singular platform to market their company. The problems with such naive reasoning are obvious and serve as a vivid reminder to companies that their marketing investments ought to be considered and planned with the same rigorous attention applied to R&D budgets, corporate strategic plans, and new product launches, with a keen eye on the long-term potential for developing value and a lasting brand, not just a short-term spike in awareness and sales.

Beyond the four elements of brand value just discussed, the diversity of Olympic sports attracts an equally diverse fan base and one can easily understand why the Olympics are a particularly attractive marketing opportunity for those companies with the financial wherewithal to participate. The temptation to be avoided is assuming a large audience equates to a good business opportunity. Developing awareness is important, but translating that awareness into measurable financial improvement in the short-term is far harder to achieve. Large-scale events such as the Olympics are useful marketing opportunities if companies recognize that a critical determinant of marketing success is based on intentionally planning and expecting a longer-term horizon to achieve positive results. Traditional promotions-based marketing in which a specific offer is made to a target audience may spike short-term sales, but such an approach may not work with fans of the Olympics. Part of the reason is that Olympic audiences are involved more in the athletic contests and are less interested in being sold products, as the blatant commercialism detracts from the Olympic appeal. Less direct appeals, while still intended to create a positive impression with audiences, do not intrude as overtly into the fans experience watching the sports. However, this simplifies the marketing activities. To make the Olympics sponsorship investment useful, marketers must approach it as they would any other marketing effort: understand the different audiences, identify their needs, create programs that appeal to their interests, and deliver and vary the message based on the marketing vehicle used. The benefits in awareness alone can be significant. Figure 12-3 is based on a survey conducted by The Ogilvy Group. Conducted for the 2004 Olympics, 100 Athens residents between the ages of 18 and 65 were asked about their awareness of companies. Ogilvy said that "official sponsors ranked the highest, especially those with long-lasting marketing communication activities prior to and during the games."

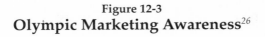

Figure 12-3
Olympic Marketing Awareness[26]

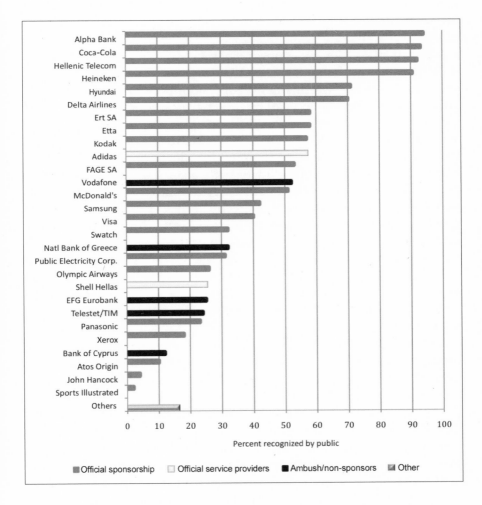

We will examine four TOP program sponsors in particular, selected because each has been involved with the Olympics for a different length of time, and each has different strategic intentions and tactical implementations:

- **Coca-Cola:** Olympic sponsor since 1928
- **Visa:** Olympic sponsor since 1986
- **John Hancock/Manulife:** Olympic sponsor since 1994
- **Lenovo:** Olympic sponsor since 2004

Case Brief: Coca-Cola

In April 2008, at the annual shareholder meeting, a member of the audience asked Neville Isdell, CEO of Coca-Cola, "Will you tell the IOC to stop taking the Olympic Torch Relay into Tibet, because Tibet belongs to Tibetans?" Isdell responded, "The torch relay has symbolized openness, it has symbolized hopes. I don't believe that stopping the torch run is in any way over the long-term going to be the right thing to do."[27]

Needless to say, Olympic TOP sponsors face controversial issues and protests regularly at the Olympics. In Coca-Cola's case, China is an important market, with first quarter 2008 results showing a 20% increase in unit case volume sales in the country and a 19% increase in net income to $1.5 billion. Approximately 5% of Coca-Cola's revenue is from China. Case unit sales are estimated to grow another 40% in 2008. Sponsoring the Beijing Olympics would seem to be good business.[28]

But Coca-Cola has been supporting the Olympics far longer than just in 2008. In fact, Coca-Cola has the longest continuous sponsorship relationship with the Olympics, having first been associated with the Games in 1928. While there is little question the company's decision to sponsor the Games is significantly influenced by conventional corporate financial objectives to grow market share and increase revenues and profits, there has also been historical strong management emphasis in building a company that is a responsible corporate citizen.

The Olympic Games are filled with symbolism and Coca-Cola is well aware of this fact. As an iconic American brand with a well-known global reputation, Coca-Cola works hard to keep its brand associated with positive lifestyle values and images. In 2005, Coca-Cola agreed to continue sponsoring the Olympics until 2020, which will make the relationship at that time 92 years old,[29] one of the longest-running corporate marketing programs in the world. The announcement of the sponsorship extension occurred at the Great Wall of China and included Jean-Claude Killy of France, winner of three gold medals in skiing in 1968, and Wu Min Xia, a Chinese diver who won a gold and silver medal at the 2004 Athens Olympics.[30] The symbolism surrounding the announcement was important in a key way: it connected the rich traditions of the past with the promise of the future. Holding it at the Great Wall echoed China's, and the Olympics', shared multi-thousand year histories while sparking interest in the 2008 Games, and also reminding the public of Coca-Cola's long-standing commitment to the Olympic Movement. The attendance of Jean-Claude Killy and Wu Min Xia brought wisdom together with youth, underscoring two key themes of the Beijing Olympics while simultaneously associating Coca-Cola with these same characteristics.

Coca-Cola's commitment to this marketing effort underscores the potential for substantial long-term gain for company management teams interested in building sustainable value. As one of the most recognized and successful consumer brands in the world with the highest brand value of all companies (in 2007, BrandFinance valued Coca-Cola at $43 billion; Interbrand valued Coca-Cola at $65 billion)[31] and vast global distribution plus loyal consumers, a reasonable question might be why Coca-Cola would want or need to invest the sizable sums required to be a TOP sponsor. One could argue that the money might be more effectively invested in research and development, or acquisitions, or vertical/horizontal integration.

One of the reasons for Coke's extraordinary brand success over time is the care and attention paid to building the company's brand equity. In March 2008, Coca-Cola's balance sheet indicated the value of the company' assets to be US$43.27 billion (this includes short-term assets like cash, syrup and other inventories and long-term assets like plant and equipment). At the same time, its market capitalization was $140.3 billion, indicating a significantly favorable investor premium, much of which is attributable to brand value. If Coke were focused merely on selling caramel-flavored, carbonated sugar water, then it is likely the consumer interest would be diminished, as would investor interest and, ultimately, brand value. Instead, Coca-Cola has been a rigorous brand builder over the decades, choosing to associate its name and trademark products with consumer lifestyles, creating strong consumer loyalty and powerful brand imagery in the process. Over the past 100 years, Coke has honed a solid, virtually unchanged reputation (with the exception of the well-known "New Coke" debacle of the 1980s) as a representative icon of American values. As the U.S. economy expanded in the twentieth century, particularly after World War II, so did Coca-Cola. A defining characteristic of this expansion was the company's use of imagery in promoting its namesake flagship cola beverage. People, from everyday consumers to the military to famous stars, were pictured enjoying themselves and their lives, sending a positive, uplifting message that consumers found appealing. With the Olympics enjoying a similar reputation for celebrating life, Coke's ongoing Olympic support seems, in retrospect, a natural fit and a logical brand association.

In describing its sponsorship of the Olympic Games, Coca-Cola states that part of the rationale is that the company's values are similar to those of the Olympics, "…which embody the discovery of one's abilities, the spirit of competition, the pursuit of excellence, a sense of fair play, and the building of a better and more peaceful world."[32]

Certainly many companies would assert similar sentiments. Indeed, declaring these values is important for putting a stake in the ground and saying "this is what we stand for." Coca-Cola's sponsorship undertakings strongly suggest a genuine commitment to bringing the company's values to life, beyond words on paper.

Coca-Cola's Olympic Sponsorship Activities

To take advantage of this unrivaled sports event, Coke has engaged in a wide range of marketing activities designed to promote the positive brand values the company represents. With direct involvement in every Olympic Games since 1928, Coca-Cola has used the Olympic sponsorship to broaden the company's appeal through innovative programs, direct athlete and team support, fan contests, and digital media, as well as more traditional marketing programs using print and broadcast media. The company's example is more about marketing innovation that leads to long-term brand value than it is about short-term sales increases. Coca-Cola takes advantage of the Olympics' emotional appeal by using imagery and promotions designed to convey vitality and imagination. Indeed, Coca-Cola has been deeply involved in more than just the commercial aspects of sponsorship. The company was involved in CSR through its Olympics relationship long before CSR became fashionable for companies to pursue. Historically, and through present times, the company has been keenly aware of the increasing emphasis consumers, government organizations, community groups, and society overall place on corporate responsibility. Each of Coca-Cola's Olympic sponsorship activities, represented in Figure 12-4, are closely tied with the company's own values and, as company management believes, those of the Olympics.[33]

Figure 12-4
Coca-Cola Olympic Sponsorship Activities

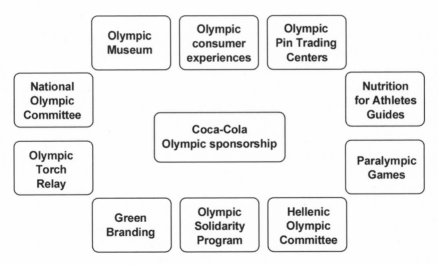

Olympic Torch Relay
The carrying of the Olympic flame in modern times started in 1928 and it took several decades for it to evolve into the transcontinental event involving thousands of runners from around the world that we know today. The Olympic flame symbolizes the ancient Greek tradition of keeping a flame or fire burning throughout the duration

of each Olympiad. The relay promotes each forthcoming Olympic Games, and by carrying the torch through multiple countries, the IOC hopes it helps connect people emotionally with the spirit of the Olympics. The torch relay is a powerful and symbolic event that not only attracts the public, but also draws the attention of protestors that see the flame as a visible means to use the surrounding media coverage to raise awareness of their cause. Coca-Cola began sponsoring the Olympic Torch Relay at the 1992 Barcelona Olympics, and the 2008 Olympic Torch Relay (ironically called the "Journey of Harmony," given the accompanying Tibetan protests) will be Coca-Cola's sixth. Coke and the other Olympic Torch Relay sponsors (Lenovo and Samsung in 2008) each pay an additional fee of $5–$15 million, separate from the TOP sponsorship fee. The company's sponsorship of the Olympic Torch Relay provides a memorable opportunity to create awareness not just for the Games, but for the corporate sponsors as well.[34]

Green Branding

The 2008 Beijing Olympics are an important, indeed pivotal, milestone for China. Rapid economic growth has given the country confidence, and the Olympics are seen within China as a chance to show the world that the country has arrived as a formidable global player. Part of the country's efforts has included the construction of iconic Olympic venues that blend ancient Chinese traditions with modern design and state-of-the-art facilities. The Beijing National Stadium is the site of many of the Olympics main events. Also known as the "Bird's Nest" stadium for its unusual steel framing that resembles the structure of a bird's nest, the stadium used an enormous amount of steel in its construction, some of which remained unused. Coke will be using some of the unused steel to create Coca-Cola-branded Olympic trading pins. The benefits are straightforward: the pins reduce the amount of leftover steel by putting it to use, while also creating memorable souvenirs that promote both the Olympics and Coca-Cola. As Table 12-10 later in this section illustrates, Coke developed its first Olympic trading pin for the 1980 Winter Olympics in Lake Placid. In 1988, the company established the Olympic Pin Trading Center, which has been a regular component of Coca-Cola's Olympic sponsorships ever since. These centers have been popular with fans, both those who collect trading pins and those seeking a keepsake of their Olympic visit. And with global concern over environmental issues, repurposing the unused stadium steel matches well with society's needs today while also continuing Coke's long-standing commitment to being a responsible corporate citizen.

Support for the Hellenic Olympic Committee

Aside from its substantial TOP program participation, Coke announced in October 2007 that it would donate $2 million to the Hellenic Olympic Committee to aid in restoring ancient Olympia, the historic Olympic site. The summer of 2007 brought devastating fires to this area that Coke's donation, along with other contributors, will help repair and restore.

Minos Kyriakou, president of the Hellenic Olympic Committee, said, "We cordially congratulate The Coca-Cola Company for its significant initiative and thank the Company and its employees for always demonstrating their commitment to the Olympic values and ideals."[35]

Support for National Olympic Committees (NOCs)

An important piece of Coca-Cola's Olympic sponsorship is its support for over 200 NOCs around the world. One of the challenges for world-class athletes with the ambition to compete in the Olympics is finding the resources to support their training, and Coca-Cola's sponsorship money (and that of other sponsors) helps support these needs. These resources include:

- Finding proper coaching
- Using the latest approved equipment
- Traveling to and from domestic and international competitions, plus food and accommodation expenses
- Paying competition registration fees

Although many athletes have lucrative endorsement contracts and related support deals, most do not. Consequently, this funding is vital to ensuring athletes have an opportunity to compete in the Olympics.

Olympic Solidarity Program

The Olympic Solidarity Program was started by the IOC in 1983 and a portion of Coca-Cola's sponsorship money funds this program. The funds support training programs for each NOC as well as scholarships for athletes. In addition, this program helps fund the construction of sports facilities and related infrastructure in NOC countries, particularly those ravaged by war. Academic programs devoted to understanding the Olympic Movement and how to host and execute successful sports events provide NOCs with vital knowledge and skills-building insights that can benefit countries for years following an Olympic Games.

Olympic Consumer Experiences

Coca-Cola markets and sells its products at the Olympics, which is to be expected given its business. But the consumer products are one dimension of the consumer experience. Coca-Cola has regularly run promotions that give away free tickets to fans around the world in an effort to connect consumers more directly with the Olympic Games. This effort has included tours of the Olympic Village; meet and greet sessions with athletes; and special Coca-Cola Olympic fan centers designed to provide fans a place to rest, have refreshments, and watch live coverage of the Olympics. Large-scale exhibits such as the Coca-Cola Olympic City at the 1996 Atlanta Olympics (an interactive venue adjacent to the Olympics); Coca-Cola RedFest Celebrations at the 2000 Sydney Olympics (featuring live, big-screen broadcasts of the Games, plus live music, entertainment, food, and dancing); Powerade-Aquarius Training Camp in Sydney (behind-the-scenes tours designed for teens); Coca-Cola "On the Ice" at the 2002 Winter Olympics in Salt Lake City (including winter sports simulations, luge course, and hockey rink); Coca-Cola Live multimedia shows; and Coca-Cola "O.N. Air in Athens" at the 2004 Olympics (featuring themed entertainment, music, and live sports reporting) are all created to directly engage and involve spectators and consumers in the energetic atmosphere of the Olympics while also reminding the public that Coca-Cola was the company that made this possible.

Olympic Museum

Coca-Cola sponsors the Olympic Museum in Lausanne, Switzerland, a facility devoted to Olympic history. Coke was the first sponsor of the museum, donating $1 million in 1987. Coke's early involvement in this museum reflects another dimension to the company's community involvement, providing the company with a more substantial link to the Olympics than just that of sponsor.

"Nutrition for Athletes" Guide
Coca-Cola's Powerade sports drink co-published this guide with the IOC. Within the guide is information about the important connection between fitness and proper nutrition. This guide has the benefit of reminding the market that Coca-Cola produces more than just cola beverages—it makes products the world's leading athletes use to enhance their competitive performance and training.

Paralympic Games
In another display of CSR and concern for the communities it serves, Coca-Cola has also sponsored the Paralympics, which follow the Olympic Games in each host city.

Companies today are increasingly expected to be engaged, supportive, and active members of society at large as well as of their local communities. The public wants companies to demonstrate their commitment to the greater good, beyond the creation of profits and wealth for a few. Coca-Cola has long seen itself as a responsible corporate citizen, and the broad set of programs it rolls out for each Olympic Games is a purposeful, and very public, demonstration of its values and illustrates that the company is serious about its role in the world as a company that offers more than a famous beverage.

Coca-Cola's Olympic sponsorship is a key part of a broad-based effort to connect with the lives of consumers. As the Table 12-10 illustrates, Coke has evolved and expanded its Olympic sponsorship activities to ensure that the company stays relevant to consumers. Through the Olympics, Coke has been able to extend the brand's presence in both tangible ways, through the introduction and sale of products, including giveaways and new launches, Olympic Pin Trading Centers, and interactive exhibits in Olympic venues; and intangible ways, through support of the Olympic Torch Relay, the Olympic Solidarity Program, and extensive consumer-experience touchpoints designed to foster strong emotional ties. While these activities could be implemented independent of the Olympics, the

Games provide a unique occasion to focus brand-building activities around an event that exudes the positive, uplifting lifestyle values Coca-Cola believes its consumers associate with the company.

Each of Coca-Cola's marketing activities directly serves the company's desire to bring people closer to the Olympics. With the Games representing peace among nations and competitive goodwill, Coca-Cola has had 80 years of Olympic association that has benefited the company's image, brand reputation, and product sales. Over the years as the Olympics have changed and grown, so too has Coca-Cola.[36]

Table 12-10 describes Olympic Games' highlights from each of the Games sponsored by Coke. The Olympic highlights provide a brief context and backdrop for each of the Olympics. Selected Coke sponsorship activities are shown alongside the year they were implemented. Note that the company started formal involvement with the Winter Olympics beginning in 1952 at the Games in Oslo, skipped the 1956 Winter Olympics in Cortina d'Ampezzo, Italy, and then renewed its involvement at the 1960 Winter Olympics at Squaw Valley, U.S.

Table 12-10
Coca-Cola and Olympics Partnership Highlights[37]

Olympics	Context	Coca-Cola Sponsorship Highlights
1928 Summer Olympics in Amsterdam	• 46 nations competed • 14 sports • 109 events • 2,883 athletes (277 women) • Gold medals were won by athletes from 28 different countries, a record that lasted until 1968 • First Olympics with competitions for women in track and field • Lighting of Olympic flame tradition was reintroduced, following tradition of ancient Greek Olympics	• Coke's first Olympic Games • 1,000 cases of Coke delivered to U.S. Olympic team • Coke sold at kiosks located throughout Olympic venues • No formal advertising or promotion used • Lighting of Olympic flame tradition was reintroduced, following tradition of ancient Greek Olympics

Table 12-10 continued

Olympics	Context	Coca-Cola Sponsorship Highlights
1932 Summer Olympics in Los Angeles	• 37 nations competed • 14 sports • 117 events • 1,332 athletes (126 women) • Number of athletes was lower due to Great Depression • 18 world records tied or beaten • A record 100,000 people attended opening ceremony • First Olympics to turn big profit, $1 million	• Coke gave away a personal record keeper that allowed fans to compare athlete performances to Olympic records • 3 million miniature sports-action cutouts, featuring Olympic records on the backs were given out across the U.S. • Coke was endorsed by former gold medal-winning swimmer Johnny Weissmuller in 1934
1936 Summer Olympics in Berlin	• 49 nations competed • 19 sports • 129 events • 3,963 athletes (331 women) • Hitler hoped Olympics would prove Aryan superiority; this failed in face of Jesse Owens' dramatic gold medals in four events • First Olympics on TV (shown on screens around Berlin) • Introduction of torch relay	• J. Paul Austin, a competitor on the U.S. rowing team, became Coke's CEO and Chairman in 1960s and 1970s
1948 Summer Olympics in London	• 59 nations competed • 17 sports • 136 events • 4,104 athletes (390 women) • First post-war Olympics • Limited financing resulted in athletes being housed in schoolrooms and army camps • First Olympics shown on home TV	• Coke shipped equipment from Scotland and Ireland to ensure the beverage could be consumed by Olympic fans and competitors • Coke logo appeared on official Olympics posters

Table 12-10 continued

Olympics	Context	Coca-Cola Sponsorship Highlights
1952 Winter Olympics in Oslo	• 30 nations competed • 4 sports • 22 events • 694 athletes (109 women) • Norway considered birthplace of modern skiing • Olympic flame lit in home of Sondre Nordheim, first famous international skier, who died in 1897 and relay-skied to Oslo with 94 skiers	• Coke used a helicopter to help in fundraising for Norwegian athletes; it was also used to direct traffic
1952 Summer Olympics in Helsinki	• 69 nations competed • 17 sports • 149 events • 4,955 athletes (518 women) • Soviet Union compete for first time, and its women's gymnastics team won team gold, starting 40-year winning streak • Considered one of the most well-organized Olympics ever	• 30,000 cases of Coca-Cola shipped to Olympics in "Operation Muscle" • Coke donated most of its product to benefit Disabled Ex-Servicemen Association • Coke printed daily menus for athletes • Sacks and cooler bags with Coke logos were distributed
1956 Summer Olympics in Melbourne	• 72 nations competed • 17 sports • 145 events • 3,314 athletes (376 women) • First Olympics in southern hemisphere • 2 boycotts: Egypt, Iraq, Lebanon protested at Israeli invasion of Suez; Netherlands, Spain, Switzerland protested at Soviet invasion of Hungary	• Coke distribute 100,000 trademarked visors • 420 vendors distributed and sold Coke products • Coke ran newspaper ads with an offer to attend Olympics

Table 12-10 continued

Olympics	Context	Coca-Cola Sponsorship Highlights
	• East and West Germany entered combined team that continued for two more Olympiads • Equestrian events were held in Stockholm, Sweden due to strict quarantine laws in Australia	
1960 Winter Olympics in Squaw Valley	• 30 nations competed • 4 sports • 27 events • 665 athletes (144 women) • Bobsledding not included because only 9 nations said they would compete in this event • Walt Disney was in charge of opening and closing ceremonies pageantry	• Coke introduce 12-ounce can for first time
1960 Summer Olympics in Rome	• 83 nations competed • 17 sports • 150 events • 5,338 athletes (611 women) • Wrestling events held in Basilica of Maxentius, historic locale of competitions from 2,000 years earlier • Pope watched rowing from window of his summer residence	• Local Coke bottlers were actively involved in supporting the Games, making thousands of 45-rpm recordings of "Arrivederci Roma" and giving them away to fans, athletes, media
1964 Winter Olympics in Innsbruck	• 36 nations competed • 6 sports • 34 events • 1,091 athletes (199 women) • Crisis initially due to lack of snow; Austrian army carved 20,000 ice bricks	• Coke published Olympic Games history, distributed to fans, athletes, media

Table 12-10 continued

Olympics	Context	Coca-Cola Sponsorship Highlights
	from nearby mountains and used them in bobsled and luge course. Army transported 40,000 cubic meters of snow to ski runs.	
1964 Summer Olympics in Tokyo	• 93 nations competed • 19 sports • 163 events • 5,151 athletes (678 women) • First Olympics held in Asia • Yoshinori Sakai, born in Hiroshima on day atomic bomb was dropped, was torch bearer • South Africa banned due to racial policies • IOC suspended Indonesia due to that country's refusal to allow athletes from Israel and Taiwan to compete in 1962 Asian Games in Jakarta	• Coke produced street signs, tourist information, guide maps, and a Japanese-English phrase book. These innovations inspired similiar offerings at the 1968 Mexico city, 1972 Munich 1972 Sapporo, and 1998 Nagano Olympic Games.
1968 Winter Olympics in Grenoble	• 37 nations competed • 6 sports • 35 events • 1,158 athletes (211 women) • First Winter Games with sex testing for women	• Coke co-sponsored ABC-TV Olympic broadcasts with other corporations
1968 Summer Olympics in Mexico City	• 112 nations competed • 20 sports • 172 events • 5,516 athletes (781 women) • Mexico City's selection was controversial due to the city's high altitude (2,300 meters above sea level), the air had 30% less oxygen as result • Many long-distance	• Coke dispensed from specially designed backpacks worn by servers who roamed the venues • Coke sponsored national TV coverage again—first time the company had sponsored national TV broadcasts of both the Winter and Summer Games in the same Olympic quadrennial

Table 12-10 continued

Olympics	Context	Coca-Cola Sponsorship Highlights
	events had slower times, collapsed athletes • Many short-distance events set world records • First Summer Games with sex testing for women	• Olympic-themed TV commercials by Coca-Cola featuring 1960 gold-medal swimmer Lynn Burke
1972 Summer Olympics in Munich	• 121 nations competed • 23 sports • 195 events • 7,134 athletes (1,059 women) • Olympics' first 10 days were successful, then tragedy: Palestinian terrorists took the Israeli team and coaches hostage, demanding the release of 200 prisoners in Israeli prisons. Two Israelis were killed initially. Battle between West German sharp-shooters and terrorists led to deaths of five terrorists and all members of Israeli team. Memorial service held in Olympic stadium, then competition resumed 34 hours later.	• Coca-Cola ran the food and beverage operation that supported all athletes, coaches, and officials • Coke created 17 commemorative medallions of "Great Olympic Moments." Proceeds donated to U.S. Olympic Committee.
1976 Winter Olympics in Innsbruck	• 37 nations competed • 6 sports • 37 events • 1,123 athletes (231 women) • Denver, Colorado was selected as host city in 1970, but voters rejected this for cost and environmental reasons. Innsbruck ultimately volunteered to host the games as a result.	• Coke produced a feature film entitled "Olympic Harmony" to celebrate the Winter Games

Table 12-10 continued

Olympics	Context	Coca-Cola Sponsorship Highlights
1976 Summer Olympics in Montreal	• Noticeably tightened security at all Olympic facilities following Munich tragedy, a practice continued at every subsequent Olympics • 92 nations competed • 21 sports • 198 events • 6,084 athletes (1,246 women) • Corruption and poor planning led to massive budget overruns, but the Games ran smoothly overall • 22 African nations boycotted due to New Zealand national rugby team tour of South Africa	• Coca-Cola bought the famous horse "Regardez" and donated it to the Canadian equestrian team

1980 Winter Olympics in Lake Placid	• 37 nations competed
	• 6 sports
	• 38 events
	• 1,072 athletes (232 women)
	• 6,703 volunteers
	• Number of media unknown
	• Second time Lake Placid hosted Winter Olympics (first was 1932)
	• Poorly run Olympics due to erratic transportation that stranded fans and prevented them access to tickets
	• IOC ordered Taiwan to use "Taiwan" name, not "The Republic of China" as had been used in years past. The IOC hoped to convince China to participate.
		• Coke raised money for the USOC through a national fund-raising tour that included a skating robot called "Kobot"
		• Launched the Coca-Cola Olympic Radio Network, announcing event results to fans
		• New promotional goods developed for these Games, including:
		  • Commemorative bottles
		  • Apparel with Lake Placid and Coca-Cola logos
		  • Frisbees
		  • Olympic pin for fans
		  • Cooler bags
		  • Key chains

Table 12-10 continued

Olympics	Context	Coca-Cola Sponsorship Highlights
1980 Summer Games in Moscow	• Taiwan boycotted instead of changing its name. • 80 nations competed • 21 sports • 203 events • 5,179 athletes (1,115 women) • Number of volunteers unknown • 5,615 media • Led by the U.S., 40–50 nations boycotted the Olympics in protest of Soviet-led invasion of Afghanistan • Despite fewest number of teams since 1956, Moscow produced more world records than the 1976 Montreal Olympics	• Coca-Cola was the official soft drink of the 1980 Moscow Olympics
1984 Winter Olympics in Sarajevo	• 49 nations competed • 6 sports • 39 events • 1,272 athletes (274 women) • 10,450 volunteers • 7,393 media • First and only Winter Olympics held in a socialist country • Games well-received for generous hospitality offered by citizens of Sarajevo	• 1.1 million cans of Coke were supplied
1984 Summer Olympics in Los Angeles	• 140 nations competed • 23 sports • 221 events • 6,829 athletes (1,566 women) • 28,742 volunteers	• Coke designed trading cards, similar to trading cards from other sports, featuring famous Olympians. Distributed with Coca-Cola beverages. • Coke launched the national

Table 12-10 continued

Olympics	Context	Coca-Cola Sponsorship Highlights
	• 9,190 media • Los Angeles was the only city that bid for the 1984 Games • Boycotted by 14 countries, led by Soviet Union • First Games since 1896 organized without government financing • Corporate funding and existing facilities were used to keep costs lower • Made $223 million profit • Became a model for future Olympics	Coca-Cola Olympic Youth Soccer Competition • Coca-Cola Olympic Games educational program for schools was introduced • Coca-Cola Olympic Youth Jamborees were developed, targeted to underprivileged children • First corporate sponsor for 1984 Games • Developed Olympic mascot called "Sam the Eagle"
1988 Winter Olympics in Calgary	• 57 nations competed • 6 sports • 46 events • 1,423 athletes (301 women) • 9,498 volunteers • 6,838 media • Games praised by athletes and spectators • Some events held on artificial snow • Horrific accident of Austrian team doctor who, after colliding with another skier, was knocked under a snow-grooming machine and was crushed	• Created the "Coca-Cola World Chorus," which performed during the opening and closing ceremonies. The chorus featured 43 youths from 23 countries. • Introduced the first Coca-Cola Official Pin Trading Center, which attracted 17,000 visitors daily.
1988 Summer Olympics in Seoul	• 159 nations competed • 25 sports • 237 events • 8,391 athletes (2,194 women) • 27,221 volunteers • 11,331 media	• 2 Coca-Cola Official Olympic Pin Trading Centers were opened in Seoul • Nationwide contest to design opening ceremony commemorative pin was sponsored by Coca-Cola

Table 12-10 continued

Olympics	Context	Coca-Cola Sponsorship Highlights
	• South Korea changed to a democracy before the Olympics • Boycotted by North Korea, Cuba, Ethiopia, Nicaragua	
1992 Winter Olympics in Albertville	• 64 nations competed • 7 sports • 57 events • 1,801 athletes (488 women) • 8,647 volunteers • 5,894 media • Controversy surrounded the Olympic venues, which were actually spread among 8 towns and resorts, so athletes could not easily meet with those from other sports	• The company introduced Coca-Cola Radio, a broadcast center from which 30 DJs from around the U.S. made daily live Olympic updates. Listening audience of 5 million people. • Pin trading grew, with 1.2 million pins traded in two pin trading centers and two Coca-Cola pin mobiles.
1992 Summer Olympics in Barcelona	• 169 nations competed • 28 sports • 257 events • 9,356 athletes (2,704 women) • 34,548 volunteers • 13,082 media • From 1988 to 1992, major international events occurred that led to more teams competing: break-up of the Soviet Union into 15 different countries; fall of the Berlin Wall; South Africa repealed apartheid; all nations were represented for first time in 20 years; Yugoslavia was only country barred from competition due to human rights and military	• Coke arranged to have 150 citizens from 50 countries in the Olympic Torch Relay. Participants were selected from Coca-Cola-sponsored programs in their home countries.

Table 12-10 continued

Olympics	Context	Coca-Cola Sponsorship Highlights
	issues. But individual athletes from Yugoslavia were allowed to compete as independents.	
1994 Winter Olympics in Lillehammer	• 67 nations competed • 6 sports • 61 events • 1,737 athletes (522 women) • 9,054 volunteers • 6,633 media • First year of IOC's schedule change that separated Summer and Winter Olympics by two years in each quadrennial cycle	• Coca-Cola introduced the polar bear animated commercial • Coke sponsored the International Torchbearers Program, featuring 30 participants from 13 countries • Introduced the "Pin of the Day," offering a different pin during each day of the Olympics

1996 Summer Olympics in Atlanta	• 197 nations competed
	• 26 sports
	• 271 events
	• 10,318 athletes (3,512 women)
	• 47,466 volunteers
	• 15,108 media
	• The "Parade of Nations" at the opening ceremony saw the athletes enter from the top of the stadium, as opposed to through a tunnel as had occurred before
	• Atlanta's organizing committee was criticized for the overt commercialism of these Olympics, with critics saying it looked more like a carnival
		• Atlanta is where Coca-Cola's worldwide headquarters are located
		• Coke was exclusive sponsor of the Olympic Torch Relay, the longest up to that time at 15,000 miles with 10,000 torchbearers from 70 countries
		• The company supported several named venues:
		  • Coca-Cola Olympic City— a 12-acre theme park with 20 attractions
		  • Coca-Cola Refreshment Plaza—an outdoor café with big screen TVs showing Olympic coverage
		  • Coca-Cola Olympic Salute to Folk Art Exhibit—art from 50 countries using the

Table 12-10 continued

Olympics	Context	Coca-Cola Sponsorship Highlights
	• Transportation and customer service problems plagued the Atlanta Games	legendary Coke bottle as the common theme • Coca-Cola Official Pin Trading Centers—more than three million pins were traded
1998 Winter Olympics in Nagano	• 72 nations competed • 7 sports • 68 events • 2,176 athletes (787 women) • 32,000 volunteers • 8,239 media • Poor weather conditions (fog, rain, snow) caused event delays • Professional hockey players competed for first time • Women's ice hockey appeared for first time	• Coca-Cola and its "Georgia" brand coffee sponsored the Olympic Torch Relay, using 550 torchbearers • Coca-Cola Pin Trading Centers continued, along with the Pin of the Day • Coke created and sponsored a Fan Plaza with drinks, food, and games • "Georgia" coffee was served to fans throughout in coffee "Hot Zones" • Coke had 50 DJs from around the world broadcast the Games • Coke created the Coca-Cola Olympic Games website, with virtual tours of the Olympics, games, and event information • Sponsored the Kirie Art Program, which focused on six themes about the Nagano region. The themes were turned into prints that were given to athletes and officials as gifts.
2000 Summer Olympics in Sydney	• 199 nations competed • 28 sports • 300 events • 10,651 athletes (4,069 women)	• Coca-Cola Radio grew to 58 stations • Coca-Cola Official Olympic Pin Trading Centers expanded to include Pin

Table 12-10 continued

Olympics	Context	Coca-Cola Sponsorship Highlights
	• 46,967 volunteers • 16,033 media • In 1999, Australian Olympic Committee revealed that it paid $1.2 million to 11 African nations just prior to the vote on host city selection for 2000, with the money to be received only if Sydney won. This was a major concern for several TOP sponsors and, along with the subsequent revelation of the Salt Lake City Olympic bribery scandal, led to rule changes from the IOC. • IOC was strict and severe on athletes using performance-enhancing drugs, stripping gymnast Andreea Raducan of Romania of her gold medal in the all-around event	Trading Schools and a Coca-Cola Pin Club • Coca-Cola selects 300 teens from around the world for participation in two programs: Coca-Cola Olympic Club; Sydney and Powerade-Aquarius Training Camp. The teens were given tours, tickets, and access to the Olympic Games. • Coca-Cola created five Coca-Cola RedFest events located in different Australian cities, which offered local fans big-screen viewing of the Olympics and also live entertainment and food.
2002 Winter Olympics in Salt Lake City	• 77 nations competed • 7 sports • 78 events • 2,399 athletes (886 women) • 22,000 volunteers • 8,730 media • In 1998–99, a bribery scandal reportedly caused some officials to consider moving the Games to another city • Corporate sponsors demanded stronger oversight from the IOC to manage member behavior and enact penalties for violators to maintain	• Coke co-sponsored the Olympic Torch Relay and selected 3,500 of the 11,500 torchbearers, from nine countries • Developed Coca-Cola Community Canvas, which were art shows featuring teen artwork in each of the torch-relay cities • Commissioned Peter Max to paint an Olympic mural that was subsequently donated to Salt Lake City • Provided Coca-Cola Ambassadors from around

Table 12-10 continued

Olympics	Context	Coca-Cola Sponsorship Highlights
	integrity of the Olympics and protect its brand reputation • Four IOC members resigned and six were expelled • New Salt Lake Organizing Committee leadership was brought in • Athletes from 18 nations won gold medals, an Olympic record	the world to provide hospitality • Hosted three Coca-Cola Olympic Pin Trading Centers that included a "Coca-Cola Live" show with interviews of Olympic legends • Launched a new attraction called "Coca-Cola on the Ice," which provided winter sports simulations that enabled fans to try out luge, hockey, curling, and other winter events • DJs sponsored by Coke from 45 countries gave Olympic broadcasts • Local residents were randomly chosen for free Olympic Games tickets, delivered via Coca-Cola Fan Vans • Introduced a 100% bio-degradable drinking cup and supported local recycling efforts
2004 Summer Olympics in Athens	• 201 nations competed • 28 sports • 301 events • 10,625 athletes (4,329 women) • 45,000 volunteers • 21,500 media • Olympics returned to their historic home • In the years and then months leading up to the Games there was increasing concern about the readiness of the venues.	• Coca-Cola supported the Olympic Torch Relay on its five-continent, 30-city tour with more than 11,000 torchbearers • Coca-Cola Olympic Pin Trading Centers continued • Created Coke O.N. Air, a multimedia program used by Greek youth who sent Olympic-themed messages via traditional and non-traditional media • Coca-Cola Radio featured DJs from around the world again

Table 12-10 continued

Olympics	Context	Coca-Cola Sponsorship Highlights
	Design adjustments were made on some venues to meet the deadline. • Transportation and security concerns, particularly in the wake of global terrorist activity, were additional concerns • The Olympics went well and experienced no significant problems	

2006 Winter Olympics in Turin	• 80 nations competed
	• 7 sports
	• 84 events
	• 2,508 athletes (960 women)
	• 18,000 volunteers
	• 2,688 media
	• Financial concerns raised in the months prior
	• Low local fan interest in the weeks leading up to the Games. Former Italian Olympians vocal that the Games could have been better promoted.
		• Supported presentation of the Olympic Torch Relay
		• Created Coca-Cola Torch Exhibition Tour, an interactive road show
		• Coca-Cola-sponsored school and community programs were developed to select torchbearers
		• Developed "Get Caught Living Olympic" programs in Italy that featured:
		  • Talking cans
		  • Coca-Cola Polar Bear
		  • Automobile prizes
		  • Event tickets
		  • Coke's Italian website featured Olympic Games timeline and history, 2006 events calendar, daily torch relay information
		• Coke created full integrated marketing platform that included:
		  • Outdoor messages
		  • Special musical anthem
		  • Olympic Pin Trading Center
		  • Historical exhibits
		  • Sports simulators

Table 12-10 continued

Olympics	Context	Coca-Cola Sponsorship Highlights
		• Video-game kiosks • Postcard email booth • Mobile Coca-Cola Cruisers that gave away Coke products • 200 volunteers from 20 countries that rewarded random acts of kindness • Created "The Coca-Cola Award: Live Olympic" that celebrated people from around the world who lived the Olympic ideals every day • Developed "Torino Conversations," a blog supported and written by university students who did interviews and posted regular updates about the Olympics • Developed program whereby fans in other cities could win trips to future Winter Olympics • Created Internet "Win Your Olympic Dream" contest in Austria; "Win Winter Fun" event in Switzerland; fundraising drive in Sweden; mobile phone contest in Belarus and Russia; "Georgia" coffee promotion in Japan; "Drink. Watch. Cheer. Win" contest in the U.S.

Table 12-10 continued

Olympics	Context	Coca-Cola Sponsorship Highlights
2008 Summer Olympics in Beijing (projected data)	• Up to 205 nations to compete • 28 sports • 302 events • 10,800 athletes (4,000–5,000 women) • 70,000 volunteers • 21,600 media • Human rights practices raised as issue by protest groups, particularly with respect to Tibet • Chinese investment—military and oil, human rights concerns in Sudan, raised by humanitarian groups and vocal celebrities. Steven Spielberg, creative advisor to Beijing Olympics, withdrew his support in protest of China's Sudan policies. • Concerns about China's plan to curb air pollution during the Olympics • China hopes this Olympics shows the world the tremendous progress the country has made since economic liberalization began • Substantial investments made in city-wide infrastructure improvements • Spectacular new sports venues anticipated	• Known Coca-Cola activities • Coca-Cola Olympic Pin Trading Center • Olympic Torch Relay; it will travel around the world for the 2008 Olympics • Other details not known at time of writing

Case Brief: Visa

Visa illustrates one of the most detailed examples of sports sponsorship. When Visa began sponsoring the Olympics in 1986 it was one of the three primary competitors in the payment services industry, along with MasterCard and American Express, in addition to lower-tier competitors such as Diners Club and Discover. Visa had a good, if unspectacular, reputation for reliable and convenient cashless payment products. Company marketers had a basic objective driving their early Olympic sponsorship activities in the 1980s: build awareness through advertising; and the Olympics provided a solid and recognizable vehicle for doing so. Building awareness was only a starting point, however. As sports marketing group IMG managing director Andrew Hampel said, "Sports sponsorship may give you the right to talk to customers, but if you want to say anything worthwhile about your brand, you have to engage them at a number of levels."[38]

As Visa gained experience from its early Olympics sponsorships, the company's objectives changed, becoming more ambitious, and it adjusted its marketing efforts accordingly, reflecting Andrew Hampel's observations about meaningful brand development. This included organizing its sponsorship investments according to three stages of market development:

- Emerging—characterized by awareness-building primarily through name recognition
- Maturing—when growth and expansion were reinforced through advertising
- Mature—when differentiation was emphasized, particularly through product innovation and communications through new media

In effect, Visa shifted over time from simple awareness-building toward differentiating its brand from the competition, including strategies to extend the benefits of the Olympic sponsorship before and beyond the 17 days of the Olympics itself. As a key Visa senior marketing executive stated in 2003, "Our campaign for the 1988 Calgary Olympics was all about branding and we focused on the 17 days surrounding the games. Then in 1994, we saw that Visa was going to have to adapt its marketing to make it closer to tourism and spread its efforts over a much longer period. We realized that we had to work with the Olympic city before, during, and after the Games in order to derive the best benefits for our members. We asked ourselves why host cities bid for the games and we realized the answer came down to showcasing the city to the world. Not only do the games bring tourists to the Olympic city, but also create a large halo effect that lasts beyond the games. Prior to the 1992 Olympics, Barcelona was the 16th most popular tourist destination in Europe. In 1993, it was the third. There was a similar kind of lift in Australia after the 2000 games."[39]

For example, at the 2000 Sydney Olympics Visa launched a four-year destination marketing program that created $40 million in additional marketing value in Australia and led to a 7% rise in tourism.[40] According to a 2003 Stanford Business School case study, "Unaided consumer awareness of Visa's sponsorship after Sydney was an unprecedented 72%, and research shows sponsorship awareness drives Visa brand preference."[41] These initiatives reflected the company's plan to shift from a commodity to a specialty position, a concept also known as the bent-arrow theory of marketing (see Figure 12-5).[42]

Figure 12-5
Bent-Arrow Marketing

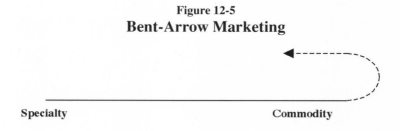

Specialty   Commodity

While this is an obvious concept to understand and present visually, the bent-arrow theory is a simplification of the S-curve/lifecycle graph familiar to business students everywhere, as shown in the Figure 12-6.

Figure 12-6
Lifecycle with Bent-Arrow Overlay

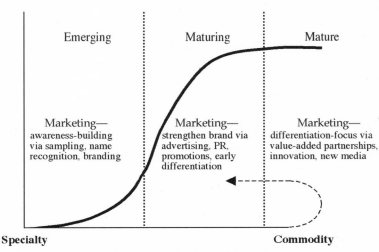

Visa marketing over time & development stage

The S-curve, so named for the shape of the graph, stylizes the stages of growth for a brand/business/product. In the early emerging stages, the new offering is unknown, often having unique or specialty characteristics partly due to sheer novelty. As the offering starts maturing, growth increases, as do competitor offerings that enter because the former novelty has demonstrated that a healthy and profitable market demand exists. As the market hits maturity, the number of competitors and offerings has grown further, creating a market with many look-alike products. Price is usually the key differentiator in the mature stage, signaling a commodity market. The savvy competitor seeks to distinguish its offerings by focusing on value-added enhancements and innovation in order to recapture a specialty status, command premium profits, and, differentiate its offerings once again.

Branding success in most businesses is dependent on clear differentiation that customers recognize and find relevant. As one can imagine, this is a common but challenging objective to execute, particularly in the payment-services industry where products are often seen as interchangeable and new features are easily and rapidly matched. Differentiation for Visa was therefore based on associating with the Olympics as a renowned, external event with a prestigious reputation and exclusive stature. Management hoped the positive brand attributes of the Olympics would create a halo effect over Visa. Visa did not approach this naively or with false hope. Management saw many parallels between the Olympics and Visa. Visa established sponsorship selection criteria to ensure the Olympics and any other company sponsorships had the right ingredients to support a large marketing investment (these (see Figure 12-7) criteria are a useful starting point for almost any company considering a sports sponsorship investment):

Figure 12-7
Visa Sponsorship Criteria[43]

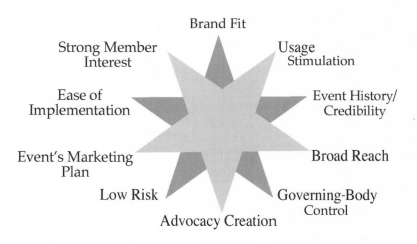

Brand Fit

Strong Member Interest

Usage Stimulation

Ease of Implementation

Event History/ Credibility

Event's Marketing Plan

Broad Reach

Low Risk

Governing-Body Control

Advocacy Creation

Brand Fit
Effective marketing includes reasonable (perfection is not critical) alignment between the sponsor and the event. Visa believed that the two organizations were leaders in their respective categories; represented excellence; and enjoyed widespread awareness, global reach, and local impact.

Usage Stimulation

Visa's members are the network of financial institutions and merchants around the world. Attracting customers and convincing them to buy are two of the key imperatives of most marketing campaigns. Visa saw the Olympics sponsorship as a catalyst for inspiring consumers to use the card more frequently, which would directly benefit Visa's members as a consequence.

Event History/Credibility

Marketing activities and marketers confront a challenging marketplace today. Associating their companies with events (or other media, for that matter) requires more than finding a popular vehicle and pouring money into it hoping to attract customers. Consumers today are more skeptical of traditional marketing, perceiving it as insincere and slick. Therefore, marketers must study the event they wish to sponsor to assess its reputation and whether sponsoring it would be consistent with their own company's reputation. The first part of this book explored highlights of the rich and storied history of the Olympics to provide readers with a greater appreciation for the appeal of the Games, beyond the common perceptions that exist. Visa saw more areas of commonality than differences, plus the obvious global clout, as net positives for its marketing investment.

Broad Reach

In advertising terms, reach refers to the total number or percentage of an audience reached by a single ad / exposure during a specified time. With respect to the Olympics, broad reach describes the size of the total audience that will see the Olympics at least once during the duration of the event. Of course, most fans watch multiple events throughout the 17 days, creating a much larger cumulative reach, representing a significant audience for Visa to establish, solidify, and enhance its position.

Governing-Body Control

Marketers must ensure their counterparts at the event under consideration are reliable and effective. A strong, competent governing body conveys professionalism and gives sponsors confidence that the event will be well-managed. Visa makes a sizable investment in each Olympic quadrennial, so governing-body control provides the company with reassurance that sponsorship commitments will be honored and, more broadly, that the integrity of the Olympic Games will remain strong and intact.

Advocacy Creation

Marketing success relies on strong public support (this is not to suggest government support, although that may be a component) in which individuals and societal institutions perceive the event favorably, and in this context Visa's leaders want to know that the public continues to view the Olympics positively. The Olympic Movement has been a driving force for developing grassroots support for the Olympics throughout much of the modern era. Furthermore, the Olympics are deeply meaningful to fans and athletes, creating a powerful emotional connection that reinforces the Olympic ideal.

Low Risk

Well-run events with positive reputations and respected governing bodies create an attractive, low-risk investment opportunity for a marketer, which represents the event's half of the relationship. The other half pertains to the sponsor. Sponsors face additional risks related to their own management of their event marketing effort, including: unclear objectives, misalignment between the sponsor and the event, and poor marketing execution. Marketers must be accountable for their activities, as should any manager. Visa's 22-year sponsorship of the Olympics has grown in sophistication, minimizing the investment risk, even as the Olympics have confronted challenges including scandals. Fortunately, the IOC has demonstrated reasonable competence in addressing these challenges and preventing any lasting harm to the Olympic brand.

Event's Marketing Plan

An event may satisfy the criteria thus far, but if the event's own marketing plan is inadequate, then marketer's should think twice before sponsoring. The event's management must present a clear plan that describes how they will market the event and how they will use the sponsorship monies. The IOC has developed a detailed, methodical plan for marketing the Olympic Movement overall and for each Olympics quadrennial, including sponsorship levels and criteria, strict Olympics-related identity usage and guidelines, and general quality control in marketing communications. Visa is familiar with the IOC, NOCs, and OCOG, and their role in supporting and marketing each Olympics globally, nationally, and at the host city, which gives the company added confidence in proper and professional execution of the Olympic image.

Ease of Implementation

Sports events are complex. Coordinating premarketing, athletes, event timing, sponsors, venue logistics, fan movement, ticketing, food, security, scoring, officiating, and more for thousands of people requires extraordinary management skill and deft planning. Most Olympics are well-run, successful events despite the innumerable variables that can affect the smooth operation of the Games. Over 100 years of experience in the modern era have resulted in practices and controls enabling each succeeding Olympiad to operate relatively smoothly. This success reflects well on Olympic management and governing-body control. As a sponsor, Visa wants to ensure that its own marketing efforts are equally well run.

Strong Member Interest

At the risk of conveying the obvious, a successful sports event should attract the attention of fans. The Olympics' broad range of sports, plus the thousands of participating athletes, offer something for almost every kind of sports fan. For Visa, Olympic fans may also become Visa customers. Therefore, Visa's sports sponsorship must be seen as beneficial and actively supported by its member institutions. Otherwise, the sponsorship investment is one of awareness development only, and not terribly effective as a result. But this member interest cannot be imposed or mandated by Visa. Much like a product is differentiated only if the customer recognizes the difference and finds it relevant, for sports sponsorships to be truly successful Visa's members must see the event as useful and appealing. Of course, the advantage of the Olympics as the event being sponsored is that they are well known, understood, represent common values, and have universal appeal. Visa's member institutions find more benefit than not, otherwise they would not have supported the event as actively as they have over the past 22 years.

Assuming a sport meets Visa's sponsorship criteria, the company then leverages the investment across several marketing "platforms," which are a modified version of classic marketing techniques. These platforms provide Visa with a framework for dividing its marketing efforts into specific activity areas in each phase (pre-, during, and post-Olympics as shown in Figure 12-8.)

Figure 12-8
Visa Sponsorship Marketing Platform Framework

Visa Sports Marketing Platforms											
▼			▼			▼			▼		
Advertising *build awareness*			**Promotional** *increase usage*			**Corporate Relations** *integrated message*			**Product** *highlight innovation*		
Pre	*During*	*Post*	*Pre*	*During*	*Post*	*Pre*	*During*	*Post*	*Pre*	*During*	*Post*
Programs *Traditional* • Print • TV • Radio • Outdoor *Non-traditional* • Viral • Digital media • Online • Mobile			**Programs** • Special offers • Limited time • Discounts • Loyalty programs • Contests • Partnering and co-marketing			**Programs** *External* • Integrated barnd message • Customer experiences • Touchpoints *Internal* • Internal branding • Employee programs			**Programs** • New product • New features • New markets (segments, geographies) • Packaging • Merchandising • Bundles • Support • Service • Warranties		

Note: The programs listed above are examples of typical programs in each marketing category and are not meant to suggest that these are Visa's actual programs.

Advertising

The objective of Visa's advertising platform is to build awareness. When marketers focus on building awareness, broad-based messages and universally appealing imagery are among the approaches considered, assuming the objective is to appeal to the widest possible audience. Building awareness is, in many ways, an effort to introduce the brand or, in Visa's case, a new storyline, since the company is already known.

Promotional

Visa's promotional platform is focused on increasing usage of the Visa payment service, and partnering with respected brands, such as Disney. The benefits are obvious: increasing usage improves the financial returns for Visa and its member institutions; and partnering with well-known brands adds credibility to Visa's products since it is unlikely another powerful brand would partner with Visa if the company's payment services were not both ubiquitous and beneficial to consumers. Plus, any promotional activity undertaken by the partner has the potential to benefit Visa as well.

Corporate Relations

The corporate relations platform is used to strengthen the power and impact of Visa's numerous marketing programs (including those outside of sports marketing) by integrating them toward a more cohesive brand message to the market. This platform also benefits Visa's employees because the company markets its various programs and partnerships to its own employees. This internal marketing is a powerful example of company-culture building. Visa wants its employees to be aware of the many different marketing efforts it is undertaking, believing that informed employees work more effectively together and will ultimately benefit member institutions and consumers as well.

Product

Visa uses this platform to launch new products and technologies. Part of the promotional platform investment discussed above implies infrastructure investment to support the anticipated usage increases. These infrastructure investments include the addition of ATMs, transactions and processing equipment, and a combination of new temporary and permanent distribution points and accompanying support for Visa member institutions.

Visa's marketing plans are tailored to each of these platforms, enabling the company's marketers to focus their planning and execution efforts around tightly defined marketing sub-activities. Visa's marketing organizational efforts are thorough and precise, affording marketers the luxury of specialized attention and detailed planning specific to the needs of each platform. While such diligent planning does not guarantee success, it reduces uncertainty about direction and it creates a clear roadmap about marketing activities and responsibilities. No plan is infallible. Indeed, the test of success is often seen during a crisis or surprise, when management has to respond in the absence of a detailed plan. But the Olympics sponsorship planning effort engages the marketing organization, sharpening its focus around a single, albeit enormous and complex, event.[44]

Have the more than 20 years of Olympic sponsorship been worth it? Visa certainly provides one of the more compelling examples of how sports sponsorship can ultimately create value for the company. Recall Figure 12-2, the Dimensions of Brand Value:

Figure 12-2
Dimensions of Brand Value

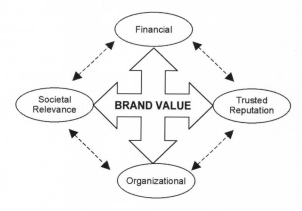

Financial

Let's look at the TOP program revenues since the mid-1980s:

Table 12-11
TOP Program Evolution[45]

Quadrennal	Games	Partners	NOCs	Revenue
1985–1988	Calgary/Seoul	9	159	US$96 mil
1989–1992	Albertville/Barcelona	12	169	US$172 mil
1993–1996	Lillehammer/Atlanta	10	197	US$279 mil

Table 12-10 continued

1997–2000	Nagano/Sydney	11	199	US$579 mil
2001–2004	Salt Lake City /Athens	11	202	US$663 mil
2005–2008	Turin /Beijing	12	205	US$866 mil

Simple arithmetic indicates that Visa's Olympic sponsorship since 1986 (the year its Olympic relationship began) has been approximately $238 million. But recall that this amount paid buys only the right to sponsor the Olympics and that each sponsor spends three to four times that amount in executing its sponsorship properly, including money spent on creative design, media placement, logistics, and implementation. Therefore, one can deduce that Visa's total Olympic investment since 1986 is probably in the range of $715–$952 million, depending on the multiple.

Visa has witnessed a significant increase in financial and market performance since it initiated its Olympic sponsorship efforts in 1986. Visa's 2007 operating revenues were $5.84 billion,[46] and while figures are not available for 1986, one can surmise that revenues have grown. The number of credit cards issued has grown from 137 million to over 1.4 billion and transactions volume (the total amount of payments and cash flowing through Visa payment services) has increased from $111 billion to $3.48 trillion. Since 2002 alone, the total number of transactions using Visa credit cards has grown from 34 billion to over 46 billion. Visa's global market share has increased 33% to 54% (MasterCard has 29% share, American Express has 13%, and Discover has 4% during this time). One of Visa's original reasons for sponsoring the Olympics in the mid-1980s was to increase awareness. As of the 2004 Olympic Games in Athens, Visa attained 87% consumer awareness, the highest level of awareness among all sponsors, indicating the power and strength of the Visa brand and the success of its Olympic sponsorship efforts. In March 2008, Visa went from a private company to a public company, with the largest initial public offering (IPO) in U.S. history, valued at $17.9 billion. As of March 2008, Visa's market capitalization was $48 billion, which was eight times 2007 sales. These results are due to more than market momentum, population growth, favorable economic conditions, or dumb luck. After all, neither MasterCard nor American Express witnessed the same degree of success during this time, although both have had financial success (including MasterCard's own successful IPO in May 2006 that raised $2.4 billion. MasterCard's 2007 revenues totaled $4 billion and its market capitalization as of March 2008 was $28.5 billion, 7 times 2007 sales. Note also that MasterCard lost its sponsorship of the 2010 and 2014 World Cup to Visa).[47]

Trusted Reputation

Since 1986, Visa management has viewed sports as something valued and shared across cultures, bringing people together to celebrate competition and athletic achievement. By aligning the company closely with the Olympics (and Visa's other sports sponsorships— Paralympics, football World Cup, and rugby union World Cup), Visa management believes that the halo effect from these renowned events will cast a favorable glow over Visa. Of course, the company has done far more than attach its name and logo to internationally recognized sports events. Visa gets deeply involved in each community where an event occurs. The net benefit is that Visa has shifted its market position from a commodity product to market leader with a premier reputation. Not only did its market share increase 33% as shown above, but its rating as "best overall card" rose to 50%. The growth and solidifying of its reputation has been the result of a patient, long-term, strategic effort to position Visa as a reliable, convenient, and vital contributor to the lifestyle of its customers, exemplified by its 22-year relationship with the Olympic Games.

Organizational

Organizational value is best exhibited when employees are directly and regularly engaged with their own company and its business activities; can clearly understand what the company is trying to achieve; and can see how, why, and where they fit in. Visa developed internal programs that involved employees in the Olympic effort, from contests to win tickets to various Olympic Games to benefits provided by Visa's other corporate partners, from Disney to Taco Bell to Clearview Cinemas. These corporate relationships connect Visa to other highly regarded brands with strong reputations, fostering confidence internally that the company is respected by recognized companies in other markets. Visa's success in winning the right to sponsor the World Cup in 2010 and 2014 provides another source of inspiration for its employees, as does the company's aforementioned efforts with the Paralympics and rugby union World Cup.

Societal Relevance

Visa's Olympic sponsorship has provided over $120 million in support for Olympic teams and athletes around the world, including the U.S. gymnastics team, U.S. track and field team, Team Visa Europe (Summer and Winter teams), the U.S. ski and snowboard teams, and the Canadian bobsled and skeleton teams. In previous years, Visa sponsored the Japanese ski-jumping team and the Russian hockey team. Additionally, Visa has sponsored selected individual athletes in figure skating and snowboarding. Visa has also created a children's art program called "Visa Olympics of the Imagination." Launched in 1994, the program teaches children between the ages of 10 and 14 about the Olympic Movement. Concurrently, the children are entered into an art competition, and selected winners have a chance to go to the Olympics, sponsored by Visa. According to company figures, more than 1 million children have competed, and 181 from 48 countries have attended the Games. Readers are encouraged to visit the following website to see examples of the winning artists: http://sponsorships.visa.com/olympic/voi/voi_gallery.jsp. The pictures from this program are a vibrant reminder of the power and imagery associated with the Olympics, with many of the themes already discussed in this book reflected in the descriptions, from unbridled optimism to hero worship to national pride. They also highlight the vivid imaginations of children as they envision the Olympics as a unifying event that allows the world to forget its troubles, if only for a couple of weeks every two years. Visa's "Olympics of the Imagination" are also an excellent illustration of non-traditional marketing, connecting children to the Olympics by channeling their energy and creativity for the purpose of conveying a hopeful image of the world, inspired by the possibility of actually attending the Games, yet also enabling Visa to use the resulting artwork to promote both the children's program and the company's support for the Olympics.

Equally important, Visa is the first global sponsor of the International Paralympic Committee and supports numerous national Paralympic sports federations. This effort included the first Paralympic website, usable by people with hearing, sight, and other disabilities. Visa has actively and visibly supported and encouraged both fan and

213

athlete involvement in the Paralympics. For example, Visa's support of the British Paralympic Association (BPA) sent over 300 athletes and staff to the 2004 Paralympic Games in Athens. The Athens Games saw Visa partner with regional Paralympic groups to encourage attendance by Visa customers. Additionally, Visa helped provide accessibility to the disabled who attended the 2004 Athens Paralympics. There are numerous other similar examples of Visa's deep and genuine social commitment to the Paralympics around the world since 1996.

Visa management acknowledges that a direct link between Olympic sponsorship and performance results is not always perfectly clear, but they firmly believe that the Olympics have been a key factor in the company's success and growth over the past two decades. Visa has learned a great deal about sports sponsorships in its two decades of Olympic efforts, developing expertise in leveraging a trusted event with several thousand years of tradition into an invaluable partnership that has changed the fortunes of the company for the better. Visa's early objectives of developing awareness succeeded and were then superceded by even more ambitious goals of building market share, increasing transactions volume, growing its financial success, improving its reputation with customers and members, and building measurable brand value—each of which was achieved, setting a firm foundation for growth as globalization continues. As Michael Lynch, senior vice president of event and sponsorship marketing, stated, "Obviously, not all of that is from the Olympics. But we're finding that those who are aware of our Olympic sponsorship are more likely to use the Visa card than those who are unaware."[48]

His colleague, Becky Saeger, executive vice president of brand marketing, reinforced the impact of Visa's Olympic marketing investments:

At Visa, we frequently review our efforts to ensure a return on investment for our members. Since 1986, no single property has allowed us to build our brand and drive use better than the Olympic Games...Since 1986, Visa volume has grown at a compounded annual rate of 16%. Unaided consumer awareness of Visa's sponsorship after Sydney was an unprecedented 72%, and research shows sponsorship awareness drives Visa brand preference. Finally, the 2002 Games scored record ratings for NBC, enabling Visa to reach a larger, more diverse audience than ever before.[49]

Visa's Olympic sponsorship marketing has been ongoing since 1986 and the company's performance during this 22-year period demonstrates many of the benefits it has derived from its carefully crafted Olympic marketing.

Case Brief: John Hancock/Manulife

John Hancock began sponsoring the Olympics in 1993 and continued this relationship until its acquisition by Manulife in 2004, whereupon Manulife has since continued as one of the TOP program sponsors. John Hancock senior management estimated that its $40 million Olympic sponsorship had led to a $50 million increase in sales.

Like Visa, John Hancock developed sponsorship criteria to help evaluate an event's attractiveness (Figure 12-9):

Figure 12-9
John Hancock Sponsorship Criteria[50]

Brand Relevance

Will associating with another well-known brand reflect well on John Hancock? Does the company share common values with the sponsored event? Are the company's various touchpoints integrated and consistent, minimizing confusion in the marketplace? There is increasing research indicating the importance of customer touchpoints. Bernd Schmitt, a respected scholar and branding expert from Columbia Business School, is an authority on "experiential marketing," which describes that customers today do not just buy products, they buy experiences. Having positive experiences with companies and products involves successfully integrating and managing multiple touchpoints, from the customer environment (retail, B2B, transactions space, etc.) to traditional communications to reputation to digital media, and more. Knowing how to manage your company's touchpoints is both complicated and necessary to ensuring a higher quality customer experience. The converse is a disconnected set of activities (such as products that don't match the company's claims, poor merchandising, inconsistent pricing, etc.) that serves to undermine the customer's experience, not enhance it. As company management considers its growth opportunities, creating a positive and engaging customer experience ought to be at the forefront. Furthermore, it must be relevant to customers. Apple's success since 1997 illustrates how a company can create a compelling adventure for customers that goes well beyond the products by integrating directly with the consumer's lifestyle. Such success appears easy in hindsight, but it is a painstaking effort to successfully manage every touchpoint every day so that it looks effortless and makes the customer's life easier.

Business Development

John Hancock wants to ensure that sponsorships have the potential to yield leads and sales. Implied is that a sponsorship must be productive and not for appearances. Indeed, one of the reasons for event-marketing failure is that companies do not put enough thought into developing new business directly from the event. Whether trade shows, conferences, or sports events, the common denominator is that large numbers of people participate and, therefore, it is incumbent upon company representatives to have a strategy for capturing potential leads and transforming them into profitable and loyal customers. Spending money on sponsoring a sports event or a trade-show exhibit requires more than having a physical presence manifested through signage, logos, and product demonstrations. A plan must be developed for both prospective and existing customers such that a logical follow-up path is created, initial customer interest is nurtured, and positive momentum is developed.

Marketing Platform

Just as Visa developed its four marketing platforms, John Hancock assesses sponsorship viability not just on the merits of the event itself, but also on integrating a wide range of marketing activities from strategic to tactical. At the highest level, company leadership must ensure that an event's reputation reflects well on its own reputation. Visa showed through careful self-scrutiny, that its values aligned closely with those of the Olympics. John Hancock applies a similar rationale, focusing the company's marketing efforts around the sweeping themes and emotions that surround large-scale sports events. At the tactical level, marketing professionals must design programs, from promotions to direct marketing, that are consistent with the overarching strategy. Even informal activities, such as grassroots and/or viral-marketing campaigns, should carry some of the same themes and messages, even if the imagery and execution are modified to fit the medium. For example, a global brand-positioning campaign with a simple message and associated imagery should bear some resemblance to tactical programs at the individual consumer level. This is not meant to suggest that frontline marketing and sales people parrot the same message and slogans as a global ad campaign, but that they design their own communications and presentations used for direct customer interactions to further explain and amplify the generally simpler messages of the strategic campaign. John Hancock wants to ensure that the benefits of the Olympic sponsorship extend beyond the strategic brand message and are translatable to local, and sometimes more informal, tactical promotions.

Motivates Employees

John Hancock wants its sports sponsorships to have direct benefits for its own employees, typically through trips to the Olympic Games. From rewards for top-performing sales people to client entertainment, John Hancock uses the sponsorship as a motivational tool. This has an obvious practical benefit of inspiring people toward more ambitious achievements in the hope of being one of the fortunate few to attend the Games. There is a more intangible benefit as well. Similar to the halo effect sponsors seek when associating with the Olympics, employees see John Hancock's sponsorship support of the Games as a prestigious and noble cause, with the undoubted psychological benefit of knowing your company is one of only a few global companies sponsoring the world's most respected and revered sports event.

Long-Term Benefits

John Hancock wisely sees the Olympics as having a lifespan beyond the 17 days of the Games, similar to Visa's pre- and post-Olympics activities. There is a natural point when international interest declines, with the steepest fall in interest occurring almost immediately upon the conclusion of the Games. However, many of the more successful athletes and teams enjoy post-Olympic celebrations and media appearances, sustaining the interest in the Olympics for weeks and months after the official conclusion. As Visa's destination marketing program demonstrates, Olympic host city tourism grows, enabling the company to leverage the infrastructure investment made for months or even years after the event. John Hancock evaluates their sports sponsorships with an eye toward potential post-event benefits. Like other TOP sponsors, John Hancock invests in infrastructure in the host city's market, including relationship development with local and regional companies that may be important partners and channels for the company's products, so leveraging this investment over a longer timeframe is an important consideration. This represents an important consideration for many other companies considering a sports sponsorship too, whether it is a globally recognized event such as the Olympics or a local event such as a marathon.

Quantifiable Results

Marketers ought to be accountable, and a sports sponsorship is no different. John Hancock seeks to quantify its results to assess whether the investment paid off. This is a more complex issue than it appears on the surface. There is no single magic formula that perfectly measures a sports sponsorship. The measures depend on the company's objectives, sponsorship strategy (like Visa's and John Hancock's marketing platforms), and specific tactics. Much like the layers of an onion, marketers must peel away the underlying details of the objectives to gain a more detailed understanding of what is required to successfully implement their sponsorship. For example, if the objective is simply to raise awareness, then company management needs to first know current awareness levels so that goals can be developed for the sponsored event. Management can then plan which marketing programs would be most effective in raising awareness. Following the event's conclusion, a survey can then be employed to update the awareness results and reveal whether the original goals were achieved. If they were not, then each step of the planning process can be evaluated to see where improvements can be made in the future. If goals were achieved, then it is incumbent on marketers to learn from the success by doing a detailed review to determine if it is repeatable, or unique for this one event. Either way, the task of measurement requires methodical planning, goal setting, implementation, and review.

John Hancock Olympic Objectives
In addition to its sponsorship criteria, John Hancock also has five objectives specifically for the Olympics sponsorship (see Figure 12-10):

Figure 12-10
John Hancock Sponsorship Objectives[51]

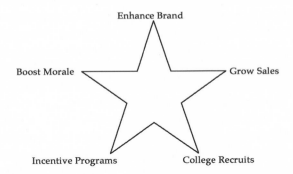

Enhance Brand
When co-branding is handled properly, then the two organizations, respective reputations should be strengthened. For John Hancock, the benefits are quite clear. The reputation of the Olympics is unrivaled and serves to boost John Hancock's own brand image and reputation. For the IOC, it receives the benefit of the sponsorship money and the visible support of a leading, trusted corporation in its industry.

Grow Sales
John Hancock's Olympic sponsorship rights, indeed those of any TOP sponsor, provide for specific usage of the Olympic name and identity

for select, approved functions, including company events. Use of the various Olympic identities attaches certain positive attributes to the company event (prestige, uniqueness, integrity, competitive virtue) and serves to create a special experience for John Hancock's customers. The simple use of the Olympic identity may attract more customers than non-Olympic company events and it may also attract a higher quality customer. Olympic-sponsored events connote a higher-class occasion, giving the event an exclusive appeal that may favorably impress customers further, prompting additional interest in John Hancock's products and services.

College Recruits
The insurance industry depends on a large pool of fields agents whose job is to market insurance and financial products to customers (both consumers and businesses). Recruiting young, smart college graduates enables John Hancock to train promising people at an early age, learning the company's products and developing both a client base and a camaraderie with their fellow new hires (as well as building relationships with seasoned veterans). The Olympics adds *cachet* to the John Hancock name and business, which may appeal to a broader range of college graduates than the company could otherwise attract in non-Olympic years.

Incentive Programs
Insurance agents, like many field-based marketers and sales professionals, are motivated by reward and incentive programs that recognize achievement. Of course, top agents earn sizable incomes and bonuses, plus they are building a base of annuity-paying loyal customers. In addition, agents thrive on recognition based on total sales (or total value of premiums sold), with many companies establishing tiered performance levels for top performers, such as "million dollar" clubs (or the equivalent high-value designation). Status is affirmed with these programs each year because only a limited number of the very best performers achieve these designations. Offering Olympic-related incentives would be a valuable motivation for achievement-driven agents. More specifically, Hancock attributes $50 million in new sales to the Olympic incentives.

Boost Morale

It is human nature to highlight our strengths and minimize our weaknesses. We want others to view us favorably. In the business world, success is partly predicated on establishing a recognized, unique position and reputation. Business professionals want to succeed and they want to be part of organizations that are recognized for their accomplishments. "Bragging rights," such as number-one market share, best-rated products, and industry awards, are examples of how companies differentiate their offerings from those of the competition. Plus, these distinctions lift morale because employees believe they are doing something unique. Being associated with the Olympic Games is an exclusive right—no other insurance company can be a TOP sponsor because John Hancock is the only one allowed from that industry, just as Johnson & Johnson is the only pharmaceutical company, Visa is the only payment-services company, and Coca-Cola is the only beverage company. John Hancock stated that roughly 95% of all employees attended an event related to the company's Olympic sponsorship, and 85% said they were proud of the company's sponsorship.

John Hancock management believes that the Olympic investments have paid off and indicate that their various sponsorship criteria have been met. For the 10-year period between 1993 and 2003, the insurance industry saw sales decrease by 4% while John Hancock's increased 14%. In 1994, a John Hancock survey of 5,000 people before the Lillehammer Olympics revealed that 58% were willing to buy Hancock products. A post-Olympics survey showed that this had increased to 70%. Equally impressive was the 40+% improvement in consumer perceptions of John Hancock as a leader in the financial-services industry. To complement its primary Olympic sponsorship, Hancock also invested in supporting directly USA Hockey, USA Gymnastics and, indirectly, Olympic figure skating.[52]

USA Hockey

The company invested $300,000 to sponsor the John Hancock USA Hockey Tour, which preceded the 1994 Olympics. The tour was designed to bring the U.S. ice-hockey team closer to the fans, promote the upcoming Olympics, and generate fan support and goodwill. By bringing the ice-hockey team to various U.S. cities, John Hancock made the team and players seem more accessible and human, fostering a closer bond with the fans. This bond was reinforced by clinics that were conducted by the players for kids in each of the 24 cities on the tour. Additionally, John Hancock agents in each locale were available to meet with local parents to discuss John Hancock products and services. The tour generated more sales leads for John Hancock's field-based agents and, by being associated with the U.S. ice-hockey team and the Olympics, created a more memorable and positive association for the company.[53] The tour required more from John Hancock than merely paying money for sponsorship rights. The company made a determined effort to be directly involved in the sponsorship and the sport. While John Hancock's expertise is insurance products, it displayed remarkable organizational agility in rallying employees to support the tour as it traveled from city to city. Furthermore, John Hancock agents departed from their normal schedules to spend time at each of the tour's stops. This effort was also intended to soften John Hancock's image from that of a giant company to one with a more personalized approach and a human touch. John Hancock's CEO at the time, David D'Alessandro said, "…the key to a successful Olympic sponsorship is not making a big splash once, but instead, finding a direct and emotional way to bring the Olympics home to consumers year after year."[54]

D'Alessandro's comment is revealing about his personal perspective on not just the value of sponsoring a large sports event such as the Olympics, but also that successful marketing requires a strategic orientation that provides guidance for effectively leveraging the sponsorship over a longer time horizon. John Hancock's subsequent investments in USA Gymnastics and Olympic figure skating further demonstrate D'Alessandro's thinking.

USA Gymnastics[55]

In 1995, gymnastics was the most popular of the Olympic sports for American audiences. Furthermore, gymnastics fans fit the basic John Hancock target customer profile, particularly their income and education. John Hancock's investment went deeper than just USA Gymnastics by supporting nine top gymnastics clubs, as well as several major collegiate teams. John Hancock also sponsored a USA Gymnastics tour of 20 cities, bringing gymnastic stars and Olympians from around the United States to perform for regional audiences in shopping malls. The Olympics sponsorship was a major draw for fans around the country, and John Hancock used these events to disseminate information about its products and services. Also in 1995, the company sponsored the "John Hancock Tour of World Gymnastics Champions," a more sophisticated, theatrical effort akin to a professional production that cost the company $1.5 million to sponsor. Following the success of the 1996 gold-medal-winning U.S. women's gymnastics team, the John Hancock Tour of World Gymnastics Champions embarked on a 34-city tour in the fall. Another 23 cities were added in early 1997. John Hancock invested further still, becoming the title sponsor of NBC's televised coverage of the 1997 tour. Each of the tour cities provided John Hancock with the opportunity to meet directly with any prospective customers, as well as use each of the tour stops for corporate hospitality events for the company's best customers. The company's marketing activities at each tour stop included extensive use of the John Hancock name in a variety of marketing vehicles:

- Signage inside and outside the arena
- Event programs
- John Hancock name on arena marquee
- Promotional materials
- Merchandise
- Post-event hospitality attended by the tour's gymnasts

The results of the 34-city tour were impressive:

- 90% average capacity in all arenas
- 500,000 people attended
- 460 news articles were generated
- $2.9 million in equivalent PR value created
- 10,000 sales leads

With the Olympics over, the subsequent 23-city tour was less well attended, with average overall capacity of 50–60%. However, John Hancock's overall success with the gymnastics tours convinced senior management that a four-year sponsorship of USA Gymnastics (USAG, the national governing body) at $1 million per year was a logical and important next step. Entitled the "John Hancock USA Gymnastics Championships," this was the culminating competition that determined the US national team. As with the gymnastics tours, sponsorship of the championships gave John Hancock unprecedented exposure in a variety of media and venues:

- Broadcast advertising
- Tickets with the John Hancock name and logo
- Signage throughout the championship arena
- Repeated exposure at the awards ceremonies
- Local marketing for the John Hancock regional agents
- Hospitality tickets and venues
- Extensive PR coverage
- John Hancock had the rights to use USAG's membership list for marketing

John Hancock co-hosted the US Gymnastics Trials in 1996 with the Massachusetts Sports Partnership, a competition that determines the final U.S. Olympic team. As with the gymnastics tours, John Hancock leveraged its trials investment by using several marketing tools to reach its target audience, including:

Public relations
In addition to the typical press coverage that accompanies national events of this stature and importance, John Hancock was directly responsible for handling all media relations for the trials, providing the company with direct and immediate contact with key media representatives.

Athlete photo opportunities
Hancock arranged to have photo and autograph sessions for the fans with the athletes. This gave the company an important and visible event that brought fans closer to their favorite competitors and generated goodwill for John Hancock.

Complimentary tickets
The sponsorship provided 1,000 tickets for John Hancock's use, which the company donated to the Boys & Girls Clubs of Boston. The

sponsorship also allowed John Hancock employees to purchase a similar number of tickets if they so desired, effectively providing them with a right of first refusal—a nice gesture given the popularity of the event.

Hospitality
Corporate hospitality events are typically part of most sponsorship packages, in the form of special tents or similar venues located on or near the sports event itself, and often a certain amount of catering and/or support services. John Hancock used the trials as an occasion to give its best customers additional attention.

Advertising and related awareness-generating activities
When corporate sponsors invest large sums such as those by John Hancock and Visa, the event's organizers ensure that selected media placement is made available, including:

- Premium placement in event publications and programs
- Signage via banners, announcements, flyers
- Sponsor name placed on athlete apparel
- Exhibit booths for John Hancock employees to use for displaying company products and services, giving presentations, and meeting with visiting customers
- Award presentation exposure

John Hancock's emphasis on branded events related to the Olympics, such as the figure-skating and gymnastics tours, is a conscious effort to make the company and the athletes more human and accessible, with the intention to foster strong emotional ties with its customers as a result. Each of these marketing vehicles requires thorough planning to ensure proper implementation. Management needs to understand what the objectives are with each marketing tool being used, determining what the desired outcome or result should be, creating a timeline with set dates and milestones for completion, and clearly assigning responsibilities directly to specific people and/or teams to ensure proper accountability. Upon conclusion of the event, a post-event review involving all relevant team members and partners is advisable, enabling people to see what worked well, which areas need improvement in future events, and what overall lessons were learned.

Olympic Figure Skating[56]

Figure skating has historically been one the most popular Winter Olympic Games sports, and it is similar to gymnastics in its combination of athletic and artistic ability. John Hancock saw figure skating as a logical complement to their support of gymnastics, so the company sponsored a tour called "Champions on Ice," featuring the best figure skaters from around the world, not just the United States. John Hancock became the title sponsor in 1998 for four years, agreeing to pay $2 million per year. The tour visited 40–50 cities per year from April to July, more stops than either the gymnastics or hockey tours, and provided John Hancock with still more marketing vehicles, from merchandise to signage to tickets to public address announcements to TV. The title sponsorship included an $80,000 media package for every city on the tour, providing a professionally produced, rich array of printed materials, giveaways, and goods for John Hancock's use. This is a sizable and highly useful promotional resource, designed to help journalists learn about the highlights of the tour, the athletes, the cities, and information about John Hancock and its role in a range of sports sponsorships. Hospitality events in which tour athletes would appear were another key feature of the tour, providing fans, John Hancock customers, and media closer access to the athletes and, like both the hockey and gymnastics tours, creating a more personal connection with the fans. This latter point is important in sports marketing activities. Without access to the athletes, companies are relegated to using athlete visages and quotes in print or broadcast media only, reducing the human element and emotional connections that can arise from direct appearances and turning a unique opportunity into a more prosaic marketing event, an approach that generates fewer and fewer returns due to increasing skepticism from consumers weary of traditional marketing appeals.

John Hancock management stated that its Olympic sponsorship has generated thousands of business leads over the years. The company has created its own "Olympic Games Effect" by supporting three of the most popular Olympic sports—gymnastics, figure skating, and hockey—and bringing them directly to the fans. As the company's president said,

The Games allow us to reach a public that is no longer easily persuaded by traditional advertising. Let's face it, consumers are getting too sophisticated for jingles and self-serving pitches. Try to show people a commercial, and they're off the couch and on their way to the refrigerator. However, allow them to rub elbows with an Olympic athlete—or invite them to bring their kids to a clinic run by gymnastics legend Bela Karolyi—and you have their rapt attention. You might even have their loyalty for life.[57]

As with Visa, the question of cause and effect is reasonable to consider. As D'Alessandro said,

Do I attribute all this to the Olympics? No. Do I want to drop out of the Olympics to find out? No.[58]

Reviewing John Hancock's marketing activities provides instructive insight into the many different ways the company reached out to its target customers, illustrating the complexity of the marketing communications plan the company chose. As D'Alessandro said,

Success in event marketing doesn't really depend as much on flashing the cash as on knowing where to spend it. Spend on properties that are well-run, and that are run like a business. Spend on events that you can own, manage, and measure. Spend on opportunities that enhance your brand, involve your customers, and extend your marketing reach.[59]

His comments reinforce an important, yet all-too-frequently overlooked business maxim—work with the best. Sports sponsorship success depends on the quality of the sports event and on how carefully company management both plans its brand-building efforts and allocates sufficient resources to support proper implementation. Furthermore, D'Alessandro's recommendation to select events that are run like a business may sound simple, but it is central to ensuring a sponsoring company's own reputation is not damaged and, instead, is enhanced, by the relationship. Clearly, relying on a simple name association with these Olympic events (by having the company logo on event programs, for example) is woefully inadequate if one wishes to maximize the enormous potential exposure and direct business opportunities that can be garnered if multiple, integrated marketing touchpoints are activated. With the Olympics, John Hancock is investing in a preeminent event with a storied history and globally recognized reputation. D'Alessandro summed up John Hancock's Olympic sponsorship succinctly:

In the end, the Olympic brand is absolutely unique. It remains consistently inspiring to consumers and to the sponsors themselves.[60]

John Hancock's Olympic marketing activities from 1993 to 2003 are shown in Figure 12-11. Like Visa, John Hancock envisioned, planned, and implemented these activities with a deliberate eye toward integrated marketing. These activities should be viewed in the context of Hancock's overall desire to use the Olympics sponsorship as an image-enhancing event with a life span that preceded and extended beyond the Olympic Games themselves. John Hancock maximized its Olympic investment by seeing its sponsorship as a series of interconnected activities and not as independent tactics.

Figure 12-11
John Hancock Sponsorship Marketing Framework

John Hancock Olympic Marketing Activities			
Communications	**Events**	**Products**	**Athletes**
• Public relations • Print ads • Broadcast ads • Local marketing • Flyers • Banners • Event publications • Signage	• Exhibit booths • Hospitality events • Tickets • Customer meetings	• Athletic apparel • Event giveaways	• Tours • Photo opportunities • Merchandising • Award presentations

Acquisition of John Hancock by Manulife
In 2003, John Hancock merged with Manulife. With the acquisition, Manulife inherited the Olympic sponsorship begun by John Hancock in 1994, committing to the relationship until the 2008 Beijing Olympics.

Manulife senior management saw the significance of the Olympics sponsorship and decided it was worth maintaining through the 2005–2008 quadrennial period, building on the equity gained from John Hancock's decade of Olympic investments. As Michael Huddart, senior vice president and general manager for Manulife in Hong Kong, said,

> *In general, it's exciting for our company name to be associated with the prestigious Olympic Games but it also generates a sense of pride and excitement amongst our staff and advisors. The obvious advantage of the Olympic sponsorship for Manulife is the unparalleled opportunity it provides to help us build our life insurance business and motivate our people—from Olympic-themed incentive programs for our staff and agency force to developing important relationships with our staff, top producers, and distribution partners.[61]*

Case Brief: Lenovo

Lenovo was founded in 1984 by 11 engineers from the Chinese Academy of Sciences. Known initially as NTD (New Technology Developer), the company's first technology product translated English-language operating systems into Chinese. The product, called Legend, was successful, solidifying the company's reputation with customers, who increasingly knew the company for its Legend product. In 1989, NTD changed its name to Legend and began making its own PCs in 1990. The company grew quickly and by 1999 its market share in China was 21.5%, making Legend #1 in that market. Its domestic market-share leadership continued, accelerating to 30% by 2001 and, by 2004, $3.2 billion in sales. During this time company management set a goal to become a Fortune 500 company by 2010, a target that would put increasing emphasis on global growth and expansion. To accomplish this would require an ambitious product, marketing, and operations strategy, and, in particular, the development of an internationally recognized brand. As a Chinese PC company, few consumers or companies outside of China knew of Legend. Furthermore, becoming a global brand would require having a marketable name that could be used around the world. The Legend name was already registered by other companies in different markets around the world, so keeping the name would have been problematic. In 2004, the company was renamed Lenovo, combining part of the

Legend name with that of "novo," a variation on the Latin *de novo* meaning "anew," suggesting "new."[62]

Shortly after the name change, Lenovo management announced it had officially signed on to be a TOP program sponsor for the 2006 and 2008 Olympics in Turin, Italy, and Beijing, China, respectively. Reported to have paid $80 million for the TOP program, the sponsorship would require another 2–3 times the original investment on marketing planning, creative development, and implementation, similar to Visa and John Hancock, bringing the total Olympic investment to at least $240 million (to be allocated over five years)—roughly 8% of Lenovo's total revenues (pre-IBM PC division acquisition), representing a substantial sum for a single marketing platform. Approximately 50% of the sponsorship cost would be "in-kind" or "trade-out" company products and services, so actual cash invested would be closer to $120 million, still a significant financial outlay.

Before the Olympic sponsorship announcement, Lenovo's advertising effort was focused on products, not the overall brand. Marketing spending had grown over the years and in 2005 the company invested more than $250 million on its global marketing efforts. This may seem like a substantial sum, but Lenovo trailed its key competitors, Dell and HP, which had a share of voice three times larger than Lenovo's.[63] The Olympics sponsorship offered Lenovo the chance to raise its profile rapidly and breakout of the conventional marketing approaches of its industry that relied on broadcast, print, billboard, and Internet advertising.

In December 2004, following the Olympic sponsorship investment, Lenovo purchased IBM's PC division for $1.75 billion a combination of cash ($650 million), stock (valued at $600 million), and debt (Lenovo assumed $500 million of IBM debt). The purchase gave Lenovo the right to use IBM's logo on its products for five years, and ownership of the ThinkPad (laptop) and ThinkCentre (desktop) brand names.[64] The acquisition brought together two companies that had collaborated behind the scenes for years. Lenovo had modeled much of its pre-acquisition business on that of IBM, so there was some similarity in corporate cultures, even though the companies were from two entirely different national cultures. In 2005, soon after the acquisition, several leading Dell executives that had been running Dell's Asia-Pacific operations left to join Lenovo, including Bill Amelio (Lenovo's CEO), Gerry Smith (Senior Vice President–Global Supply

Chain), David Miller (Senior President of Asia Pacific), and David Schmoock (Senior Vice President, Center of Excellence).[65] David Shaw, Director of Brand Marketing and Marketing Communications at Lenovo Asia Pacific, who joined in 2006 and was a former executive from HP, said a key challenge and opportunity for Lenovo management was how to best integrate the diverse, global employee base and wide-ranging operations the company had acquired. One of the most challenging aspects of any acquisition is the post-purchase integration—determining how to knit together different operations, job mapping, cost takeout strategy, and uniting different cultures. In Lenovo's case, while the integration was complex, the Olympics commitment provided a particularly visible platform around which employees could rally as they worked toward supporting the company's global integration and growth strategies.

Integration

Lenovo management established four objectives, shown in Table 12-12, that were seen as necessary both for short-term brand building, including ensuring a successful Olympics sponsorship effort, and long-term company health, including developing a well functioning, tightly integrated organization.

Table 12-12
Key Lenovo Integration Objectives

Clarify	Cultivate	Market	Measure
Clarify DNA and focus of the new Lenovo culture and brand	Cultivate the new culture and brand within Lenovo	Market the new brand identity externally 360°	Measure Lenovo's brand image; use findings to recalibrate, refine, reload, and recharge the brand

The measurement objective focuses on qualitative dimensions, including awareness, consideration, and image. Awareness describes whether the market knows that a company and/or its offerings exist and, if so, how strong that awareness is. Consideration refers to the exchange of value between a buyer and a seller, such as when the seller promises a certain product at a certain price and the buyer agrees by

231

giving a payment (money, in-kind, IOU). Image, in Lenovo's case, refers to the number of people (out of those already aware of the company) who rated the brand 8, 9, or 10 on a 10-point scale (1 is worst, 10 is best). These objectives provided both the guidance and the glue to help this new company begin the process of transformation to a single culture with ambitions to use its diverse assets to compete successfully around the world. As *BusinessWeek Online* said shortly after the acquisition,

> *Lenovo's new leaders will have to bridge not only the 6,800 miles from New York to Beijing but also immense cultural differences. Lenovo PCs will carry the IBM name for five years, and former IBMers will be among the product designers, but some corporate customers may not trust Lenovo to deliver the quality and innovation they have counted on from IBM. And tech combos far less complex than this one have been notoriously difficult to pull off in the past. Notes Dell Chairman Michael S. Dell: "When was the last time you saw a successful acquisition or merger in the computer industry?*[66]

To facilitate cultural and business integration, as well as prepare for the 2008 Beijing Olympic Games, the new Lenovo management team set out a multi-year cultural integration path with several key milestones:[67]

As Figure 12-12 highlights, each year focuses on a key theme that, upon completion, adds to the cultural foundation. Note that this effort is extended over four years initially, although this is not to suggest that the cultural integration will be complete by the end of year four, nor that all of the tasks assigned in each year's theme (the items listed under each theme) will be perfectly executed. The listed sub-themes are not exhaustive, but they do highlight important tasks to be accomplished.

Figure 12-12
Lenovo Cultural Integration Path

2006	2007	2008	2009
Assess and Define *The New Culture*	**Engage and Personalize** *The New Culture*	**Celebrate and Live** *The New Culture*	**Embed and Reward** *The New Culture*
Global interviews	Cultural framework cascade	All-hands meetings	Embed new behaviors in processes
Cultural framework	Culture toolkits training	Infuse CSR strategy	Measure and revise
		Leverage the Olympics	

2006: Assess and Define
Global interviews
The new management team committed to interviewing employees from the newly combined company's many global operations to learn about the company from the inside.

Cultural framework
With multiple operations coming together, establishing a new, single "Lenovo" identity would be crucial to developing a cohesive, integrated company that shared common values and objectives.

2007: Engage and Personalize
Cultural framework cascade
Once the cultural framework is set, the rest of the company needs to learn about it through active engagement. Cascading is a communication process that rolls out important company information from senior management to frontline, from headquarters to all field operations. Different people and teams are assigned from a cascade session to continue the cascading to their own region and offices. Successful engagement requires more than internal memos and official

pronouncements. A sincere effort to personalize the company's direction via direct meetings with senior management and open dialogs with fellow employees connects people in a more social manner that provides a more informal atmosphere and also communicates vibrancy and energy that can have a positive viral effect with employees.

Culture toolkits training

Toolkits typically are a compilation of summarized values, new employee policies, behavior guidelines, brand tenets, and key aspects of corporate strategy, including product direction and basic brand communication. Toolkits are disseminated worldwide to all offices and can range from physical materials such information packets to online delivery to mobile device delivery.

2008: Celebrate and Live

All-hands meetings

As implied, all employees attend these meetings, typically used to disseminate new information about company products, changes, direction, and achievements. With Lenovo's new management team, global growth ambitions, branding initiatives (including the 2008 Beijing Olympic Games), and new product direction, all-hands meetings are a necessary forum for employees to talk directly with each other and senior management.

Infuse CSR strategy

Part of Lenovo's strategy was to be a recognized leader in corporate accountability, including ethical behavior, product leadership (innovation, quality, environmental), and employee welfare. A central emphasis was placed on use of recycled materials and making products that are recyclable. Additionally, the company intended to design products that were energy efficient. These CSR practices are not unique as many companies are stepping up similar efforts, but they are an important component of Lenovo's global reputation development as the company expands into markets where consumers are environmentally active and assess corporate CSR practices with increasing rigor in their product purchase decisions.

Leverage the Olympics

Within the Celebrate and Live theme resides an attitude of enthusiasm for the future potential of Lenovo. The Olympics, while filled with ancient traditions, is very much a celebration of young athletes at their competitive best. While Lenovo is arguably a young competitor in the global PC business, despite its two-decade domestic legacy in China, it has sprinted nonstop in recent years to become a successful international company, with a diverse management team from around the world driving a new global competitiveness. The spirit of sport exemplified by the Olympics, therefore, seems particularly opportune. Using the marketer's toolkit, Lenovo sees the Olympics as a once-in-a-lifetime opportunity of enormous global importance to elevate its brand and attract an even broader following of consumers.

2009: Embed and Reward

Embed new behaviors in processes

With several years of culture building, business integration, and brand development underway, new practices and processes inevitably develop formally and informally. In this phase, the company will focus on institutionalizing the better practices adopted over the preceding recent years and reward those that represent the company's targeted ideal behaviors.

Measure and revise

Accountability is a common requirement for every area of companies today. With new practices, products, and strategic efforts underway, management needs to regularly review the business's performance to assess progress.

This multi-year plan provides an organizational roadmap for Lenovo as it combines global operations and cultures. Lenovo management implicitly acknowledges that successful integrations do not happen overnight, but over time. As mergers and acquisitions veterans know, the easier part is buying another company and mapping out the planned efficiencies. The hard part is implementation because people are involved (along with their emotions, loyalties, fears, ambitions), and there are inherent challenges in working with disparate personalities and diverse corporate cultures. The acquirer wants to retain the acquired company's

235

best employees, while the acquired company's staff is concerned about their future, including what changes will be introduced by their new management. Integration plans that look good on paper, despite not being based on thorough and thoughtful due diligence, are subjected to the real-world challenges of employee resistance, inconsistent communications, and general misunderstandings that can quickly unravel the best of plans. This can push management from proper integration and toward problem management, delaying the acquisition's benefits and creating further uncertainty for employees.

Getting these foundational brand-building components in place does not guarantee success. Careful attention to implementation detail and organizational nimbleness are required. Layered on top of this foundation are the immediate needs for Lenovo to raise its brand profile around the world. While Lenovo is and has been a leader in China and the #4 PC maker in the world behind HP, Dell, and Acer,[68] and while China is growing rapidly economically and has witnessed important socio-economic gains domestically, the company faces a skeptical consumer population outside China, particularly in the West. This skepticism is underscored by concern Lenovo has faced since the IBM acquisition that it cannot maintain IBM's quality or reputation for innovation. To Lenovo's credit, the company has garnered international recognition and awards since the IBM acquisition for both innovation and quality (including "Best of Show" at the annual Consumer Electronics Show in Las Vegas; Gold Awards from the Industrial Design Excellence Awards (IDEA); "Highly Commended" recognition by PC Pro; and favorable product reviews from *Fortune* magazine, *PC World* magazine, and numerous other international publications).[69] Of course, being associated with the Olympics further enhances this international recognition, and Lenovo took full advantage of its sponsorship beginning with the 2006 Turin Olympics.

As discussed, part of Lenovo's Olympic sponsorship was paid through in-kind product. Lenovo supplied the Turin Olympics with 350 servers, 5,000 desktops, and 750 notebooks. With the highly visible Olympics as a stage, Lenovo's fledgling international reputation was on full display for the world to see. A successful product performance would help establish a positive foundation for the company's continued emergence onto the world stage and provide an important credibility-building step as the company prepared for the 2008 Beijing Olympics. An embarrassing failure, such as computer problems that impact event results, would be potentially devastating or, at a minimum, certainly reinforce negative perceptions about the quality of the company's products, making Lenovo's future product launches and subsequent 2008 Olympic sponsorship problematic. With weather conditions at the Turin Olympics understandably cold (62 of the 200 competitions were held in sub-zero temperatures), technology failure was a reasonable risk. Lenovo placed 70 technicians onsite for the duration of the Olympics, and they provided error-free support for every single Olympic event. One of the vital components of Lenovo's technology infrastructure included the "Commentator Information System" that provided broadcast journalists and producers with updated information on athlete biographies, the latest event performance statistics, and an ongoing news stream from around the Olympics. Lenovo created seven i.lounges, essentially Internet-style cafes, in which journalists, athletes, trainers, and coaching staff could stay in contact with family, friends, and fans. Over 200 athletes from 40 countries used the i.lounges each day. Lenovo's technology infrastructure also supported over 415 hours of coverage for five broadcast networks. Lenovo partnered with other TOP sponsors, including Coca-Cola, GE's NBC broadcast division, Visa, and Bank of America, to provide technology services for their Olympic infrastructures. For example, Visa collaborated with Lenovo to provide free ThinkPad Z60m's, one of the top models in the company's notebook product line, to winners of the online video contest called "Visa Championships–Torino 2006."[70] GE's NBC broadcast division chose Lenovo to be its computer-equipment supplier in supporting broadcast coverage of the various winter events. These collaborative relationships between Lenovo and other TOP program sponsors were an important credibility-building point for the company in its efforts to convince the world that its products were trustworthy. After all, if some of the world's best-known companies entrusted Lenovo to handle their technology needs during a highly visible, high-demand event, then that would send a powerful signal to the marketplace that Lenovo is a major emerging company in the world. Lenovo's Olympic efforts succeeded, as captured by Managing Director of IT for the Turin Olympics Enrico Frascari,

THE OLYMPIC GAMES EFFECT

There is no such thing as a "second try" at the Olympic Games. Thanks to the reliable and secure PC solution developed and supported by Lenovo, we have passed a critical operational period in Torino with record-breaking performance from the technology system.[71]

These activities were necessary to successfully support the demands of the thousands of people attending and participating in the Winter Olympics, in addition to the hundreds of millions of people watching from around the world.

Lenovo Product and Marketing Strategy

To reach the world's television viewers and develop the company's brand further, Lenovo planned to launch new products and a three-part advertising strategy. First, from May to September 2005 the company's ads concluded with the name "ThinkPad." The Lenovo name was not used in this first advertising phase, a conscious choice to emphasize a known entity, ThinkPad, which required little explanation since the market knew the ThinkPad name well from IBM's years of stewarding this product line. Furthermore, using the name Lenovo so soon after the IBM acquisition in the months leading up to the 2006 Winter Olympics would require far more explanation than could be reasonably accomplished in the span of a short broadcast advertising spot.

Second, following the "ThinkPad" first phase, Lenovo launched a new ad campaign called "ThinkPad Unleashed" (unveiled for the 2006 Winter Olympics in Turin) that delivered over 1 billion impressions worldwide (an "impression" is typically defined as a single instance of an ad being displayed. A similar definition says an impression is the number of "views" m an ad receives).[72] While the "ThinkPad" campaign was designed to reassure people that the product was the same reliable one as before the acquisition, the "ThinkPad Unleashed" campaign was signaling to the market that improvements were in store for this well-known laptop. A reasonable question is to ask why Lenovo dared to improve the ThinkPad at all. After all, the product had a solid reputation with consumers and analysts. Part of the answer was to abruptly change the market's perception (and apprehensions) and alleviate any concerns about the future quality of the ThinkPad and ThinkCenter products. But a related problem was whether the ThinkPad products would continue to be innovative at all, or if they would be pushed toward the lower-cost, commodity end of the PC product continuum. Quality products are certainly possible and necessary, even in a commodity market. But product quality is increasingly a minimum cost of entry, a point of parity, to get into any market. The key question for any company trying to build a brand is determining the company's point(s) of differentiation, or whether it wants to be distinctive at all.

One of the perception problems Lenovo inherited following the IBM acquisition was how to overcome doubts about the company's ability to innovate—something for which IBM had been known, while Lenovo had little, if any, image beyond naive, inaccurate stereotypes that labeled the company as a cheaper, less-reliable manufacturer of PCs from China. The "ThinkPad Unleashed" campaign was intended to send the message that Lenovo was an innovator of a new generation of PCs, and not a caretaker of some other company's work. While many of the same engineers were involved (since they stayed with the new company following the acquisition by Lenovo), Lenovo had its own team of talented engineers as well. Successful cross-pollination would show the world that the cultural integration had not come at the expense of product quality or innovation.

What much of the world did not know was that, contrary to these doubts, Lenovo (under its prior name Legend) actually had a track record of innovation in China. They had developed the first Chinese-character card for PCs, an important breakthrough that enabled English-language operating systems to be translated into Chinese. The company introduced the first Intel® Pentium® PC in China in 1994; the first integrated LCD PC in 1998; the first Internet PC with easy-to-use single-key access in 1999; the first dual-mode PC in 2002 (it operated on both LEOS (Linux Embedded Operating System) and Microsoft Windows); the first wireless PC to use IGRS (Integrated Grouping and Resources Sharing, a standard protocol for interoperability among different equipment, such as PCs and TVs) in 2003;[73] and the first broadband PC in 2004.[74] Each of these was a significant innovation in China and was instrumental in opening the Chinese market to PCs and the Internet. Thus, despite the concerns, Lenovo's heritage was firmly rooted in innovation.

Since the new management team took over, Lenovo has been innovating in its operations as well. Led by CEO Amelio, the company is focused on a concept called "world-sourcing." As opposed to outsourcing, a term associated with locating production where labor is cheapest, world-sourcing emphasizes doing work where the expertise is best. Operating 24 hours per day, 7 days per week, complex projects are developed across three continents (Asia, Europe, North America) and four major countries with design, development, operations, and distribution teams operating in a virtually borderless world. Amelio himself operates as a roving CEO, splitting time among company offices in Beijing, Singapore, and Raleigh, as well as the rest of the world. His energetic leadership sets the tone for the rest of the company, reinforcing the drive to become both the best, and the most innovative, PC company in the world.

The third and final part of the advertising plan was to begin associating the Lenovo name more directly with "ThinkPad" and with innovation in order to build both brand awareness and credibility. Company surveys showed that Lenovo's TOP program participation had helped improve the brand's reputation. Brazil and China, in particular, responded quite favorably to the company's Olympic sponsorship. Lenovo marketers focused on a simple combination of traditional and non-traditional marketing, including Web-based advertising, television campaigns, and extensive print ads, allocating $100 million for these pieces of the Olympic marketing effort. An interesting complication was that the IBM logo could not be used in any Olympics-related advertising, even though Lenovo had the right to use the IBM logo for five years. The simple reason was that IBM was not an Olympic sponsor. Given the recent acquisition of the IBM PC division, and given Lenovo's interest in using the Turin Olympics as a key brand-building platform, this restriction gave the company a sizable challenge—how could they directly leverage the IBM name and reputation at the Olympics? This situation could have conceivably confused consumers who might have seen the ThinkPad advertising in its Olympic and non-Olympic forms—in other words, one ad campaign with and the other without the IBM logo. Fortunately, the ThinkPad brand was well established in the market, so Lenovo's Olympic advertising featured a familiar product name for consumers, even without the use of the IBM logo. Mark McNeilly, Executive Director for Branding and Marketing Strategy at Lenovo, said,

What we wanted was to maintain the ThinkPad brand and use that brand's strength to build the Lenovo brand.[75]

McNeilly's comment is noteworthy because it is a departure from conventional brand-management thinking, which emphasizes using the corporate umbrella brand to cast a positive halo over the rest of the company's offerings and, thereby, give product brands added credibility in the market. This is also known as a *branded house* approach in which the branded house is the main or master brand under which lesser-known products or business divisions are organized (if one were to view brand strategy as a continuum, then a branded house is at one end and a *house of brands*—meaning a less powerful corporate brand with well-known individual products underneath, such as Procter & Gamble, is at the other end). Company management was planning a hybrid approach : leveraging the better-known ThinkPad sub-brand to enhance the lesser-known Lenovo brand. Hybrid approaches can work, but they typically begin with a strong branded house that trickles down to strengthen sub-brands over time. Examples include the Intel® Pentium®, Toyota Landcruiser, and Creative Soundblaster. Lenovo management wanted to strengthen the corporate brand using the better-known product brand, yet they also had to ensure the product brand was not diluted or harmed by being attached to a relatively unknown company.

As discussed, management believed that part of the solution was to redesign the ThinkPad product, yet this too was a tricky proposition since management did not want to alienate ThinkPad customers. The IBM name was certainly reputable and respected, and Lenovo had good reason to continue the association in the short term while it integrated the acquisition, solidified the operation, and began building toward a long-term, differentiated brand. At some point, a transition would need to occur from using the IBM name to eliminating it entirely. Lenovo's rights to the IBM logo were based on the schedule in Figure 12-13:

Figure 12-13
Timeline for Use of IBM Logo[76]

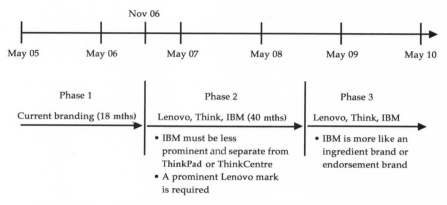

This timeline evolved slightly in the ensuing months from an emphasis on the phased-out usage of the IBM logo toward a more strategic brand approach emphasizing the phased-in usage of the Lenovo name on an accelerated basis, as shown in Figure 12-14:

Figure 12-14
Three Phases of Lenovo Brand Building[77]

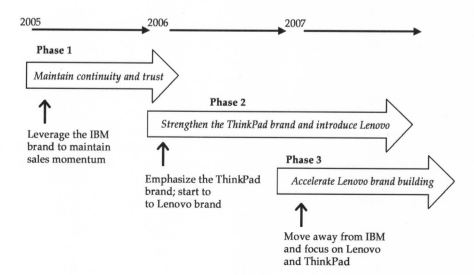

The new product, the ThinkPad Z60, was a design departure in one very obvious way: it was now offered with a titanium cover. All previous ThinkPads had been black. In addition, the ThinkPad Z60 offered new, wider 14-inch and 15.4-inch displays. The company improved the design features of the keyboard and improved the laptop's wireless capability. *Fortune* magazine commented,

> All told, Lenovo's stewardship of this brand is off to a good start, with perhaps the best ThinkPad yet.[78]

The ThinkPad Z60 was off to a promising start. But one of the keys to building a successful brand is for management, indeed the entire company, to think well past points of parity (product quality) and points of distinction (what makes you special). A successful brand must win the hearts and minds of its own employees—it must be embedded deep into the psyche, the practices, and the beliefs of the organization. Employees must feel they are part of something special, similar to having the sense that they are pursuing a cause and not just developing products for profit. Lenovo wanted to find a unique way to convey its innovation capabilities, beyond the core PC products, to serve as a source of inspiration for its own employees. At the risk of sounding overly philosophical, this was analogous to a soulful search for meaning. At the same time, the Beijing Organizing Committee sought designs for the Olympic logo and Lenovo submitted an entry. While the effort did not win, it did succeed in getting employees to begin thinking about the brand differently, opening up the idea that they could be innovative and creative beyond the world of PCs.

Undaunted by the loss, Yao Yingjia, executive director of the Lenovo Design Center in Beijing, jumped at the chance to submit a design for the Olympic torch. Over several months a team of Lenovo designers and engineers worked feverishly, finalizing a design called "Cloud of Promise." Conceived to look like a rolled-up scroll, the design was also a stylized homage to China's invention of paper. The team chose a simple yet elegant circular cloud motif in red outline, reflective of traditional Chinese art, with the circle themes that evoked the Olympic rings. The Lenovo team won the competition out of a field of 300 competitors, an unusual feat since winning designs from previous Olympics were usually awarded to design companies. This provided the internal inspiration the company sought, and sent a message to the rest of the world that Lenovo had design and innovation capability that extended beyond PCs. In trying to convey an image of innovation, Lenovo had succeeded in straddling two worlds: product and design, a combination in the PC market that has been most closely associated with Apple in recent years. This was an important milestone for Lenovo and, arguably, would not have been possible without the impetus provided by the Olympic sponsorship.

Lenovo then decided to use the torch motif to inspire a limited-edition laptop. The product's appearance is striking, with a bold exterior finish that resembles ancient Chinese lacquer boxes. While this special laptop will not be available to consumers in the mass market, more than 2,000 will be auctioned for charity, benefitting the Lenovo Hope Fund, a "donor-advised philanthropic fund... supporting the creation and growth of new businesses in distressed communities around the world, as well as innovative nonprofit organizations that serve these communities." The limited-edition laptop and the Lenovo Hope Fund burnish the company's credentials as a responsible corporate citizen while also setting the stage for future product direction. As Yao Yingjia said, "We'll continue to try laptop designs with interesting cultural and emotional appeal."[79]

This combined marketing and product strategy was important for several reasons. First, the three-part campaign demonstrated that Lenovo was committed to maintaining the innovation legacy long associated with IBM and, as the market was learning, with Lenovo. Second, Lenovo's ThinkPad innovations were incremental, not dramatic, in the hope that loyal ThinkPad customers would not be turned off. However, at the same time the changes were substantial enough to demonstrate that Lenovo was committed to continuing IBM's more visible reputation for quality innovation. Third, as the official computer supplier to the Turin Olympics, Lenovo's crucial early image development was at stake, and both the internal operational infrastructure and external communications had to be well received. Fourth, and more generally, the eyes of the world were watching to see how the transition from IBM to Lenovo was proceeding, looking for signs of success and/or failure. Clearly, there was a great deal riding on Lenovo's sponsorship of the Olympic Games because it would be the company's first significant post-acquisition launch and it was being held on the world's biggest sports stage. Lenovo was trying to fulfill a diverse range of expectations, metaphorically juggling many balls. Any dropped ball risked embarrassment and, worse, the possible loss of customers, as well as reputational and financial harm, even before the new company had a chance to take-off.

Lenovo also developed a website dedicated to its Olympic sponsorship (http://2008.lenovo.com/). The site features a customizable interface that visitors can organize based on their own preferences and country of origin. The interface offers a rich array of Olympic-specific content, including photos of the winning Olympic Torch design and the "Cloud of Promise" laptop it inspired; descriptions and videos of the athletes Lenovo sponsors; Google Earth maps of the Lenovo-sponsored Olympic Torch Relay route; a Lenovo Olympics blog; real-time Olympic news feeds; and an interactive calendar of events.

Consistent with the latest web tools, there is an "add stuff" button that takes visitors to a page of Google applications and widgets that users can add to their Lenovo Olympics website. The thinking and effort that went into the Lenovo Olympics website highlights an important point: Lenovo did not just build a static website about the Olympics, which would have been the equivalent of a one-way brochure; instead, it created a flexible, user-directed website that enables visitors to get directly involved in customizing the interface based on their own tastes. The site is well-suited to appeal to the sizable world of Web 2.0 online users who seek more interactivity and engagement with a company if they are to remain as visitors and, ultimately, customers.

Engaging customers with your brand, just as Lenovo was doing with its own employees internally, is a vital component of creating a great customer experience. When customers are involved with the brand, such as when they are able to customize their own website, then they are likely to remember it more, return to it more often, and recommend it to others more frequently.

Sponsored Athletes[80]

Aside from the marketing communications, equipment supplies, and design innovations, Lenovo is also directly involved in sponsoring 14 athletes from around the world (a 15th athlete is pending at the time of writing):

- Libby Trickett—Australia - Swimming
- Eamon Sullivan—Australia - Swimming
- Ricardo Santos—Brazil - Beach Volleyball
- Emanuel Rego—Brazil - Beach Volleyball
- Adam van Koeverden—Canada - Kayaking
- Liu Xiang—China - Athletics
- Xavier Rohart—France - Sailing
- Steffen Deibler—Germany - Swimming
- Markus Deibler—Germany - Swimming
- Shingo Suetsugu—Japan - Athletics
- Paola Espinoza—Mexico - Diving
- Gail Emms—United Kingdom - Badminton
- Kerri Walsh—United States - Beach Volleyball
- Misty May-Treanor—United States - Beach Volleyball
- *Tatiana Lebedeva—Russia - Athletics* (agreement pending at time of writing)

Lenovo created detailed profiles of these athletes on its company website, including highlights of their sports careers and videos of select performances. Many of the athletes employ innovative training methods, are actively involved in charitable activities, and enjoy wholesome reputations in their home countries—sharing values and characteristics that are consistent with Lenovo's CSR philosophy. The athletes have agreed to use Lenovo PCs to write about their Olympic adventures and Lenovo will also expand its coverage of each athlete as the games progress. This is a clever application of several marketing tactics, from athlete sponsorship to interactive online communications between fans and the athletes to thoughtful and involved corporate citizenship to general buzz-building for both the athletes and Lenovo.

Performance to Date[81]

Lenovo's revenues grew nearly 10% between 2006 and 2007, increasing from $13.27 billion to $14.59 billion. Gross profits rose during that time from $1.86 billion to $2.03 billion. Lenovo was #3 in global PC market share through the middle of 2007, behind HP and Dell. This position was relatively consistent since the IBM acquisition. However, Acer acquired Gateway in the second half of 2007, vaulting it to the #3 position and pushing Lenovo to #4, as shown by Table 12-13, from Gartner.

Table 12-13
Preliminary Worldwide PC Vendor Unit Shipment Estimates for 2007 (000's of units)

Company	2007 Shipments	2007 Market share (%)	2006 Shipments	2006 Market share (%)	2007–06 Growth (%)
Hewlett-Packard	49,434	18.2	38,037	15.9	30.0
Dell Inc.	38,709	14.3	38,050	15.9	1.7
Acer	24,257	8.9	18,252	7.6	32.9
Lenovo	20,131	7.4	16,652	7.0	20.9
Toshiba	10,932	4.0	9,198	3.8	18.9
Others	127,717	47.1	119,022	49.8	7.3
Total	**271,180**	**100.0**	**239,211**	**100.0**	**13.4**

As Gartner stated about both Lenovo and Acer in its analysis:

> *In the fourth quarter, Acer achieved solid consumer mobile PC growth in EMEA and the United States. Acer's acquisition of Gateway's consumer business boosted the shipment volume. Lenovo also well exceeded the worldwide growth average. Despite a lack or weak consumer market presence, Lenovo showed a relatively good performance in consumer sales in both EMEA and the United States during the quarter.*[82]

The fourth quarter of 2007 revealed that Lenovo was continuing to grow rapidly, near the pace of Hewlett-Packard and Acer. Dell, while growing as well, was 4–6 percentage points below that of the other three. One quarter's performance does not indicate a trend, but for Lenovo management's, which is in the midst of multiple major initiatives including the Olympics, there is at least some indication that its efforts are paying off internationally. Table 12-14 provides PC shipment information for the last quarter of 2007.

Table 12-14
Preliminary Worldwide PC Vendor Unit Shipment Estimates for 4Q07 (000's of units) [83]

Company	4Q07 Shipments	4Q07 Market share (%)	4Q06 Shipments	4Q06 Market share (%)	4Q07–4Q06 Growth (%)
Hewlett-Packard	14,411	19.0	11,691	17.4	23.3
Dell Inc.	10,977	14.5	9,381	14.0	17.0
Acer	7,243	9.5	5,912	8.8	22.5
Lenovo	5,825	7.7	4,779	7.1	21.9
Toshiba	3,004	4.0	2,590	3.9	16.0
Others	34,468	45.4	32,786	48.8	5.1
Total	**75,928**	**100.0**	**67,138**	**100.0**	**13.1**

However, one of the big challenges for Lenovo is expanding its U.S. market presence, where it is not among the top five PC makers, as show in Table 12-15:

Table 12-15
Preliminary US PC Vendor Unit Shipment Estimates for 4Q07 (000's of units)

Company	4Q07 Shipments	4Q07 Market share (%)	4Q06 Shipments	4Q06 Market share (%)	4Q07–4Q06 Growth (%)
Dell Inc.	5,345	31.4	4,651	29.3	14.9
Hewlett-Packard	4,441	26.1	4,053	25.5	9.6
Acer	1,527	9.0	1,380	8.7	10.7
Apple	1,035	6.1	808	5.1	28.0
Toshiba	900	5.3	852	5.4	5.7
Others	3,790	22.2	4,143	26.1	-8.5
Total	**17,038**	**100.0**	**15,886**	**100.0**	**7.2**

The Olympics sponsorship is not designed to directly improve Lenovo's market share in the United States, nor is that a primary strategic objective of the company. Consumer trust in brands takes far longer to win than can be reasonably expected in two years of Olympic support. Despite having taken over the IBM PC division, Lenovo still needs to prove itself as a viable, long-term competitor in the global PC market. But the 2008 Beijing Olympics provide a unique opportunity for Lenovo to stimulate customer interest further, particularly since the audience for the Summer Games is much larger than for the Winter Games. The company's success with the winning torch design, and its unique application of that design to a limited- edition laptop, suggest that Lenovo may be offering bold new products in the market following the Olympics. Assuming this occurs, then part of the inspiration for this revitalization will have been due to the laser-sharp attention paid to maximizing its Olympic sponsorship.

Each of the Olympic TOP program sponsors discussed in this section has developed its own unique approach to leveraging its association with the Games. Marketers must recognize that TOP sponsors are treating the Olympic investment as a serious strategic asset. Just as the easiest part of a corporate acquisition of another company is the purchase itself (versus the integration, which is far harder and more complex), the easiest part of a sports sponsorship is spending money for exposure. The real challenge, and opportunity, is deciding how to implement the sponsorship so that the event boosts the company's image while simultaneously avoiding undermining or damaging both organizations' reputations. Furthermore, a sponsorship's success is due to far more than a company giving money for the right to associate its name with an event such as the Olympics. As the examples in the preceding pages demonstrated, TOP sponsors have planned sophisticated brand-building efforts designed to run for many years using multiple marketing platforms. These marketing platforms are a modern analog to the four Ps of the classic marketing mix (product, price, place, promotion), except that the four Ps have been "retired" in favor of integrated marketing campaigns that introduce a wider range of today's marketing tools. Among these are digital and social media tools in particular. Using blogs, social sites, and digital and mobile downloads, companies can have direct, one-on-one communications with consumers. Each of the TOP sponsors set multiple criteria for assessing the return on its sponsorship investment, including short-term financial and long-term strategic positioning gains. Evaluating sponsorship performance using an assortment of measures is a crucial point to understand.

There are multiple ways to measure sponsorship success. A single formula does not shed the necessary light on the contributions of the full range of marketing activities employed unless a company is investing in only one or two focused areas. As the company briefs illustrate, each sponsor evaluates success using a wide range of criteria, and the audit questions at the end of each section throughout this book are designed to help management think through the strategic objectives, tactical choices, and methods of assessment. Brand value is one measure that is gaining increasing interest. As David Haigh, CEO of BrandFinance, stated, 63% of enterprise value today is intangible, which means "brand" is taking on a leading role in measuring company performance. As a brief illustration, Samsung began its TOP sponsorship involvement in 1997, the same year as the Asian financial crisis. The company initiated a major restructuring following the crisis that helped set it on the successful path that it has enjoyed since. Samsung's director-general for the sports marketing group, Sunny Hwang, said in an interview during the 2004 Olympic Games in Athens that Samsung had spent over $200 million on the Turin and Beijing Olympiads and proclaimed that Samsung was seen as the most successful TOP sponsor in Athens due to three areas: sponsorship of the global torch relay; establishment of the Olympic Rendezvous at Samsung (a gathering place outfitted with mobile communications equipment and real-time updates on competition results via TV); and sizable advertising investments. While his enthusiasm for Samsung's relative performance may be self-serving, Samsung has certainly witnessed significant growth in brand value concurrent to the increase in its Olympic investments, growing from $8.3 billion in 2002 to $12.6 billion in 2004 to $16.8 billion in 2007 (as measured by Interbrand's annual "Top 100 Global Brands Survey").[85]

Ambush Marketing

When an event is as successful as the modern Olympics it is little wonder that many companies would want to find a way to take advantage of the Olympic Games Effect. This includes seeking alternative marketing routes to receiving Olympic benefits without paying Olympic costs. Ambush marketing is a practice whereby a company attempts to associate itself with a significant event, such as the Olympics, in an unauthorized and unofficial way without paying the sponsorship fees. Official sponsors get upset, of course, plus the event risks losing credibility if it cannot enforce protection of its image and the official sponsors' rights. In preparation for the 2004 Olympic Games in Athens, more than $750,000 was spent removing and cleaning billboards throughout the city. The best billboards located near the athletic venues were reserved for authorized sponsors only. Despite similar efforts at all Olympics, unauthorized companies do find ways to leverage the Olympic juggernaut. Exhibit 12-1 highlights Olympic marketing ambush examples. Policing every conceivable location near the venues and watching each individual person carefully is not feasible, and also risks sending the message that the IOC does not trust people or companies, which would be counter to the Olympic spirit.

Exhibit 12-1[86]
Ambush Marketing Examples in the Olympics

1984 Kodak sponsors TV broadcasts, despite Fuji being Olympics' official sponsor. Fuji returns favor at Seoul 1988 Games.

1992 Nike sponsors news conferences with the U.S. basketball team in Barcelona. Michael Jordan accepts the gold medal for basketball and covers up his Reebok logo.

1994 American Express runs ads claiming Americans do not need "Visas" to travel to Norway (for Lillehammer Winter Olympics).

1996 Nike buys out billboards around Atlanta Olympic sites.

2000 Qantas Airlines' slogan "Spirit of Australia" coincidentally sounds like Games slogan "Share the spirit" to chagrin of official Sydney Olympic sponsor Ansett Air.

After the 12 TOP sponsors for the 2008 Olympic Games in Beijing are 11 lower-level sponsors that have invested close to $50 million to be associated with the Games, as well as companies signed-on as "Official Suppliers" in dozens of product categories. They, too, want their sponsorship investment protected against ambushers. At the same time, Pepsi (not an authorized sponsor of the Games) changed its can color to red from blue for the Beijing Olympics, ostensibly because red is an auspicious color in China. Nike (also not an authorized sponsor) has apparel contracts with many athletes who are required to wear the official Adidas Olympic outfit during medal ceremonies. Market research firm Ipsos conducted a survey of thousands of Chinese consumers in 2007 that revealed many think non-sponsors are "official." According to R3, a Beijing-based consulting firm, 75% of Chinese consumers "would prefer to buy products they associated with the Olympics." Ambush marketing is not cheap, however. The athlete and team sponsorships independent of the Olympics cost enormous sums of money. But that money is leveraged across all activities in which that athlete is involved, so the Olympics-specific costs are certainly lower than for a TOP sponsor. Do Coke and Adidas, for example, lose sponsorship benefits as a result of the examples described? Conceivably, yes. If consumers believe non-sponsors are actually officially part of the Olympics, then it serves to divert some attention from the TOP sponsors. Are the non-sponsors doing something illegal or wrong? Many of the ambush marketing examples seen are simply extensions of pre-existing business and marketing relationships between the company and the athlete/team. The ongoing challenge for the IOC is finding ways to minimize the effects of ambush marketers without interfering with the normal conduct of business and established contractual relationships for sponsors and non-sponsors alike. Despite these challenges, the IOC has been able to make its sponsorship programs perennially attractive, indicating that while not perfect, there is sufficient confidence in the structure of the programs to keep companies interested.

When signing a sponsorship deal, the onus is on the company to ensure that the contract language is clear about how the company's authorized status will be protected and unauthorized companies will be prevented access. While no contract can cover all contingencies, an open, upfront exchange of expectations between the event and the sponsor can at least provide strong guidance about what is and is not possible in protecting authorized sponsors from ambush marketers.

For those companies with the financial ability, an Olympic TOP sponsorship is a powerful and visible platform for expanding a company's brand image, financial performance, and market reputation. As a reminder, success as a sports sponsor involves more than giving money to have your name associated with an event. Having a plan that sets clear sponsorship objectives, tactical programs, and evaluation criteria is not a luxury but a requirement and a major responsibility. As the Olympics continue to grow and costs accelerate, the complexity of hosting an Olympiad increases. Corporate sponsors may be tempted to offset the increased sponsorship costs by implementing more aggressive product, marketing communication, and merchandising programs to boost revenues. Doing so risks accelerating the pace of overt commercialization of the Olympics, a criticism leveled against the 1996 Olympic Games in Atlanta. If the Olympics become too commercial, then the spirit of the Games will likely be harmed, reducing what was once a prestigious, exclusive, unique event to one of commercial clutter in which fans and athletes are bombarded with advertisements, distracting and detracting from the primary purpose of the Olympic Games: pure athletic competition. However, when such situations occur the ensuing public backlash has led to adjustments by the IOC and improved self-policing by sponsors, quietly guided by the reputation of the Olympic Movement and the values it espouses.

CHAPTER 13

Section IV: Sponsorship Preparation Questions

Sponsorship

1. Review audit questions from other sections to provide context.
2. What is the level of investment being made?
   a. Is the investment for the sponsorship rights only?
   b. How much are you willing to invest to activate the sponsorship?
   c. Have you prepared a budget detailing sources and uses of sponsorship monies?
3. Have you identified who is on the sponsorship team?
   a. Are responsibilities and reporting lines of authority clearly understood?
   b. Are the degrees of decision-making freedom known?
   c. Do any team members have prior sports-sponsorship experience of this kind?
4. What are the pre-, during, and post-sponsorship tactical plans?
   a. What marketing communications programs will be used for each target customer?
      i. What are the objectives/goals for each?
      ii. What message will be used?
      iii. Which media? Traditional? NT? Both? (See Section V for more details.)
         1. Frequency, reach, GRP, other?
         2. Insertion dates?
   b. How will you determine success?
      i. Identify measures and milestones.

Four Dimensions of Brand Value
Financial

1. What are your goals in deriving measurable value for the company?
   a. Improve image of the company to develop a more premium image?
   b. Enhance brand value?
   c. Review key financial objectives from audit questions at end of Section II under "Halo Effect."
2. What are your plans for highlighting the value of the products offered during the sponsorship?
   a. Optimizing price? Focusing on features? Differentiation? (Each of these ultimately affects customer perceptions of value, and the Olympics can serve as a platform for product launches, test marketing, or dramatic changes in current pricing structures.)
3. How will you measure return on your sponsorship investment?
4. Do you understand the investment required to protect and reinforce your brand image and support the massive logistic and infrastructure needs?
5. How financially stable is the event?
6. Any concerns the event does not have the required capital to successfully operate?
   a. How do you plan to learn this?

Trusted Reputation

1. What is your reputation with customers? In the marketplace in general?
   a. How do you know your perception is accurate?
   b. How will you convey your reputation?
2. Will you include your best customers as guests at the sponsored event?
   a. Will your best employees and/or partners be there?
3. What is the event's reputation?
   a. What are the factors that have created this reputation (see audit questions at the end of Section II)?

Organizational
1. Do you have recognized support from senior management?
2. Does each person involved have contact information for easy access?
3. Which internal resources/departments will be needed to support each activity?
   a. Can you deliver on support and logistics expectations?
   b. What equipment is needed and how will you get it?
4. Which outside resources will be needed to support each activity?
   a. Are there contractual relationships with clearly defined expectations and deliverables?
5. How will you communicate your sponsorship plans inside the organization?
   a. Who is responsible for communicating them?
6. What are the timing sequences for involving different resources?
7. How would you rate the event's organization?
   a. Can they provide necessary support?
   b. Who are the key decision makers and do you have their contact information?
   c. Have they provided clear guidelines and instructions?

Societal
1. What is the societal "good" your company does overall?
   a. Is this known? If so, how is it known?
   b. How are you getting feedback on the positive contributions your company is making?
      i. Do you need a more formal mechanism for tracking this?
2. What is your company's corporate social responsibility (CSR) plan relative to the sponsorship?
   a. Is it in line with the company's overall CSR efforts, or are these new initiatives?
   b. Do you intend to promote these initiatives? If so, how?
   c. Are you providing resources to get involved in the local community?

3. What is the societal benefit provided by the event?
   a. Community goodwill?
   b. Entertainment value?
   c. Superior sports product?
4. Which of the event's characteristics are most closely aligned with your company's and your expectations?
   a. Is your *sponsorship* aligned with these?

V

Training for Olympic Marketing Victory

CHAPTER 14

Customers

Investing $200–$300 million on sponsorship, a sizable sum, implies that company management has thoroughly assessed the strategic advantages and disadvantages of being associated with the Olympics and is therefore well aware of the need to fully leverage the sponsorship. Of course, having keen awareness of the sponsorship's importance is only part of the leveraging process. Translating this awareness into an actionable plan that includes determining objectives, identifying target customers, developing marketing programs, recommending resource needs, and then measuring the results are the key activities that the marketing team must undertake to safeguard the investment and maximize returns. A central challenge is identifying who the Olympic customer is. Is it an athlete? Is it a general consumer? Is it a sports fan? Is it a fan of a particular sport? Is it a businessperson or a company? Is it a not-for-profit person or organization? Is it young people? Is it old people? The answer is yes to all, which can be a frustrating answer at first glance. But as this book has discussed, the Olympics are a unique entity that represent an ideal and a set of beliefs and values that embody a sense of hope for humanity. The definition of an Olympic customer, therefore, defies and transcends more traditional business vocabulary that suggests a company's customers are tangible. Olympic customers represent a state of mind, a lifestyle, a love of fair competition, and a belief in international solidarity.

We can assert that Olympic fans are those who:

- Attend the Games
- Watch or listen to the Games on broadcasts
- Read about the Games
- Hear about the Games from others

But these descriptions offer little insight beyond the obvious. What is it that attracts people to do any of these activities? Indeed, marketers must pay attention to this question if they want to get closer to understanding the Olympic audience and, consequently, take meaningful advantage of this once-every-four-years event. Fans know that what the athletes are doing is extraordinarily hard, even if they do not have personal experience doing it. People can easily discern the challenge and skill involved and can appreciate the unique circumstances and stresses confronting the athletes. The performance is also evaluated in the context of the current competition, taking into account event conditions, the other competitors, qualifying heats, and even personal profiles of the athletes shown on TV. Yet another appeal of the Olympics is that deep knowledge or detail is not required of viewers and fans of the Olympics. In fact, many of the athletes and teams in both the Summer and Winter Olympics are not as regularly followed as more traditional sports clubs or teams, nor are the sports in which they compete always widely understood. The comfort many loyal sports fans find in knowing their athletes, teams, and leagues comes from a lifetime of devotion to attending games, sharing knowledge with fellow fans and friends, and reading the daily results from the newspaper or online. But this level of intimate knowledge is not widespread with all fans of the Olympic Games. There are certainly passionate fans, particularly of specific sports contested within the Olympics, who are well informed on the particulars of their sport and the players. There are also fans who love the Olympics simply because they are a known exclusive event with a positive reputation based on thousands of years of tradition. Knowing the specific sports, while certainly helpful, is not a defining characteristic explaining the appeal and success of the Olympics, nor is it a requirement. The Olympics have risen above the typical need for detailed knowledge of the nuance of individual sports, which suggests that they represent more than just sport—they are a celebration, a happening, an entertainment vehicle, and even a source of political tension relief. The Olympics are an escape from the world as it is to a world as it could be. This combination of factors helps attract fans and provides some guidance for marketers in tailoring their sponsorship programs, but there are additional questions companies must pay attention to if their marketing programs are to be productive.

It would be a mistake for corporate sponsors to approach the Olympics as if they were conducting a typical promotional campaign or using a narrow customer lens. While there is little question that narrower targeting would eventually reach the intended audience, there is a strong likelihood that such an intensity of focus would risk alienating the broader audience that is also watching the Olympics. Plus, such a direct, targeted emphasis may appear heavy-handed, creating a negative impression of the company and, with today's viral marketing tools, from social media such as Youtube.com and Facebook.com to the millions of blogs and podcasts, company management may quickly find itself handling a crisis it never expected and, worse, detracting from the intent of its original message. The onus is on marketing and senior management to start their customer discussions at a broad level, one that reflects the qualitative characteristics of the Olympic Movement, to guide their Olympic sponsorship strategy. The following simple questions can help guide this part of the planning process:

1. What do we hope our association with the Olympics will accomplish for us?
2. What do we want people to think about us?
3. What does our company stand for (values, beliefs) and how do these fit with the Olympic Games and its billions of fans?
4. Are we prepared to invest in proper support of our overall marketing theme?

Given this emphasis on understanding the intangible, qualitative aspects of the Olympics and the relative match to the sponsor's company, marketers might be somewhat nervous about recommending marketing activities to senior management that do not offer clear, tangible targets and outcomes. Yet this discussion of intangibles should not compel marketers to ignore the more traditional, tangible aspects of customer planning. Implicit within these marketing planning responsibilities is the fact that sports sponsorships are most effectively maximized when companies connect the high-level strategic and qualitative components of their marketing directly with on-the-ground tactical, measurable activities designed to engage the customer directly with the company's offerings. To do this, it is a marketer's responsibility to understand their customers more clearly and then use that knowledge to shape marketing programs geared toward creating memorable customer experiences. Creating customer experiences means that sponsors must engage and interact with customers through multiple touchpoints. These touchpoints include:

- Products (products, services, price)
- People (staff, athletes, suppliers)
- Marketing communications (advertising, PR, promotions, broadcast, online, digital)
- Retail environments (atmosphere, merchandising)
- Support (customer service, warranties, guarantees)
- Events (games, contests, drawings)

Each of these touchpoints, and many more, ultimately affect perceptions of a company. From the CEO on down, the entire sponsor organization must be cognizant of the need to create as positive a customer experience as possible. Therefore, marketers must know the profiles of their customers and supplement their knowledge with new research information to facilitate their understanding and knowledge of their customers.

At a minimum, useful customer information includes knowing:

- Customer segments and targets
- Relevant customer needs within
- Your market share per customer
- Your revenues and profits per customer type

These are by no means the only customer profile components marketers should know, but they provide an important starting point for determining whether a customer audience is attractive and, if so, the marketing team can then develop the most appropriate message.

Customer Segments and Targets

Segments are defined as groups of customers that share common characteristics. Classic marketing theory says that there are four segmentation approaches:

Demographics: Age, ethnicity, income
Psychographics: Behaviors, personality, lifestyle, values
Geographic location: Local, regional, national, natural boundaries
Product use: Matching customer need and product purpose

Marketers use these segmentation approaches separately, or in some combination, to identify common characteristics that could be exploited in the integrated marketing plan. This first step in customer identification should yield characteristics that a company can compare to its own capabilities, determining if a segment, while attractive at first review, is one that can be reasonably pursued using existing resources. If additional resources are required, then the company must decide whether further investment merits consideration. This is hard to determine without additional information about the customer group, so the marketing team must dig deeper to learn more.

Relevant Customer Needs Within

To begin the customer evaluation process, marketers must gather information about the different customer segments. The reason for doing this is to determine what differences, if any, exist among the segments. Market research, either company-initiated or through third-party market research firms, is highly recommended since the resulting information tells marketers if they can address the needs of each segment in their sports sponsorship marketing activities. The market research information provides the converse as well—helping marketers eliminate segments early before additional time and resources are expended on attracting them.

In this hypothetical example, our sports sponsor has identified three segments (A, B, C). Each segment has slightly different needs, as shown in Table 14-1.

Each segment's needs provide insight about the type of program and message this company ought to consider in planning its sports sponsorship activities. Segment A is most interested in service, quality, and lifestyle, which signals to marketers that this is a high-end customer group that may be willing to pay a premium for outstanding offerings. Knowing this would guide the marketing team to devise a marketing program that appeals to this segment's needs. Segment B

Table 14-1
Segments

Needs	A	B	C
Service and support	X		X
High quality	X		
Low price		X	
Loyalty programs		X	
Lifestyle fit	X		

is attracted to low price and loyalty, suggesting that if they find the right product at an affordable price, they will be regular customers. The marketing team would develop a different marketing program for this customer segment as compared to Segment A for obvious reasons: each segment's interests are both unique and in opposition to each other. Segment C simply wants great service, and this, too, provides the marketing team with useful information about how to plan a marketing approach that would best appeal to this segment. Interestingly, of the three segments in this example, Segments A and C share a common preference for quality service. If the sports event being sponsored is considered premier, such as the Olympics, then these two segments may be where the company devotes its marketing activities. The marketing team would logically deduce that Segment B may not fit in its sports sponsorship plan at this time, although Segment B may be a good fit for other marketing programs unrelated to this sports sponsorship. This needs analysis has been useful in narrowing down the customer identification choices.

Marketers must now look at the business opportunities for their company with each segment, starting with a closer review of their company's performance in penetrating each segment and the potential for future gains.

Existing performance within and future potential of each segment can be measured several ways, but for simplicity, let's focus on three key metrics, then analyze them in greater detail:

- Market share of each segment
- Revenues represented by each segment
- Profit represented by each segment

Market Share of Each Segment

Every company has customer segments whose business it seeks to attract. Understanding your market share of each customer segment can uncover useful information about the relative success of your company's product, marketing communications, and service-offerings mix compared to the competition. However, it is not always possible or practical for many companies to know their customer market shares because their own company is too small, or metrics are relatively meaningless, perhaps because the customer segments are sufficiently small and fragmented such that reliable statistics are hard to find. Assuming the data is available, market share information rarely exposes all the underlying details that led to the market status of each competitor, but as Figure 14-1 shows, marketers must look past the initial indicators and ask themselves several questions:

1. Can we gain market share versus our competitors if we succeed in winning over these customers?
2. What are the market share gains, if any, we can reasonably expect?
3. Is it reasonable to expect any market share gains in the short term?
4. What is our competition doing that is affecting their success with each segment?
5. Are there gaps or opportunities in our offering that can be addressed?
6. Are the relative market shares indicative of product quality, effective marketing communication, service delivery, or some combination of these?

Armed with this information, marketers can determine which segments might best respond to the marketing activities supporting the sports sponsorship. Market-share analysis by segment is a good start. However, there is still more that marketers can and should do to fully assess their customer base before determining the best set of marketing activities for implementing the sports sponsorship. Marketers will learn even more by reviewing the financial contribution each segment represents to the company's overall business. Combining the market-share analysis with a revenue and profit analysis gives a marketer additional information that paints a more complete picture of the customer segments, which can help the marketing team direct its planning energies.

Figure 14-1
Market Share By Customer Segment[1]

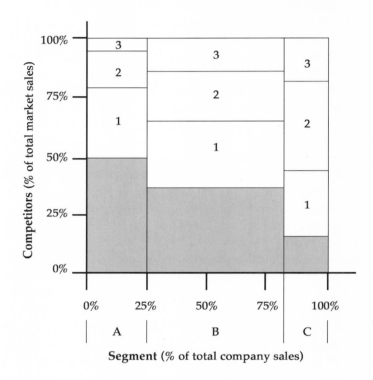

Segment (% of total company sales)

Revenues and Profits Represented by Each Segment
The marketer's task is regularly assessing how much each segment contributes to the company's total revenues and profits. Knowing this reveals not just how well the company is doing in appealing to its customer segments, but whether the financial performance can be improved. Several questions must be addressed:

Revenues
1. Is the customer group (either business or consumer) large enough that our success with one to two customers will enable us to continue developing growth opportunities?
2. If not, then is the potential for revenue growth large enough with each individual customer?

Profits

1. What is the profit we can earn from these target customers over a given period of time?
2. Are these customers high-end, high-margin customers with whom we can cultivate a premium image?
3. Or are they volume customers requiring us to secure sizable contracts to ensure a reasonable profit?
4. How will winning over these customers affect our brand reputation?

Figure 14-2 is a hypothetical illustration of how a company can graphically represent the overall contribution of its customer segments. The revenue and profit analysis for Segments A, B, and C shows the relative financial contributions of each segment to the company's overall performance. This is a useful device because it provides a convenient and informative performance snapshot that can help marketers ascertain which customer segment(s) are performing well and, therefore, which should be emphasized in the marketing activities supporting the sports sponsorship. The decision of which segment(s) to focus on may sometimes be counter-intuitive. For example, a customer segment that contributes most of the profits might seem like a likely candidate for the marketing effort since that high margin segment is willing to pay a premium. However, management may determine that the weakest-performing segment should receive most of the marketing effort, perhaps because that segment offers the best long-term growth potential despite the lower margins in the short-term. Alternatively, a segment might be emphasized because its profile most closely matches that of the sports event's target audience and the company has thus identified it as an influential segment to capture.

Let's review the implications of this particular graphic. Segment A represents 25% of the company's customer base, approximately 10% of the revenues, yet roughly 60% of the profits. Segment B is the largest customer segment overall, but its revenues are 30% of the total and its profits are approximately 15% of the total profits. Segment C is about 20% of the total customer base, yet it has more than 50% of the revenues and 25% of the profits. Given our earlier needs analysis that showed Segment A's preference for premium quality, service, and

Figure 14-2
Revenue and Profit Contribution By Customer[2]

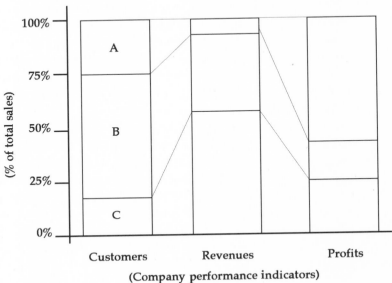

(Company performance indicators)

lifestyle fit, this analysis helps explain that while they are not the dominant segment in terms of total customers, they dominate total profits. Clearly, Segment A is the high-margin customer group that may be a best fit with the sports sponsorship opportunity, assuming that it is a premier event. The company may decide to direct its marketing efforts toward this segment and perhaps toward Segment C (whose key need is great service), but leave Segment B out of its customer marketing efforts.

However, this graphic may also reveal opportunities the company has with Segment B. How? It is conceivable that market research indicates that Segment B is trending toward more premium interests. Perhaps their low price needs are less important than their interest in loyalty, for example. In this instance, the company might choose to use the sports sponsorship to communicate that the company is aware of that customer group's changing needs, believing that the sports event might be influential enough to persuade Segment B to deepen their relationship with the company. New loyalty programs could be marketed through the sports sponsorship with the intent to convert a larger percentage of Segment B to higher-margin customers.

As this demonstrates, evaluating your segments by reviewing revenue and profit contributions can be quite helpful in guiding the final marketing plan for the sports sponsorship. Keep in mind the lesson that marketers must look beyond the summary statistics and dig deeper into the factors that created the financial picture being reviewed. Part of what distinguishes superior marketer's from the rest is their ability to see connections and relationships among various data and understand the potential implications, even though this information is not clearly delineated. It is easy to report numbers and describe trends, but it is much harder to explain what the potential causes are and where opportunities exist. Much like a general understanding that the Olympics are a prestigious sports event only scratches the surface and does not reveal the depth of the event's history and traditions, seeing market share/revenue/profit numbers only provides a glimpse of the customer results. They do not explain why these results happened, describe what the underlying influences were, or overtly review what the broader market context was. For those insights, marketers must look still deeper.

Targeting
Targeting reveals the most attractive, high-potential customers within each segment. Recall the Visa example earlier. While the company's initial overall objectives were to increase awareness and, ultimately, grow its business, a more detailed, descriptive plan was needed to take these objectives from vague generalities to concrete specifics that identified targets, actions, and measures so that everybody within the company could more easily understand where and how they contribute. Arguably, Visa's desire to increase awareness could be in reference to anybody seeking financial services, which could also be construed as a segment, however vague it may sound. This would have been insufficient and relatively uninformative since anybody seeking financial services would have been too imprecise for making meaningful marketing investment and resource allocation decisions. Within the segment of customers needing financial services are Visa's related sub-segments or targets: consumers and member businesses (non-financial and financial).

In Visa's situation, for its sports sponsorship investment to be useful in increasing awareness and growing their business, management had to decide which customers appeared to be the most attractive to target, especially in light of these general objectives. Visa's awareness could be raised to all audiences by simply being associated with the Olympics. But the awareness might quickly wear off without marketing programs designed to engage target customers more directly, and a drop-off in awareness would not likely lead to increased growth. Logically, one can assume Visa recognized the importance and interdependence of consumers and member businesses as two of its key target customer groups. Heightened consumer awareness of Visa might reasonably translate to increased demand for Visa-brand financial products such as credit cards. Consumers might also increase their purchase of products and services from businesses that use the Visa card. In concert with these consumer-led demands might also be a related decline in consumer patronage of businesses that do not honor the Visa card, possibly compelling many of those businesses to begin accepting Visa in the hope of recapturing lost customers and gaining new ones as well.

How should a sponsor determine the most attractive targets within a segment? The answer requires an understanding of marketing planning fundamentals. When launching a new product or a new brand campaign, marketers must first understand their segment evaluation criteria. This includes asking:

1. What are the characteristics of the target segments and/or markets?
   a. Are they large enough to warrant our attention for this event?
   b. Higher revenue/profit potential?
   c. Market share growth potential?
   d. Early adopter/late adopter?
   e. Price sensitive/inelastic?
   f. Better ROI?
   g. High cost/low cost entry?
   h. Risk of competitor retaliation?
   i. Fast/slow growing?
   j. Risk-taking/risk-averse?
   k. Limited means/wealthy?
   l. Fair-weather/casual/devoted sports fans?

m. Functional/emotional orientation?
n. Interests/behaviors/needs?
o. One-time/loyal?
2. How closely does this segment match our company's capabilities?
   a. Can we deliver on promises we make?
      i. Infrastructure?
      ii. Support?
      iii. Meet demand?
      iv. Necessary financial resources?
      v. Previous experience with this market?
   b. Do we fit (loosely) the target customer's characteristics?
      i. If so, is the customer aware of this?
      ii. If not, do we believe our efforts will create the awareness needed?
      iii. Do they buy our products currently?
      iv. Will our effort be seen as credible?
      v. Is our reputation positive with this customer? Negative?

These represent a selection of the many questions company management should ask when evaluating their segments to determine the most attractive targets. Each of the target customer's characteristics and company capabilities can be turned into a single factor that can be rated by marketing to help in the target market selection process. Figure 14-3 shows a ratings scale that can be used for each customer characteristic and company capability:

Figure 14-3
Customer Profile Ratings Scale[3]

-3	-2	-1	0	+1	+2	+3
unacceptable	much worse	worse	equal to better markets we now are in	better	much better	superior

Once the target customer analysis has been completed, several sets of segment data will be available for a comparison. The marketing team can select the ideal target customer(s) based on the resulting scores. A higher, positive score is obviously desired. There will be a temptation to select all customer groups, particularly with an event such as the Olympics, which has a significant global reach and reputation that appeals to a diverse range of people. But upon closer examination, as we saw in the earlier examples of Coke, Visa, John Hancock, and Lenovo, each company uses the sponsorship for a multi-platform approach that reaches both a broad audience as well as more focused customer groups within. This is an important finding of sports sponsorships, particularly large-scale events. Awareness is created by appealing to a broad audience often through a lifestyle, feel-good message that reflects the qualities embodied by the sports event. However, as we saw with the TOP program sponsors, their multi-platform marketing effort included a wide range of tactics designed to involve customers more directly with the company's products. Coca-Cola has sold its products throughout the Olympics at various venues and supplements this with unique programs such as Olympic Pin Trading that show consumers a different side of the company. Visa offered host city destination getaways. John Hancock (now Manulife) has brought its local field agents to the Games to meet directly with customers. Lenovo built lounges for athletes and fans to use for their computing needs. In each case, these companies combined the strategic message with tactical programs to create an extensive customer experience.

This sequence of customer planning around segmentation and targeting may seem like hard work, and it is. To have a chance at sponsorship success requires hard work. But as the saying goes, chance favors the prepared mind. Or in this case, the prepared marketing team. Leveraging the Olympic sponsorship meant that the companies had to think about the best ways to capture the imagination of their customers. Some managers will stop when they have developed a clever advertising campaign, thinking that marketing and sports sponsorship is primarily an effort in attaching logos to signs around the event. Of course that is both limiting and naive. Whether or not your company has the same resources as the Olympic TOP partners is irrelevant because the key lesson from these companies is not derived from their size, but from their ingenuity and implementation. Arguably, any sports sponsorship should compel companies to undertake similarly thoughtful efforts. Inarguably, a sports sponsorship costs time, resources, and money (or the in-kind equivalent), so it behooves marketers to think thoroughly about their customers and how best to attract them. Knowing your objectives and identifying the best customers then allows the marketing team to focus on creative execution.

CHAPTER 15

Creative Execution

Creative activities are among the most visible and common components of marketing. When asked what marketing is, many people reply that it is about clever advertising, and this is partly because marketing has long been associated with the brand-building efforts of companies which, in turn, have historically been the responsibility of advertising agencies. When the business world was simpler (nostalgically and essentially, anytime before the present), the marketer's job was to advertise their products using messages created by an ad agency and deployed in print publications or via TV and/or radio broadcasts. Companies had a great deal of power while consumers did not. Of course, the world has not been that simple for years and, in recent years, consumers have grown increasingly skeptical of advertising claims. Furthermore, consumers are armed with information from Internet searches, blogs, podcasts, and social media well before they decide to purchase a product. They might pay attention to an advertisement, but only after their skepticism has been overcome through their own research. Power has shifted from companies to consumers (or any customer, for that matter), which makes creative execution much harder. In fact, creative execution has expanded from an emphasis on graphic design and ad copy to include an emphasis on innovative distribution, merchandising, corporate identity/logo programs, mascots and, more broadly, integrated marketing platforms. A key driver of this shift is the desire to create the aforementioned customer experiences, and not just clever advertising, which, in isolation, is not nearly as effective as it was in decades past. As discussed in Chapter 12, the annual Super Bowl game in 2000 saw over a dozen dot.com companies spend $2.2 million each for a 30 second TV ad that featured a cavalcade of odd sights including dancing chimpanzees and sock puppets. Many of these ads were bizarre, having little to do with the companies or their products, but the hope was that the cheeky cleverness would distinguish these hot upstart companies from all others and consumers would flock their way thereafter. While there is nothing wrong about using such unique imagery—it can work in some cases—it did not work for the 2000 Super Bowl dot.com advertisers, most of which subsequently went out of business (their demise was more the result of poor business plans and a lack of customers than due to the one Super Bowl ad, but the ads certainly did not advance their cause).

Another example of provocative creative that was memorable, but yielded little or no long-term benefit, was a television ad for a dot.com called Outpost.com.[1] The ad featured a gentleman in a suit sitting in a leather chair. Next to him was a large ship's cannon with another person standing alongside firing gerbils (a small rodent) from it toward a sign on the wall that said "Outpost.com." The man in the chair said to the camera, "Hello, we want you to remember our name, Outpost.com, that's why we've decided to fire gerbils out of this canon through the 'o' in Outpost..."

While he was speaking the camera panned over to the cannon with the other person firing away. The first gerbil missed, hit the wall and fell to the floor, scampering off screen. The man in the chair said in response, "cute little guy," then nodded his head toward the person next to the cannon and said, "fire," whereupon several more gerbils were fired, each missing the hole in the "o." When the last gerbil went through the hole, a red light and siren went off and the man in the chair nodded his head in approval. The ad ended with the following onscreen words set against a black backdrop: "Send complaints to Outpost.com. The place to buy computer stuff online."

This TV ad was certainly memorable, but it also left many viewers scratching their heads in wonder. While it was clever, did it boost awareness and, ultimately, sales? Awareness was boosted, but not of the company—only of the gerbil being shot out of a cannon. There was some recall of the company name, but not what the company did. The company was eventually acquired in 2001 for $8 million (roughly 25 cents per share) by a regional U.S. electronics retailer called Fry's. Outpost.com was started in 1995 and claimed to have 1.4 million customers, but its sales had been declining in the years leading up to the acquisition. While relating the creative execution of Outpost.com's advertising to its decline and then eventual sale to Fry's is problematic at best, it is clear that Outpost.com's advertising might have benefitted from a more direct message.[2]

For creative execution to succeed today requires much more than a simple emphasis on bold visuals for building awareness. In fact, bold visuals may have little or no impact, as the dot.com examples illustrate. As tempting as daring creative might be, it must be used in the context of longer-term strategic objectives. Companies must evaluate their sports sponsorships cognizant of the reasons for investing in the first place and the possible benefits to be derived. The benefits will include increased awareness, and superb creative can facilitate this. Coca-Cola's Olympic sponsorship marketing campaigns since 1928 illustrate the many different ways it used creative execution to improve and reinforce awareness. Visa's use of captivating sports imagery was in alignment with both the Olympics and the values of individual achievement that Visa's financial services celebrate. John Hancock's imagery was similar to Visa's, tapping into the strong fan following for gymnastics and figure skating. Lenovo's creative design of the Olympic torch inspired the design of the limited-edition laptop, and both suggest that the company is taking risks to improve its standing on the world stage, just as athletes are taking risks when they compete in the Olympics. Each of these TOP (The Olympic Program) partner sponsors have used creative tastefully and innovatively, but not garishly or in an attempt to shock or provoke the market. When the creative is disconnected from the company and/or the event, as it appears to have been with the dot.com ads from the 2000 Super Bowl and the Outpost.com example, then any potential benefits rapidly disappear, leaving a cautionary footnote about the dangers to a company's reputation from ill-conceived creative execution, but little or no evidence of success in growing the business or building a brand.

To help describe uses of creative execution, we will briefly highlight examples and descriptions of message, imagery, identities/logos/landmarks, and mascots.

Message

Creative imagery is considered one half of the core advertising concept, with the other half represented by the message, often more commonly known as ad copy (the actual verbal descriptions). Well-conceived ad copy says a great deal in a few words and does so in a way that paints verbal pictures that complement the imagery used. Simplicity is key. Or, to summarize a quote attributed to the American writer Mark Twain, "I didn't have time to write a short letter, so I wrote a long one instead."[3]

As almost anybody in a professional capacity knows, it is far harder to write and/or speak concisely (whether the communiqué is an e-mail, a business plan, a proposal, or a verbal presentation) than it is to communicate excessively. Part of the magic in successful message campaigns is in creating sweeping, positive themes that attract people magnetically while also presenting a persuasive point of view. Dense, detailed messages may well be informative, but the deep content can be counter-productive.

Marketing messages will differ in execution, depending on whether they are written (print, online) or verbal (broadcast, speaking engagements). Written communication, particularly print advertising, affords greater latitude in message since more detail can be provided. Verbal communication, particularly broadcast (radio, TV) is more appropriate for less verbose messages. However, while these are general guidelines, they are not hard-and-fast rules. With the advent of the Internet in the 1990s and the subsequent growth of online and digital tools that has led to blogs, podcasts, and social media, traditional guidelines have become increasingly situational, as will be discussed in the section on non-traditional marketing.

There are four requirements for developing a successful message: *relevance, resonance, distinction,* and *simplicity.*

Relevance

The message must connect directly to the target audience. Whether the goal is a simple, three-word slogan, or a multi-layered product description, or an even broader "understanding" one has of a company, the customer must be able to clearly understand it and say "that is important to me." Without relevance, the message is unlikely to be successful, no matter how creative or lyrical it sounds.

Resonance
The message must evoke important and/or emotional imagery or sensation. Customers must feel that the message or information is right and has meaning for them.

Distinction
The message must reinforce to customers why a company is different and what distinguishes a company and its products. Furthermore, customers must recognize this distinction. This is not always a literal description, as it could be a combination of evocative images as well.

Simplicity
The early reference to Mark Twain captures the key point—a convoluted and/or verbose message risks boring or confusing the market, or both.

Focusing on one or two without the others handicaps the message, making it incomplete. The challenge of developing a successful message should be readily apparent—it is not about being funny, loud, verbose, or different.

Apple is recognized for having all four requirements and for paying attention to Twain's advice. The company's iPod products, for example, are relevant to customers who believe that having control over their listening choices is important to them. Their products resonate because they evoke a sense of personal freedom and imagery of an individualistic lifestyle. And their products are distinctive from visual (well-known iconic designs), functional (they are famously easy-to-use), and socio-cultural (they are considered cool and hip) perspectives. Apple's messages are simple, and often have no words at all, just images that reinforce what the public already associates with the company. When a brand such as Apple is so well known that it can develop message campaigns by not using words, then it has reached a rare position—that of being universally understood. The Olympics are relevant to fans around the world because of the love of unfettered, genuine athletic competition. They resonate with fans because of the emotional intensity they feel for their favorite athletes and sports. The Games are distinctive because of their unrivaled traditions and diversity of contests. And like Apple, there is little question the Olympics are universally understood, requiring little or no explanation.

For Visa then, designing its marketing activities to attract more consumers and member businesses, the two customer targets discussed in the customer section, was a sensible conclusion. Past Visa Olympic marketing campaigns did just this. With its nearly two-decade marketing campaign "It's everywhere you want to be," Visa was conveying convenience and access. At times, this campaign was supplemented by a message that stated more businesses accepted Visa cards than any other credit card, and that it was the only card accepted at the Olympic Village.

The implications of the message were clear: for consumers to ensure financial security they should have a Visa card, and for businesses to ensure more customers they should accept the Visa card. This campaign lasted nearly 20 years and saw Visa's market share, revenues, profits, and overall brand reputation grow, while it also diversified its product offerings from consumer products (credit cards, debit cards, prepaid cards) to consumer services (ATM locators, exchange rates, lost cards, lost traveler's checks) to commercial solutions (small businesses, mid-to-large companies, government). In 2006, Visa changed its message to "Life Takes Visa" to reflect the changing nature of its offerings from simple credit cards to the broader range of financial solutions it had expanded into. The design of the message was deliberately intended to convey that Visa is essential to almost everything in life. Visa also hoped the new message would connect more emotionally with the market.[4]

Visa's successful customer-targeting efforts over the past 20 years, along with its targeted marketing communications, enabled the company to increase its market-leadership position as measured by awareness, market share, revenues, profits, total transactions, and the number of cards issued.

To a greater or lesser extent each of the 12 TOP sponsors has attempted to create a message for its Olympic sponsorship, as shown in Table 15-1. Note that these messages are often not the current advertising slogan. Instead, these are themes described in the Olympic Games sponsorship sections of their respective websites.

Table 15-1
TOP Sponsor Olympic Messages[5]

Sponsor	Industry category	Message theme
McDonald's	Retail food services	*Bring the games to life*
Lenovo	Computing equipment	*Celebrate and live*
Manulife	Life insurance/ annuities	*Bring their dreams to life*
Coca-Cola	Non-alcoholic beverages	*Bringing unique Olympic experiences*
Panasonic	Audio /TV / video equipment	*Sharing the passion*
Kodak	Imaging	Message not known
Atos Origin	IT services	*For the spirit*
Visa	Consumer payment systems	*Celebrating human achievement*
Johnson & Johnson	Health care products	*Caring for others*
Samsung	Wireless communication	*Everyone's an Olympic Games champion*
GE	Diverse offerings	*Leaving a legacy*
Omega	Time pieces/ timing systems	*Official timekeeper*

Customers will ultimately determine each sponsor's success, although a weak message does not portend an unsuccessful sponsorship. By this point readers should be well aware of approaching the sponsorship from a multi-dimensional set of activities and not dependent on one or two elements, such as message, for determining success. Each of the TOP sponsors is investing in numerous activities, related to its known expertise, to create a memorable experience for Olympic fans, athletes, and business partners.

Imagery

Choice of visual imagery is an important tool in the marketing mix since well-chosen images can become easily recognized as related to a brand. Great imagery is powerful and evocative. However, this does not mean bright, outlandish images are the only choices that work best in marketing communications. Even simple images can have significant influence on awareness and recognition. When determining choice of imagery, note that success here has similar requirements to successful messages, particularly an emphasis on resonance and relevance. Consider Apple again—for years the iPod imagery has had a distinctive black silhouette of a person dancing to music wearing the iconic white ear buds, set against a single color background. We instantly associate these ads with Apple iPod. Nike's advertising imagery is replete with athletic scenes, as are UnderArmor's (a rapidly growing athletic-apparel maker). McDonald's is known for showing people, particularly families and kids, enjoying themselves. Disney's castle and Mickey Mouse are classic images for which the company is widely known, as are many of their best-known characters. Singapore Airlines has the renowned Singapore Girl. Manchester United's ubiquitous red color is used with creative identities targeted to different fan groups, with "Fred the Red" focused on kids and "The Red Devils" targeted to adults, not to mention the club's extensive merchandising, advertising, and online communications efforts, all tied together thematically by the color red. Benetton is known for its "United Colors of Benetton" advertising that frequently uses arresting, controversial images. The Olympics, of course, have the flame.

Identities/Logos/Landmarks

Imagery encompasses corporate-identity marks such as logos. The world's leading brands have instantly recognizable logos. This is not by accident, but by careful planning in marketing communications choices, including sports sponsorships. When we see a logo, even without the company name, other images and associations as well as emotions bubble to the surface.

Logos are also part of a detailed corporate-identity program that describes appropriate use of all logos and trademarks, from corporate stationery to podcast logos to sales literature to advertising. Corporate identities and logos are legally protected from unauthorized or improper use, as designated by each organization. The IOC has strict guidelines for proper and consistent usage of all imagery associated with the Games. Doing so protects the Olympic trademarks and the sponsors since the risk of non-approved usage is reduced due to the legal penalties for violators, ensuring that official sponsors will have the appropriate support when using Olympic images in their marketing. Even the order of colors in the Olympic rings must be presented a specific way to prevent a multitude of confusing variations in the marketplace (the blue, black, and red rings are always across the top; and the yellow and green rings are along the bottom.) Imagery is linked to locations. We do not have to see the name of a city or a country to know its name once we see a world-renowned landmark.

Seeing recognized logos and landmarks immediately conjures images of their organization and location, triggering a flood of associations. The power of these images acts as an information filter, helping us evaluate how we feel about them. Marketers have a significant opportunity and responsibility to think carefully about how to use imagery to take full advantage of the enormous exposure they will receive when sponsoring the Olympics, or any other sports event. An easy starting point for planning imagery is to write down the top two to three associations you would like target customers to have, then consider the innumerable choices available that convey those associations.

Mascots

What is the purpose of a mascot? To be technical, a mascot is intended to help put a colorful, memorable face on the organization it represents. Sports teams, particularly from North America, although they are used increasingly around the world, use mascots to inspire fans during games and for public appearances via community outreach events to bring the public closer to the organization. Mascots range from animals (such as the Chicago Bears) to gastropods (the University of California at Santa Cruz Banana Slugs) to birds (such as Tottenham Hotspur's Chirpy Cockerel). Sports mascots have been a source of controversy, particularly when they appear to be caricatures of an ethnic group, and a few more extreme observers have suggested the banning of mascots altogether because they serve as little more than a PR stunt that does not affect how players play. Yet no such elimination has occurred.

Consumer marketing has long relied on mascots as a device for attracting young customers. Think of Ronald McDonald and images of a yellow-suited clown in red floppy shoes with flaming red hair instantly appear. Mars' M&Ms candy has turned the round, green candy-coated chocolate treat into a much-sought after toy, complete with its own website where visitors can make their own M&M's characters and then send them to friends (www.becomeanmm.com). Mascots, or a variation of them, can go viral, demonstrating another clever method marketers can use to reach the public. Jollibee, a popular Philippines-based fast-food chain, has a giant bee in a red blazer and chef's hat as its mascot and main corporate identity. NTTDoCoMo, the Japanese telecommunications company, has Docomodake—the smiling mushroom, as its mascot. Arguably, Disney has perhaps been the most responsible for turning mascots into their own industry with stuffed toys, action figures, cartoons, and a dizzying array of related merchandise.

The Olympics have been using mascots since 1968, when "Schuss" the skier was introduced at the Grenoble Olympic Games. The tradition continues to this day with the 2008 Beijing Olympics' mascot called "Fuwa," which is actually five different figures symbolizing a gesture of greeting and peace. The five characters are: *Beibei* the Fish, *Jingjing* the Panda, *Huanhuan* the Olympic Flame, *Yingying* the Tibetan Antelope, and *Nini* the Swallow.

According to the website for the 2008 Beijing Olympics (http://en.beijing2008.cn/), when the five names are combined, *Bei Jing Huan Ying Ni*, it means "Beijing Welcomes You." The 2010 Winter Olympic Games in Vancouver feature three mythical creatures: Miga, the mythical sea bear that is part-bear and part-killer whale; Quatchi, a sasquatch; and Sumi, an animal spirit with the wings of a hummingbird, the legs of a black bear, and the hat of an orca whale (www.vancouver2010.com). While having an anchor in reality is not a requirement in creating a mascot, having a sense of fun and whimsy is. Mascots allow organizations to make themselves more playful, perhaps even more human (despite the general lack of anything remotely human in most cases), to endear themselves to fans. Mascots help the Olympics attract younger audiences, add another dimension to each host city's personality, and provide a symbol that loosely represents the host nation's culture. Mascots, of course, can also be turned into merchandise that increases the pool of revenues flowing into the International Olympic Committee (IOC).

For Olympics sponsors, mascots are another Olympic identity that can be leveraged for hospitality events, particularly community outreach programs and youth-oriented activities. Corporate sponsors do not typically design their own mascot for the Olympics as there really is no reason. Plus, such an effort might serve to undermine the Olympic mascot effort. Table 15-2 summarizes the Olympic mascots since 1968:

Table 15-2
Olympic Mascots[6]

Olympic Games	Mascot(s)	Description
1968 Winter Olympics in Grenoble	Schuss	Skiing man—first unofficial mascot
1972 Olympic Games in Munich	Waldi	Dachshund—head and tail were blue and the body had 3 vertical stripes featuring Olympic colors
1976 Winter Olympics in Innsbruck	Schneemann	Snowman
1976 Olympic Games in Montreal	Amik	Beaver—meant to symbolize hard work
1980 Winter Olympics in Lake Placid	Roni	Raccoon—Roni replaced "Rocky," who was an actual raccoon that died just before the Olympics
1980 Olympic Games in Moscow	Misha	Bear—mascot's full name was "Mikhail Potapych Toptygin"
1984 Winter Olympics in Sarajevo	Vucko	Wolf—representing friendship with animals

Table 15-2 continued

Olympic Games	Mascot(s)	Description
1984 Olympic Games in Los Angeles	Sam the Eagle	Eagle—designed to appeal specifically to children
1988 Winter Olympics in Calgary	Hidy and Howdy	Bears—symbolizing Canadian friendliness
1988 Olympic Games in Seoul	Hodori	Tiger —designed to show the friendly side of a tiger…and Korea
1992 Winter Olympics in Albertville	Magique	Snow Imp—replaced "Chamois" the Mountain Goat as the mascot
1992 Olympic Games in Barcelona	Cobi	Surreal dog—became successful TV show
1994 Winter Olympics in Lillehammer	Haakon and Kristin	Boy and girl dolls from Norwegian folklore— two actual children who looked similar traveled the world as Olympic ambassadors
1996 Olympic Games in Atlanta	Izzy	Nondescript blue blob—one of the least understandable mascots
1998 Winter Olympics in Nagano	Sukki Nokki Lekki Tsukki	All four are snow owls—they replaced "Snowple" the Weasel
2000 Olympic Games in Sydney	Olly Syd Millie	Kookaburra—representing generosity Platypus—representing the environment Echidna—representing the millennium
2002 Winter Olympics in Salt Lake City	Powder	Snowshoe hare— symbolizing speed

Table 15-2 continued

Olympic Games	Mascot(s)	Description
	Copper	Coyote—symbolizing highest performance
	Coal	Black bear—symbolizing strength
2004 Olympic Games in Athens	Athena and Phevos	Brother and sister— looked like ancient Greek dolls
2006 Winter Olympics in Turin	Neve Gliz Aster	Snowball Ice cube Snowflake
2008 Olympic Games in Beijing	Beibei Jingjing Huanhuan Yingying Nini	Fish Panda Olympic flame Tibetan antelope Swallow
2010 Winter Olympics in Vancouver	Miga Quatchi Sumi	All three are mythical creatures based loosely on local folklore

Whether they are absurd, surreal, or cute and cuddly, mascots are not a rocket-science project designed to inspire deep thinking about the organization they represent. Mascots are simply a marketing device, nothing more or less. They are intended to help reinforce the organization's identity by making it more memorable.

Merchandising

The IOC's Olympic merchandise is controlled by its licensing program. Companies that become official Olympic licensees must adhere to the IOC's strict requirements, including product quality, product type, and approved use of the various Olympic symbols and marks. An ongoing education program informs licensees and the public about the legal protections the IOC has in place, plus enforcement and monitoring procedures. The Olympic licensing program is designed to protect the integrity of the Olympic brand and the rights of licensees and sponsors by ensuring unauthorized "knock-offs" and copies are kept to a minimum. Tables 12-6 and 12-7 in Chapter 12 show the licensing revenues since 1988. The strongest-performing Olympic licensing program was during the 1996 Olympic Games in Atlanta, although such a strong performance resulted in heavy criticism about the over-commercialization of the Olympics, sacrificing some of the spirit and values that are associated with the Games. Since then, Summer Olympics merchandising revenues have been roughly 30% lower. Licensed merchandise revenues from the Winter Olympics have been in the mid-$20 million range since the 2002 Salt Lake City Games.

For corporate sponsors, merchandise programs can extend into a wide range of offerings, from apparel to office supplies to household items. There is no magic set of guidelines that says which types of merchandise are best and which are to be avoided—each company needs to determine the items that lend themselves most effectively to extending its brand. But there is a possible lesson in the Olympic merchandising experience: too much can lead to public disenchantment, which might ultimately undermine the image of integrity associated with the Olympics. For companies, a similar effect may very well harm their brand as well.

CHAPTER 16

Marketing Communications

Marketing communications is a broad discipline with numerous tools available for reaching target customers. They encompass traditional and non-traditional components, ranging from broadcast advertising to blogs. Whereas companies used to treat marketing's different tools as separate areas of expertise, the past 15–20 years have seen an emphasis on integrating these pieces together through a concept called integrated marketing. Integrated marketing guides marketers to take advantage of the company's investment in strategic positioning, customer targeting, product development, and messaging by creating a consistent approach that ensures the entire marketing effort creates a memorable experience for customers. Done well, integrated marketing minimizes the chances of different marketing programs contradicting each other or misrepresenting the company's offerings since everyone involved knows the common objective, so their efforts are focused on adapting that objective to the unique strengths of each marketing tool.

As we saw with the four TOP (The Olympic Program) sponsors in particular, their sponsorship activities were designed around common themes, and then executed differently depending on the marketing tool used. For example, 30-second television spots do not work well on the Web. But a short clip with a similar theme might easily find a viral effect on Youtube.com. An elegantly worded print ad would not translate well to a billboard or text message, yet techniques exist that convey the same meaning without the depth of content. Sports marketing success is predicated on marketers identifying the target audience, selecting a marketing tool to reach them, and adapting the company message to fit that tool. Visa's four marketing platforms— advertising, promotional, corporate relations, product—are broad theme areas under which are specific marketing activities supporting each theme. Its marketing has consistently followed a central theme supported by advertising, PR, merchant programs, hospitality, and destination programs in an integrated program tailored to the Olympics.

Traditional Marketing

Companies considering a sports-sponsorship investment, such as the Olympics, would do well to review the experiences of the companies featured in this book and then determine what marketing mix is most appropriate for their specific situation. The audit questions throughout this book and the marketing checklist at the end are designed to help marketers plan their marketing activities around the needs of their target audiences. Traditional marketing represents the classic communication elements most often associated with large-scale media in television, radio, and print, although it also includes additional mix elements such as hospitality tents, team sponsorships, and outdoor advertising. Traditional marketing is usually one-way communication from the company to the market. Non-traditional marketing describes the newer marketing vehicles that have developed over the past 15 years as a result of advancements in technology that led to the commercial uses of the Internet, mobile technology, and social media. Also, unlike its traditional forerunner, non-traditional marketing is comprised of two-way, even simultaneous, communication between the customer and the company.

The past few years have seen a tremendous power shift from companies to customers, requiring marketers to rethink their communication priorities in a way that is relevant to how today's consumers seek information. In preparing for sports sponsorships, marketers would be well advised to use this, or a similar template, in planning their marketing activities. In the following hypothetical example, a marketer has determined through research that her six primary target audiences (A, B, C and X, Y, Z as shown in Tables 16-1 and 16-4, which highlight traditional and non-traditional media, respectively) respond to the marked media best.

Table 16-1
Traditional Marketing

	TV	Radio	Print	Product	Signage	Outdoor	Tickets	Hospitality	Athlete/Team sponsorship
Target Audience A	X	X	X		X				
Target Audience B					X		X	X	
Target Audience C					X	X		X	X

Target audience A pays attention to classic media such as TV, radio, print, and outdoor signage, whereas target audiences B and C respond to different marketing tools. A marketer must develop a communications program that best fits the profile of each audience (assuming the company has the luxury of investing in multiple marketing vehicles to reach different customer groups). Table 16-2 is an example of a Marketing Activity Planning Worksheet that can serve as a useful guide:

Table 16-2
Marketing Activity Planning Worksheet
(Traditional Marketing)

Media Type	Target Audience	Message	Reach	Frequency	Insertion date	Ad length or size	GRP (gross rating points)	Total cost (creative, media buy)	Project outcome
TV	A	"Go for Gold"	20%	6x	Aug 1	30 sec.	225	3 m	10%^ awareness
Radio	A	‖	40%	12x	July 1	15-30 sec.	300	300k	‖
Print	A	‖	25%	8x	June 15	1 page	75	225k	‖
Signage	A	‖		3 mth contract	June 1	5 billboards	un-known	125k	‖

This company has chosen "Go for Gold" as its message for the Olympics and it uses this theme consistently across the media types targeted to audience A. Note that the key goal is to increase awareness of the company 10% by the time the campaign has ended. This can be measured using surveys before, during, and after this marketing campaign. "Reach" measures the number or percentage of people that were exposed to a single ad during a specified period of time.[1] "Frequency" measures the number of times members of the target audience are exposed to the same ad during the specified period of time.[2] "GRP" (gross rating points) are the result of Reach x Frequency, and they describe the total number of ad exposures a marketing campaign will generate during a specified period of time.[3] To calculate these figures requires data about the size of the customer audience from each of the media companies. Insertion date refers to the start date of the particular media type used. Ad length/size is self-explanatory. Total cost includes the cost of creative (producing the creative content either in-house or through an outside ad agency), the cost of media (fees charged by the media type to place an ad with them in a specified size, location, and time slot), and related support costs (other professional services). Determining the project outcome is both science and art. A company may have historical data that shows the impact on awareness (or whatever goal is used for the project outcome), which should guide the marketer's goal setting. If the company has historically seen awareness grow 1%, then setting a goal of 95% increase in awareness would be too ambitious. But settling for 1%–2% suggests a lack of effort. This is where the art comes in since part of the entire marketing effort directed to each target audience is predicated on judgment born of other experiences.

The actual cost of TV coverage depends on the size of the expected audience and the demographics of the broadcaster's country of origin. When broadcasters set advertising rates in the United States, for example, they base the rates on the size of the expected audience at each viewing time. The most expensive TV advertising time slots in the United States are during prime time, between the hours of 7 pm and 11 pm, since that is when most Americans tend to watch TV. Viewing habits in the United States have changed significantly over the past 25 years due to more choices, such as cable and even the Internet, while the traditional big television networks (ABC, CBS,

NBC, and, more recently, Fox) have seen steady viewership declines. Nevertheless, the big networks broadcast the Olympics and have added to their core media business by acquiring or adding cable and Internet-based offerings. Table 16-3 shows the changes in U.S. television coverage along with the growth of the Olympics:

Table 16-3

Olympic Games Since 1960 and U.S. Television Coverage[4]

Olympics	U.S. TV network	Average prime time rating*	Total network hours	Number of nations competing	Number of olympic events
1960 Winter Olympics in Squaw Valley.	CBS	NA	NA	30	27
1960 Olympics in Rome	CBS	NA	20	83	150
1964 Winter Olympics in Innsbruck	ABC	NA	17.5	36	34
1964 Olympics in Tokyo	NBC	NA	14	93	163
1968 Winter Olympics in Grenoble	ABC	13.5	20	37	35
1968 Olympics in Mexico City	ABC	NA	43.75	112	172
1972 Winter Olympics in Sapporo	NBC	17.2	26	35	35
1972 Olympics in Munich	ABC	24.4	62.75	121	195
1976 Winter Olympics in Innsbruck	ABC	21.5	27.5	37	37
1976 Olympics in Montreal	ABC	23.9	76.5	92	198
1980 Winter Olympics in Lake Placid	ABC	23.6	35	37	38
1980 Olympics in Moscow	NBC	**	**	80	203
1984 Winter Olympics in Sarajevo	ABC	18.4	41.5	49	39
1984 Olympics in Los Angeles	ABC	23.2	180	140	221
1988 Winter Olympics in Calgary	ABC	19.3	95	57	46
1988 Olympics in Seoul	NBC	17.9	176	159	237
1992 Winter Olympics in Albertville	CBS	18.7	107	64	57
1992 Olympics in Barcelona	NBC	17.5	148	169	257
1994 Winter Olympics in Lillehammer	CBS	27.8	110	67	61
1996 Olympics in Atlanta	NBC	21.6	164	197	271
1998 Winter Olympics in Nagano	CBS	16.3	124	72	68
2000 Olympics in Sydney	NBC	14.2	441	199	300
2002 Winter Olympics in Salt Lake City	NBC	16.9	375.5	77	78
2004 Olympics in Athens	NBC	15.5	1,210	201	301
2006 Winter Olympics in Turin	NBC	12.2	416	80	84
2008 Olympics in Beijing	NBC	TBD	3,600 (est.)	205 (est.)	302 (est.)

*   Average prime time rating: each point represents 1.1 million U.S. households
** The United States boycotted the 1980 Summer Games; NBC's coverage was limited to highlights and two anthology-style specials after the Games were completed, though the network still paid the full rights fee.

The prime time ratings for Olympiads held outside the United States decrease due to time zone changes, so that many U.S. fans end up watching tape-delayed broadcasts, or skip viewing events entirely, unless they are both of interest and shown live during prime time hours. There is a significant jump in the total network hours broadcast starting with the 2004 Olympics in Athens. The increase is due to NBC choosing to broadcast 24 hours per day 7 days per week, using the network's various broadcast, Internet, and cable properties. The 2006 Turin Olympics' network hours broadcast increased over the previous Winter Olympics by over 300%. The network broadcast hours for the 2008 Olympics in Beijing are estimated to total 3,600 hours, representing a substantial increase in coverage. The U.S. television audience is large, which is why corporate sponsors are attracted. The challenge for them is timing their ads during peak viewing hours and, with more broadcast choices available now, this increases the complexity of the sponsor's advertising mix, including reach and frequency decisions. Corporate sponsors may also buy advertising time on foreign broadcast networks, assuming they sell commercial air-time, which many do not. But the total possible range of TV advertising options is large.

Marketers must plan each activity carefully, just as we saw from each of the companies earlier, starting with strategic objectives—such as Visa's initial desire to raise awareness in the 1980s—to tactical goals that identify specific marketing programs targeted to specific audiences with a message designed to yield a specific outcome—such as Visa's increases in transactions volume, credit cards issued, and increased financial-institution membership.

Non-traditional Marketing

Non-traditional (NT) marketing describes new media and/or unconventional marketing communications choices. The term NT will no doubt be obsolete soon since these various alternative media are becoming well established, but the term is useful for descriptive purposes and also highlights the increase in interesting new-media choices available to corporate sponsors. The growth of NT is dramatic, illustrating the massive change occurring as more consumers around the world opt for the newer communications tools as they slow their usage of traditional media. NT marketing tools can be less expensive up front. For example, many blog and podcast applications are available for free or very low prices, reducing the expense of media placement (in the case of these two media types). Of course, NT marketing requires companies to rethink their marketing approaches if target customers are to find the message credible. Traditional marketing is one-way communication, from the company to the market, whereas NT marketing is two-way and often simultaneous. The public increasingly views traditional marketing with skepticism since one of its key tools, advertising, is the company's effort to push its message across to customers with no direct feedback (in the short-term), therefore it is often perceived as unsubstantiated claims in the eyes of consumers. NT marketing can be started anywhere by anybody—it does not have to be generated by the company. Customers view NT marketing as more genuine and authentic because it is unedited communication among and between people, sharing opinions. When good (or bad) news is reported about a company and its products, NT marketing enables the message to grow virally extremely quickly and, conceivably, reputations grow or change rapidly as well. John Deighton, a professor at Harvard Business School, who has studied the impact of new media and related digital tools on marketing, suggests that the old style of bombarding consumers with messages simply won't work anymore. His research, which included analyzing Dove's "Real Beauty"campaign that featured actual consumers and not models, says marketers must get comfortable suggesting a topic, then let customers respond. Deighton states, "When a brand adopts a point of view, rather than simply making a claim for softer skin, for instance, it can become a lightning rod for discourse. You have to be confident that your message can withstand reinterpretation."[5]

The important point for sports marketers is to use both traditional and NT tools in their sponsorship planning since the world is comprised of audiences familiar with each, but some are more comfortable with one versus the other. Furthermore, successful integrated marketing is about leveraging a common theme across a variety of marketing programs, and combining traditional and NT marketing can offer the potential for maximum impact with target audiences.

Returning to our hypothetical example, the marketer has determined that target customers X, Y, and Z respond to NT marketing best, as shown by Table 16-4:

Table 16-4
Non-traditional Marketing

	Multi-media	Web-site	Banner	Blogs	Pod-casts	Social media	Mobile	SMS
Target audience X	X	X	X	X				
Target audience Y		X		X	X	X		
Target audience Z		X					X	X

In this example, a marketer would create a worksheet for each media type (web, banner, etc.), with specific metrics as goals for the specific sports-sponsorship campaign. The company, in this case, is using the "Go for Gold" message in its NT marketing tactics, just as it did with traditional marketing, and this worksheet displays a possible way to evaluate the performance of the sponsorship's Web-specific campaign. The website campaign choices range from special sports-specific offers on the company's existing website, to an entirely new and separate website (or a site within a main website). A campaign planning worksheet is shown in Table 16-5:

Table 16-5
Marketing Activity Planning Worksheet (NT Marketing)

	Target audience	Message	Direct URL access	Engage-ment	Abandon-ment	Cost (US$)	Purchase goals
Web	X	"Go for Gold"	5k^ per week	20%^ in time spent on site	15%˘ in shopping cart abandon-ment	250k	15%^ in pur-chases

The company's marketers have set specific goals using select Web metrics. Direct URL access describes the number of customers that access the company's website by directly entering the URL, versus linking to it from another site. This can tell marketers how well known and sought after their company is. The company wants to increase the number of people who visit the site using direct URL access by 5,000 per week. Engagement refers to the length of active time a visitor spends on a website (versus idle time, indicated by a page that sits for hours because a user has walked away). Our company wants its sports-sponsorship website to drive a 20% increase in engagement (as compared, for example, to other company website unrelated to the sports sponsorship). Abandonment describes the instant when a visitor leaves your website, which could be during the act of ordering a product.[6] Here, the company is targeting a 15% decrease in shopping-cart abandonment (perhaps a feature of the shopping cart has been improved that streamlines the ordering process). While these numbers are for illustration purposes, the goals companies actually set must be done in the context of the overall sponsorship strategy and must be grounded in reality.

Each NT tool will have its own goals and objectives because each is used differently. Blogs are another fast-growing activity. "Blog" is a shorthand word for Web logs, which are online articles, often opinion pieces, written by anybody. For example, many of the most popular blogs are comprehensive, lengthy pieces. Of course, blogs are not usually used like traditional print advertising. But the bloggers (the term describing people who write blogs) often discuss companies, products, services, politics, and much more. Many of the most popular blogs are seen as more credible than a company's advertising because the information is coming directly from customers. Also, the most popular blogs have thousands or even millions of fans and readers who regularly spread the message from the blogs through online sharing, also called viral marketing. Viral marketing is a form of marketing, but it is not easy for companies to control. Nevertheless, it has become one of the new communication tools in recent years and, unlike traditional print advertising, it is two-way communication since anybody can respond to the comments online in full view of the world.

A blog's success can be analyzed using website metrics plus a review of changes to the number of RSS feed subscribers, the number of RSS to e-mail subscribers, top posts, top feed readers, trackbacks, and replies (RSS is short for Really Simple Syndication, and it is a easy way for people to be automatically notified of content changes to their favorite blogs and websites without initiating their own search). Posting videos on the Web has become a popular tactic for getting messages out to market. Youtube.com provides statistics on views and even a basic five-star viewer ratings system. A small group of Lenovo employees produced several short, whimsical video spots about the superior qualities of their laptop computers that they uploaded to Youtube.com (such as the "Lenovo Skywalker" video). They set a goal of getting around 900,000 views (200,000 views is considered very good and 1,000,000 views is considered excellent) and did not inform their colleagues or senior management about their "project." Total views came to more than 3,000,000, indicating a major success. Senior management then noticed, illustrating to them the potential power and reach of NT marketing.

While referred to as NT marketing, these are not fringe media anymore —they are becoming mainstream. The growth is impressive and it is driven by enormous changes in the way individuals and companies use NT marketing. Global advertising patterns are changing as well as the NT marketing tools become increasingly common. ZenithOptimedia, a media research firm, cites the following general advertising trends:[7]

- Ad expenditure growth will be 3.8% in 2008 in Europe and North America and 11.1% in the rest of the world
- Developing markets will keep global ad-expenditure growth above the 10-year average
- Share of global ad market will increase from 27% to 33% for developing markets, and these markets will be responsible for 63% of total global ad growth
- The Asia-Pacific region will overtake Western Europe by 2010
- Internet advertising will grow from 9.7% of total global ad expenditures in 2008 to 12.3% in 2010

Table 16-6 shows total ad expenditures by region:

Table 16-6
Ad Expenditures by Region—Major Media[8]
(newspapers, magazines, TV, radio,
cinema, outdoor, Internet)

	2006	2007	2008	2009	2010
North America	181,816	186,667	193,606	197,921	202,605
Western Europe	103,576	108,287	112,559	117,253	122,249
Asia-Pacific	91,811	98,842	106,980	113,937	122,520
Central and Eastern Europe	24,124	28,756	34,010	39,527	45,143
Latin America	22,725	25,627	29,025	31,941	34,540
Africa/M. East/ROW	13,480	16,657	18,715	21,976	26,063
World	**437,531**	**464,837**	**494,895**	**522,555**	**553,119**

Note: Figures shown are in millions US$ using 2006 currency average rates. ROW means "Rest of the World."

The trends in advertising spending are clearly evident in Table 16-7, showing the differences in growth of each advertising medium. A quick calculation will show that ad expenditure growth for Internet is 132% from 2006 to 2010, the largest percentage growth rate of all mediums.

Table 16-7
Global Advertising Spending by Medium[9]

	2006	2007	2008	2009	2010
Newspapers	122,795	125,030	126,327	127,583	130,070
Magazines	53,795	55,437	57,151	59,338	61,566
Television	161,633	171,823	184,212	193,673	204,559
Radio	35,834	37,251	38,587	39,927	41,246
Cinema	1,882	2,013	2,197	2,410	2,700
Outdoor	26,802	28,952	31,676	34,475	37,330
Internet	28,818	37,795	47,544	57,106	66,903
World	**431,561**	**458,301**	**487,695**	**514,512**	**544,375**

Note: Figures shown are in US$ millions using 2006 currency average rates. The totals here are lower than the totals in the previous table of ad expenditures by region, since that table includes total ad spend figures for a few countries for which spend is not itemized by medium. That table also excludes some advertising that does not fit into the above media categories.

Reviewing where the fastest ad-expenditure growth is occurring reveals significant variation among countries, as Table 16-8 illustrates:

Table 16-8
Top 10 Contributors to Global Ad Spend Growth Between 2007 and 2010[10]

Country	Growth %	Country	Growth %
Russia	92.1	South Africa	45.8
China	61.5	South Korea	21.6
Pan Arab	54.2	UK	19.5
India	52.2	U.S.	8.3
Brazil	46.6	Japan	5.7

Note: Pan Arab generally refers to the Middle East, excluding non-Arab states.

The information contained in these tables is beginning to tell a story to marketers about trends in traditional and NT marketing.

NT Marketing Tools Growth Areas

Helpful additional information at this stage would include specific penetration/usage patterns of selected media. To illustrate, let's look at broadband data in Figures 16-1 and 16-2.

Figure 16-1
Total Number of Broadband Subscribers in Q3 and Q4 2007[11]

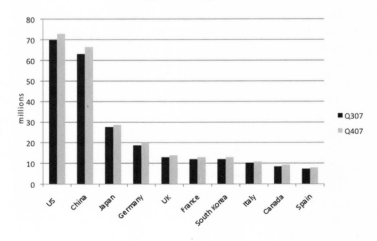

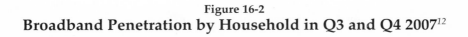

Figure 16-2
Broadband Penetration by Household in Q3 and Q4 2007[12]

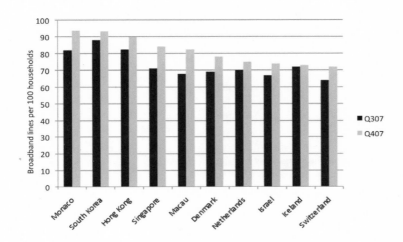

Clearly, broadband penetration is increasing. Knowing that a medium is growing is helpful. Now marketers should turn their attention to learning why customers are online, what they are doing, and which applications should be considered in a marketing campaign (this rationale is not limited to broadband as marketers would conduct a similar analysis for other NT and traditional marketing areas).

Figure 16-3 shows how consumers are spending their leisure time. Online and digital activities have become a sizable percentage of the average person's leisure time. In fact, data from 2006 shows both the attractiveness and uses of online. Overall, 48% of the average person's leisure time was spent online. Broadband usage and penetration statistics provide an excellent guide for corporate marketers as they weigh their tactical marketing decisions in support of sports sponsorship. Online usage is shown in Figure 16-4. Knowing how target customers spend their time when online helps marketers determine the type of message, which websites, and message location. Varying the message and location by website can provide additional detailed data on which approach yielded the most effective response rates from customers.

Figure 16-3
Allocation of Consumer Leisure Time[13]

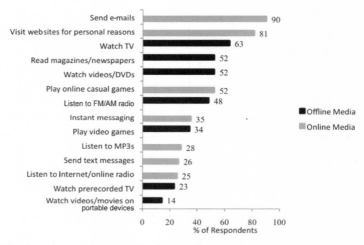

Number of respondents=4,190   Base: All respondents

Figure 16-4
Allocation of Total Time Spent Online[14]

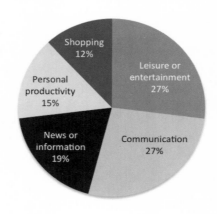

Number of respondents=4,190   Base: All Respondents

Since the Olympics involve athletes from nations from around the world and attract their fans, the diversity of the target audience is extensive. Corporate sponsors should pay careful attention to the consumer statistics in each country or region, as much as possible, since marketing can then be specifically tailored based on the traditional and NT marketing levels of acceptance within. Knowing contextual statistics such as those on the following charts can help marketers pinpoint which countries would be most receptive to an online message, for instance. Note again the differences in Figures 16-1 and 16-2—the United States has the largest number of broadband users, followed closely (and gaining rapidly) by China, whereas in the household penetration numbers the top 10 countries change significantly. Marketers should use data such as this to help adapt their sports sponsorship marketing communications tactics accordingly.

The preceding charts provide important data on market statistics and trends. Segmentation is useful to apply here since such information adds detail to the profile of target customers. Marketers can identify areas of opportunity when looking at these and similar statistics. From here, marketers should look at the specific target audience profiles in the key countries where the marketing effort will concentrate and try to link target-customer profiles to advertising trends to see if there is a large enough audience justifying the marketing investment and choice of medium.

The demographics of the audiences using new media are attractive since 50% are in their peak income years (35+) and are well-educated, as Table 16-9 shows.

Corporate sponsors of the Olympics would find this demographic breakdown helpful when developing their specific marketing tactics since this audience responds favorably to NT marketing tools, thereby focusing the sponsor's marketing-communications decisions around related media.

Table 16-9
New Media Consumer Demographics[15]

Demographics	
Age	**%**
12–17	18%
18–24	11%
25–34	21%
35–44	22%
45–54	16%
54+	12%
84% college education	
24% advanced degrees	

Of course, online usage is one of the many NT marketing tools. A quick review of mobile entertainment, blogs, podcasts, and social media lends further credence to the increasing acceptance and use of NT marketing.

Mobile Entertainment

According to Juniper Research, mobile entertainment is forecasted to grow to $47.5 billion by 2010 from $20 billion in 2007. China and the Far East are the largest market, contributing 41%, and they will remain in the lead through 2012 when the total mobile market will be $64 billion, contributing 33% at that time. Sports marketers may consider developing marketing programs that work effectively in mobile entertainment, such as games, small-profile videos, and real-time delivery of sports statistics, along with the sponsorship message.[16]

Blogs

In 2007 there were 71 million blogs in the world and 120,000 new blogs created every day. There are 1.4 million blog postings added each day (58,334 per hour), and more than 50% of *Fortune 500* companies blog. Blogs are growing because they enable anybody to have a voice online. Many of the blog tools are free, so cost is not an important consideration. For the lucky few, a blog that catches on does so quickly and can become an influential source of information.[17]

Podcasts

The number of podcasts grew impressively, from 4,000 in 2004 to 61 million in 2005 and 266 million in 2006. Podcast ad spending is growing globally, particularly in the United States, due to the sheer number of Internet users and the maturity of the online customer market overall. Spending is forecasted to grow from an estimated $240 million in 2008 to $435 million in 2012, nearly doubling in four years. Podcasting is growing rapidly because of increasing awareness of it as a medium for information and entertainment, relative ease of use and ubiquity, the substantial concurrent growth in portable media players, and the affordable cost structure for content creation and deployment.[18]

Social Media

Companies in this space grew dramatically in 2007. Youtube.com grew approximately 1,000% in 2006 and was acquired by Google in October of that year for $1.65 billion. Facebook grew 200% in 2007, had between 40–50 million users in December 2007, and was adding one million new users per week at that time. Investors valued the company at $15 billion. MySpace grew 72% to 120 million users in 2007. Friendster grew 65% in 2007, to 25 million users. Juniper Research forecasts revenues rising in this market from $572 million (2007) to $5.7 billion in 2012, a CAGR of 59%.

Looking at Facebook's data more deeply, over 40% of its customers are over the age of 35, college-educated, white-collar professionals, indicating that social media are not just for the young. The average visitor stays on the site for 20 minutes each time, suggesting the social commitment level is high. Facebook has over 10,000 applications deployed, many suggested by users and designed to make the site even more useful and customized. Its largest markets are in North America and Europe.[19]

Why are the social media sites growing so rapidly? According to Forrester, a technology and market research firm, social media sites have become a central communications hub for users, as shown in Table 16-10.

As the center of social activity, these sites, along with blogs and podcasts, have become trusted sources of information. Trust, or Trusted Reputation, as was discussed in **Section IV: Winning Marketing Gold**

Table 16-10

Social Media Usage[20]

See what my friends are up to	86%
Sent a message to someone	79%
Posted/updated my profile	70%
Looked at profiles of people I didn't know	65%
Searched for someone that I used to know	59%
Send a friend/connection request	53%
Listened to music	47%
Read a blog or journal	51%
Wrote on someone's profile page	55%
Watched a video	40%

in the explanation of the Dimensions of Brand Value, is essential to the long-term success of a brand. For sports sponsors, knowing that a large number of customers are using online media for reasons of trust should inspire thinking and planning on how to use these social-media tools to connect to these customers.

CHAPTER 17

Is Your Company in Shape for Olympic Marketing?

Your Company's Competitive Fitness

The audit questions at the end of Sections I–IV are a highly recommended starting point for assessing your company's competitive fitness. It may seem like a lot of work, and it is. But so is the preparation and work an Olympian does well before competing in the Games, let alone winning a medal. So is the effort the TOP (The Olympic Program) sponsors put in to create a successful sponsorship. As described within this book, successful sponsorships are multi-part, multi-year commitments. Only a few organizations end up putting in the rigor required to succeed. But for those that do, the rewards can be substantial.

Sports Sponsorship Checklist

Three areas should be on every company's sports-sponsorship checklist:

1. Objectives
2. Deliverables
3. Post-Event Evaluation

1. Objectives

Management must ask itself why it wants to sponsor a sports event, whether the Olympics or otherwise. Answering this question will begin the process of identifying what are sensible and practical objectives to set forth for guiding the sponsorship. These will vary according to each company's individual needs, but may include:

- *Revive, renew, or enhance company reputation*
  Sports events are visible and established ones such as the Olympics have the potential to cast a favorable glow over the sponsoring company.

- *Grow awareness*
  Awareness includes recall (can the company be named without prompting?) and recognition (is the company remembered once a respondent is prompted?).
- *Improve sales*
  Sales can be measured in units or dollars and are frequently an objective. The challenge is tying long-term sponsorship efforts to short-term sales expectations. It may be better to measure sales over the long term unless a specific offer is made during the sponsorship event.
- *Convert new customers*
  Awareness helps attract customers, so a logical objective would be converting the newly "aware" to actual customers.
- *Reinforce company personality*
  Consumers connect to companies that exhibit a human face. Use the sponsorship to foster a more genuine, likable company image.
- *Expand social responsibility efforts*
  Help the public see a different side of the company by demonstrating community involvement, society-building, and/or environmental programs.
- *Inspire employees*
  Successful brand building requires a strong internal organization that rallies behind and supports company objectives. A sports sponsorship is a fun and engaging way to increase employee interest and involvement in the company.
- *Distinguish from competitors*
  Associating with a major sports event creates a visible and memorable distinction from competitors.

2. Deliverables

Exhibit 17-1 will help companies identify deliverables they should consider as they investigate and negotiate their sponsorship contract. There are many other possible benefits a sponsor may seek, but this provides a useful starting point:

Exhibit 17-1
Sports Sponsorship Deliverables[1]

Pre-Event Deliverables	Event Day and Related Deliverables
• Access and usage of event images and trademarks • Publicity support by event management • Detailed event and venue guidelines for signage and other sponsorship exposure vehicles	• Tickets/tickets in preferred zones • Hospitality suites/facilities • Access to off-limit areas • Access to event management, support, and logistics
Association Type Deliverables • Name association recognition—"official sponsor" • Sport association recognition • Athlete association recognition	**Athlete/Team/Facility Deliverables** • Athlete appearance deliverables • Athlete endorsement deliverables • Athlete image deliverables • Use of facilities for corporate events
Visual Image Deliverables • At event site • At event surroundings • On direct transmission of event • On replays of events • Use in advertisements/promotions	**Ambush Marketing Protection** • Aggressive stance against "ambushers" **Post-Event Deliverables** • Review and audit with event management • Preparation for next event/stage in relationship

3. Post-Event Evaluation

The pre-event objectives serve as the guide for setting detailed performance goals. Each of the objectives is reviewed along with the more specific tactical programs that were deployed in support of the sponsorship. Actual results compared to projected results should be closely reviewed to see what lessons can be learned. Aside from reviewing pre-event objectives, additional measures might include:

- *Marketing communications effectiveness*
  This includes all media used, comparing media placement metrics with actuals. Surveys of consumer feedback will supplement this review.

- *Market share (a longer-term measure)*
  One-time sponsorships are not likely to create market share gains, but sustained sponsorships, such as those represented by many of the Olympic TOP sponsors, can track market share changes over time.

- *Brand value (a longer-term measure)*
  Similar to market share, appreciable changes in brand value are more likely to occur over time than overnight. Determining if the sponsorship is the sole driver of brand value changes is less likely to be confirmed, but part of the entire sponsorship effort discussed in this book is a microcosm of ongoing, corporate brand-building activities anyway, so a well run sponsorship may noticeably accelerate positive brand-value changes.

CHAPTER 18

Key Lessons from 100 Years of Olympic Marketing

Benefits to Olympic Sponsors and Non-Olympic Sports Sponsors

Respect and honor traditions

The 2,700 year review of Olympic highlights that started this book is intended to show the enormous diversity of influences that shaped the traditions we now commonly associate with the Olympics. While other sports do not have a several-thousand-year history, most have rich traditions that have carried on for decades, inspiring generations of fans. Understanding the traditions will help companies develop a sponsorship plan that does not violate society's understanding of the sport and its deeper meaning. Athletes pursue the Olympics because they love what being an Olympian means and what it might confer on them.

Seek common values

Every organization stands for something far beyond making money. Each athlete has a personal code of conduct and a set of values by which they live. Identifying and knowing core values of both the company and the sports event will help avoid artificial or forced match-ups.

Self-assess

As athletes become more successful, they specialize. Over time, they have built a skill set and expertise in their event. Business schools teach the virtues of developing a recognized expertise and a set of skills and competencies to support it. Knowing what you are good at doing will assist the process of identifying sports sponsorship opportunities that offer the best potential. Tobacco companies, as mentioned earlier in this book, would have a hard time developing a convincing and successful sponsorship plan if they were to sponsor the Olympics. While they may share a few values in common, such as desire to be the best, their expertise would be in contradiction to that of the Olympics.

Focus on strategic benefits

The long-term is important. Short-term sales and profits can be increased, but are often temporary in the absence of a guiding set of objectives that provide a sense of direction. An athlete looks at their long-term goals, such as winning a gold medal, and keeps that objective at the forefront of their thinking where it serves to inspire them. Looking at a sponsorship as a strategic investment in the growth and development of the firm's value ensures the sponsorship is supported and viewed seriously, rather than as a one-time expendable tactic. Adjustments can and should be made, as was shown with the TOP (The Olympic Program) sponsors—each made changes in its event-specific marketing programs as they learned more about which activities worked best—but they should be made in the context of moving toward the long-term objective.

Develop a pre-, during, and post-event plan— outlining tactical implementation

This is where daily accountability is rooted. Long-term strategy is realized when short-term tactics are executed effectively. Mistakes will be made, but successes must outweigh failures for a strategy to work. Athletes know that aiming for a gold medal does not make it happen. They have to train rigorously, vary their preparation, compete against the very best, perform in different locations, all in an effort to achieve their strategic goals. The athlete's daily training routine is the equivalent of a company's sponsorship marketing tactics. This is where many managers and marketers get into trouble. Successful planning requires not just descriptions of what is to be done, but assignment of responsibility, setting of deadlines and accompanying deliverables, establishing measures of success, and preparing options if and when programs need adjusting. Managers must "own" their piece of the plan and teammates must be accountable to each other and to the company's overall objectives. Reviews of the plans at pre-determined stages must occur if accountability is to have any teeth.

Be flexible, but don't compromise core principles

Every plan faces risks, challenges, and possible disappointments. Planning a risk- or failure-free event may be politically attractive, but it is impractical if not impossible. Instead, the options mentioned above may be put to use here. Alternatively, and more likely, the hundreds and thousands of judgment calls made every day will determine success. The only rule of thumb is a simple one: if it is illegal, unethical, immoral, or simply against the organization's normal principles, then don't do it (no matter how attractive the short-term benefits might be). Athletes know there are no compromises or shortcuts that can be made to achieve ambitions. When compromises are made then the long-term dream suffers, such as from using performance-enhancing substances, or may even be irreparably damaged, as happened with the U.S. sprinter Marion Jones. The Olympics have a formidable reputation because, fundamentally, their caretakers over time have kept Olympic ideals at the forefront of their decisions and the Olympic Movement. When crises occur, public opinion simply won't let the Olympics be compromised. You know you have a strong brand when your own customers, your fans, help keep you focused on the ideals for which you stand.

Commit to excellence

Sports sponsorships are unlikely to fail when organizations and responsible people within commit overtly and privately to excellence. There is a simple choice each one of us faces every day, as do, more broadly, our organizations: you can choose to be world-class. Or not. Success comes when people dedicate themselves to being world-class. Just ask any Olympic athlete.

CHAPTER 19

Section V: Sponsorship Preparation Questions

Customers

1. What segments are you targeting?
   a. What do the customers have in common?
2. What do you know about them?
   a. What are their needs?
   b. Your market share?
   c. Their contribution to revenues/profits?
   d. Does the segment match your ability to deliver?
3. Have you evaluated each customer target and scored/rated them?

Creative Execution

1. Is your message clear?
   a. Is it designed to be funny/memorable/professional/instructional/other?
2. Is your message succinct?
   a. Can you describe it in a few words or seconds?
3. Is it relevant to the needs of the target customers?
   a. How do you know?
4. Does it resonate with them?
   a. How do you know?
5. Is the message distinctive?
   a. Is the distinction recognized by customers?
6. Is it simple?
   a. Do people "get it?"
7. What images/imagery do you want associated with the message and your company (follow the relevance/resonance/distinctiveness guidelines from above)?

8. What logos and trademarks will be used?
   a. How will they be used?
   b. Are they following corporate guidelines?
9. Mascots and merchandise?
   a. Will you be using either or both?
   b. What is the purpose of the mascot in your specific situation?
      i. Will it enhance or help your sponsorship plan?
   c. How is the merchandise plan being handled?
      i. Design
      ii. Vendors
      iii. Quantities
      iv. Quality
      v. Price
      vi. Distribution
10. What are the equivalent answers to these questions for the event and for other sponsors?
    a. Are you comfortable with how these activities and plans are unfolding (as far as you known them)?

Traditional and NT Marketing

1. What is your mix of traditional and non-traditional marketing?
   a. How will they be deployed?
   b. Who is in charge of media planning and purchase decisions?
   c. Is there a media insertion schedule?
      i. Who is responsible for it?
      ii. Who monitors the execution?
   d. Do you have digital media expertise in-house, or do you need to source for it?
   e. Are all logos and trademarks designed in appropriate formats for use in all media?
   f. Is your corporate and/or product image being properly conveyed?
2. Are your various marketing media integrated?
   a. Who overseas and coordinates this effort?
3. What are your contingency plans if a media provider does not deliver?
4. What is your perception of the event's equivalent marketing efforts?

a.   Are you confident they can deliver a great overall message in support of the sport?

Final Word

While this book was written in a specific sequence in order to provide a proper contextual backdrop for evaluating sports sponsorship opportunities, the audit questions at the end of each section may ultimately be addressed in a different order. Those covered in this book are not exhaustive and you will undoubtedly create your own list. Obviously, it is important to know who your target customers are as you plan, so the questions you ask and the data you receive may come earlier in the planning process. Perfect planning with all information known up-front and all potential problems addressed before they start is not a reasonable expectation. Such "analysis-paralysis" thinking will miss any marketing opportunity. The most important point is to keep asking questions as you go through the sponsorship planning and execution process. Oh, and since it is ultimately a sports event you will be sponsoring, be sure you enjoy it!

Endnotes and Credits

Introduction
1. Official website of the Olympic Movement. (n.d.) Retrieved October 29, 2007, from http://www.olympic.org/uk/organisation/facts/programme/sponsors_uk.asp.
2. Helm, Burt. "An Olympic PR Challenge." *BusinessWeek*, June 21, 2007. Retrieved October 21, 2007 from http://www.businessweek.com/globalbiz/content/jun2007/gb20070621_511854.htm.
3. Official website of the Olympic Movement. (n.d.) Retrieved October 3, 2007, from http://www.olympic.org/uk/organisation/facts/programme/sponsors_uk.asp.
4. Olympic Marketing Fact File 2008 Edition, p.24. Retrieved February 23, 2008, from www.olympic.org.
5. The IOC 2008 Marketing Fact File describes total viewer hours as "a statistic that measures the number of hours of Olympic programming that have captured the attention of the global television viewing audience during the period of the Olympic Games. Viewer Hours per program is measured by multiplying the duration of the program by the number of viewers in the audience. Total Viewer Hours for the Olympic Games and Olympic Winter Games is the sum of all Viewer Hours per program." Olympic Marketing Fact File 2008 Edition, p.24.
6. Wilson, Stephen. "Athens Olympics Draw Record TV Audiences." *USA Today*, October 12, 2004. Retrieved November 24, 2007, from http://www.usatoday.com/sports/olympics/athens/news/2004-10-12-athens-tv_x.htm.
7. Slack, Trevor. *The Commercialization of Sport*. (London: Frank Cass Publisher, 2003).
8. Multiple sources: The NDP Group. "Global Sports Market Growing." September 24, 2007. http://www.itsasurvey.com/artman2/publish/sports Global_ Sports_Market_Growing. shtml and http://www.sportsandplay.com/news/npd_estimates_2008_low.pdf, slide 21.

SECTION I
2,700 Years of Olympic Tradition, 100 Years of Olympic Marketing

Chapter 1–The Olympic Dream
1. Blais, Eric. "Quebec and 2010." *Marketing Magazine*, 11964650, 11/12/2007, Vol. 112, Issue 21.
2. Foster, George, and Victoria Chang. "Visa Sponsorship Marketing." Case: SPM-5 p.5. Stanford University Graduate School of Business ©2003.
3. Tufts University, Perseus Database. (n.d.) Retrieved October 28, 2007, from http://www.perseus.tufts.edu/cgi-bin/ptext?doc=Perseus%3Atext%3A1999.01.0162.
4. Kuntz, Tom. "The Guy Who Ate a Cow and Other Olympic Stars." *New York Times*, July 14, 1996. Retrieved December 11, 2007, from http://www.nytimes.com/specials/olympics/cntdown/0714oly-review.html.
5. Tufts University, Perseus Database. (n.d.) Retrieved January 4, 2008, from http://www.perseus.tufts.edu/cgi-bin/ptext?doc=Perseus:text:1999.04.0004:id=pindar.

6. Dio Chrysostom. *Dio Chrysostom, I, Discourses 1–11*, Cohoon, J.W., translator. Loeb Classical Library, Harvard University Press. Retrieved February 26, 2008, from http://www.hup.harvard.edu/catalog/L257.html.
7. Fowler, Robin, "Pherenike the Trainer." Ancient History. (n.d.) Retrieved February 24, 2008, from http://ancienthistory. suite101.com/article.cfm/pherenike_the_trainer.
8. Kyle, Donald G. "Winning at Olympia." *Archaeology*. April 6, 2004. Retrieved October 28, 2007, from http://www.archaeology.org/online/features/olympics/olympia.html.
9. Verrengia, Joseph B. "The Ancient Olympics Had its Own Scandals." July 28, 2004. Retrieved October 30, 2007, from http://www.msnbc.msn.com/id/5467740/.
10. Miller, Stephen G. *Ancient Greek Athletes*. (New Haven, CT: Yale University Press, 2004).
11. University of Pennsylvania Museum of Archaeology and Anthropology. "The Athletes: Amateurs or Pros?" (n.d.) Retrieved October 28, 2007, from http://www.museum.upenn. edu/new/olympics/olympicathletes.shtml.
12. Young, David C. "Imagine That! Olympic Games in Greece!" Columbia University. (n.d.) Retrieved February 18, 2007, from http://www.greekembassy.org/Embassy/content/en/Article.aspx?office=1&folder= 30&article=11574&hilite=David%20Young.

Chapter 2–How the Olympics Make Us Feel

1. Wallechinsky, David, and Jaime Loucky. *The Complete Book of the Winter Olympics Turin 2006 Edition*. (Toronto: Sports Media Publishing, Inc., 2006), pp. 3-10.
2. Ibid.
3. Official website of the Olympic Movement. (n.d.) Retrieved October 29, 2007, from http://www.olympic.org/uk/games/pastindex_uk.asp?OLGT= 2&OLGY=2006.
4. Majid, Kashef; Ramdas Chandra and Annamma Joy. "Exploring the Growing Interest in the Olympic Winter Games." *Sport Marketing Quarterly*, Volume 16, Number 1, 2007.
5. Davis, John. *Measuring Marketing: 103 Key Metrics Every Marketer Needs*. (Singapore: John Wiley & Sons (Asia) Pte. Ltd., 2006) p.153. Author's note: My research over the past seven years has reviewed the brand practices of over 200 organizations from around the world in numerous industries. Those that perform best in brand valuation and awareness are relatively consistent in viewing their approach to external (market-facing) brand development in remarkably simple and clear terms. Equally important was the management and execution of their internal brand-building efforts. In effect, the internal and external emphases ensured these companies delivered on their promises.
6. Author's note: a "touchpoint" is defined as any point of contact between an organization and the customer. An example of a tangible touchpoint is a physical product, whereas an intangible touchpoint would be service or, even more abstractly, one's perception of the organization.
7. Majid, Kashef; Ramdas Chandra and Annamma Joy. "Exploring the Growing Interest in the Olympic Winter Games." *Sport Marketing Quarterly*, Volume 16, Number 1, 2007. p.30.
8. Smart, Barry. Article—"Not playing around: global capitalism, modern sport and consumer culture." p.10; in *Globalization and Sport*. Edited by Richard Giulianotti and Roland Robertson. (Oxford: Wiley-Blackwell, 2007).
9. Corral, Conrado Durantez. *"Pierre De Coubertin, The Olympic Humanist."* (Lousanne: The IOC and the International Pierre De Coubertin Committee, 1994), p.65.
10. Hofmann, Verlag Karl. *"Pierre De Coubertin, The Olympic Idea."* Edited by Carl-Diem-Institut. (Karl Hofman Verlag, 1967), p.100.
11. Majid, Kashef; Ramdas Chandra and Annamma Joy. "Exploring the Growing Interest in the Olympic Winter Games." *Sport Marketing Quarterly*, Volume 16, Number 1, 2007, p.30.
12. Ibid.
13. Davis, John. *Measuring Marketing: 103 Key Metrics Every Marketer Needs*. (Singapore: John Wiley & Sons (Asia) Pte. Ltd., 2006), p.xiv.
14. Majid, Kashef; Ramdas Chandra and Annamma Joy. "Exploring the Growing Interest in the Olympic Winter Games." *Sport Marketing Quarterly*, Volume 16, Number 1, 2007, p.30.

15. Smart, Barry. Article—"Not playing around: global capitalism, modern sport and consumer culture." p.22; in *Globalization and Sport*. Edited by Richard Giulianotti and Roland Robertson. (Oxford: Wiley-Blackwell, 2007).

16. Official website of the Olympic Movement. (n.d.) Retrieved January 16, 2008, from http://www.olympic.org/uk/games/past/index_uk.asp? OLGT=1&OLGY=1972.

17. Young, David C. "With Hands or Swift Feet—The ancient Greek city-states were rarely as united as they were at the Olympic Games." This article has been adapted from Young's book *A Brief History of the Olympic Games*. (Oxford: Blackwell Publishing, 2004). Retrieved January 30, 2007, from http://www.naturalhistorymag.com/0704/0704_feature.html.

18. Fiegal, Eric. "Vick sentenced to 23 months for dogfighting." *CNN*. December 10, 2007. Retrieved December 17, 2007, from http://edition.cnn.com/2007/US/law/12/10/vick.sentenced/index.html.

19. Tufts University, Perseus data base (n.d.). Retrieved October 28, 2007, from http://www.perseus.tufts.edu/olympics/amat.html.

20. Young, David C. "With Hands or Swift Feet—The ancient Greek city-states were rarely as united as they were at the Olympic Games." This article has been adapted from Young's book *A Brief History of the Olympic Games*. (Oxford: Blackwell Publishing, 2004). Retrieved January 30, 2007, from http://www.naturalhistorymag.com/0704/0704_feature.html.

21. Hyde, Walter Woodburn. "Greek Literary Notices of Olympic Victor Monuments outside Olympia." *Transactions and Proceedings of the American Philological Association*, Vol. 42, (1911), pp.53–67. (Article consists of 15 pages). Published by: The Johns Hopkins University Press. Retrieved December 12, 2007, from Stable URL: http://www.jstor.org/stable/282573.

22. Poliakoff, Michael B. "Melankomas, ek klimakos, and Greek Boxing." *The American Journal of Philology*, Vol. 108, No. 3 (Autumn, 1987), pp.511–518. Publisher: The Johns Hopkins University Press. Retrieved December 12, 2007 from Stable URL: http://www.jstor.org/stable/294676.

23. Mylonas, George E. "The Bronze Statue from Artemision." *American Journal of Archaeology*, Vol. 48, No. 2 (Apr. - Jun., 1944), pp.143–160. Publisher: Archaeological Institute of America. Retrieved December 12, 2007, from Stable URL: http://www.jstor.org/stable/499921.

24. Carney, T.F. "Content Analysis and Classical Scholarship." *The Journal of Hellenic Studies*, Vol. 88, (1968), pp.137–138. Publisher: The Society for the Promotion of Hellenic Studies. Retrieved December 14, 2007, from Stable URL: http://www.jstor.org/stable/628678.

25. Author's note: Avid fans are encouraged to read David Wallenchinsky's comprehensive Olympics books, *The Complete Book of the Summer Olympics* (Toronto: Sport Media Publishing, 2004) and *The Complete Book of the Winter Olympics* (Toronto: Sport Media Publishing, 2005 co-authored with Jaime Loucky), as these books provide thoughtful detail on the innumerable Olympic athletes of the modern era.

26. Review: "America's Shame—Review of Heroes without a Country: America's Betrayal of Joe Louis and Jesse Owens by Donald McRae."*The Journal of Blacks in Higher Education*, No. 45 (Autumn, 2004), pp.125. Publisher: The JBHE Foundation. Retrieved October 3, 2007, from Stable URL: http://www.jstor.org/stable/4133637.

27. Litsky, Frank. "Bob Mathias, 75, Decathlete and Politician, Dies." September 3, 2006. *The New York Times*. Retrieved October 13, 2007, from http://www.nytimes.com/2006/09/03/sports/othersports/03mathias.html.

28. Schwartz, Larry. "Boy-wonder Mathias elevated decathlon." *ESPN.com*. (n.d.) Retrieved October 13, 2007, from http://espn.go.com/sportscentury/features/00016202.html .

29. Official website of the Olympic Movement. (n.d.) Retrieved October 13, 2007, from http://www.olympic.org/uk/athletes/profiles/bio_uk.asp?PAR_I_ID=77534.

30. Mutliple sources: Official website of the Olympic Movement. (n.d.). Retrieved October 13, 2007 from http://www.olympic.org/uk/athletes/profiles/bio_uk.asp?PAR_I_ID=44503; and supplemented by Miller, Toby. "Competing Allegories: An Introduction." Social Text, No. 50, The politics of Sport (Spring, 1997), pp. 1-Publisher: Duke Universiaty Press. Retrieved October 15, 2007 from Stable URL: http://www.jstor.org/stable/466811, http://www.bartandnadia.com.sg, http://www.nadiacomanceci.com.

31. Multiple sources: Official website of the Olympic Movement. (n.d.) Retrieved October 12, 2007, from http://www.olympic.org/uk/athletes/profiles/bio_uk.asp?PAR_I_ID=43395 and supplemented by http://news.bbc.co.uk/sport2/hi/olympics2000/bbc_team/859595.stm, http://www.timesonline.co.uk/tol/sport/article537461.ece, and http://www.independent.co.uk/news/people/sebastian-coe-you-ask-the-questions-556162.html.

32. Multiple sources: Ibid. Retrieved October 12, 2007, from http://www.olympic.org/uk/athletes/profiles/bio_uk.asp?PAR_I_ID=33546 and http://www.nba.com/history/dreamT_moments.html.

33. Multiple sources: Ibid. Retrieved October 12, 2007, from http://www.olympic.org/uk/athletes/profiles/bio_uk.asp?PAR_I_ID=75787 and http://www.katarina.de.

34. Multiple sources: Ibid. Retrieved October 12, 2007, from http://www.olympic.org/uk/athletes/profiles/bio_uk.asp?PAR_I_ID=20272, http://www.markspitzusa.com/ and http://www.goldmedalgreats.com/athlete.asp?userID=77.

35. Multiple sources: Tyan, Tina. "Scott Hamilton's baby is all grown up." Skate Today. January 26, 2006. Retrieved October 12, 2007, from http://www.skatetoday.com/articles0506/012606.htm and http://edition.cnn.com/2005/US/09/12/cnn25.hamilton.tan/index.html.

CHAPTER 3–The Ever-Changing Olympics

1. NBC Sports. "Qatar lures athletes with citizenship, cash—Country importing athletes to help win medals at Asian Games." December 8, 2006. Retrieved December 2, 2007, from http://nbcsports.msnbc.com/id/16113525.

2. Isidore, Chris. CNN/Money senior writer. "Time to pay Olympic winners: U.S. medal winners get prize money, but most Olympians are true amateurs who get nothing for a win." August 20, 2004. Retrieved December 2, 2007, from http://money.cnn.com/2004/08/19/commentary/column_sportsbiz/sportsbiz/index.htm.

3. Brennae, Mark, and Meagan Fitzpatrick. CanWest News Service. "Canadian athletes to get cash for Olympic success." November 19, 2007. Retrieved December 19, 2007, from http://www.canada.com/globaltv/national/story.html?id=2a36c58a-ac62-4815-8d56-d815d71d9843&k=69958.

4. BBC Sports. "Russian winners promised windfall." July 12, 2000. Retrieved December 16, 2007, from http://news.bbc.co.uk/sport2/hi/athletics/830528.stm.

5. Ibid.

6. ChinaDaily. "Comaneci no longer inspires Romanian gymnasts." March 27, 2008. Retrieved March 30, 2008, from http://www.chinadaily.com.cn/sports/2008-03/27/content_6569757.htm.

7. Singapore National Olympic Council. "Multi-Million Dollar Awards Program." Retrieved December 15, 2007 from http://www.snoc.org.sg/mmdap.htm.

8. The Japan Times. "JAAF offers rewards for medal winners." June 15, 2004. Retrieved December 15, 2007, from http://search.japantimes.co.jp/cgi-bin/so20040615a1.html.

9. Li, YongYan. "Chinese Athlete: 'I owe it to the party.'" August 26, 2004. Asia Times Online. Retrieved December 16, 2007, from http://www.atimes.com/atimes/China/FH26Ad05.html.

10. Taylor, Scott. "Slow swimmer a crowd favorite." September 20, 2000. Deseret News. Retrieved December 16, 2007, from http://deseretnews.com/sydney/view/1,3466,195015385,00.html.

11. Baker, Mark. "Olympics 2004: For Some Athletes, Behind the Medals Lies Real Gold." Radio Free Europe/Radio Liberty. August 6, 2004. Retrieved December 16, 2007 from

http://rferl.org/featuresarticle/2004/08/7c76e915-dd8a-452e-a788-22d90d0bf6a2.html.

12. Author's Note: Endnotes 2–11 were a subset of over two dozen references to payments for Olympic medalists from different nations. Not all nations pay their medalists. Furthermore, there is some variation in the ranges. To the extent there was consistent agreement from multiple sources, those figures were included in Table 3-1. http://bbs.comefromchina.com/forum22/thread271376.html.

13. Multiple sources: Official website of the Olympic Movement. (n.d.) Retrieved February 3, 2008, from http://www.olympic.org/uk/games/torino2006/backstage/backstage_photo_uk.asp?LngId=2&RubId=2&PicId=73 and http://translate.google.com/translate?hl=en&sl=de&u=http://www.michael-greis.de/&sa=X&oi=translate&resnum= 1&ct=result&prev=/search%3Fq%3Dmichael%2Bgreis%26hl%3Den.

14. Multiple sources: Ibid. Retrieved October 12, 2007, from http://www.olympic.org/uk/athletes/profiles/bio_uk?asp?PAR_I_ID=136177 and http://wwwmichaelphelps.com/2004/english.html0. Henderson, John. "Phelps ready to strike more gold." *The Denver Post.* April 12, 2008. Retrieved April 1, 2008 from http://www.denverpost.com/sports/ci_8907515.

15. IOC Charter. "Programme of the Olympic Games." pp.86–95. Retrieved from http://www.olympic.org/uk/organisation/missions/charter_uk.asp.

16. Multiple sources: Official website of the Olympic Movement. (n.d.) Retrieved January 7, 2008, from http://www.olympic.org/uk/games/index_uk.asp. "IOC approves new sports for Beijing Olympics." October 27, 2005. *CBCSports.* Retrieved January 7, 2008 from http://www.cbc.ca/sports/story/2005/10/27/iocmeetings051027.html.

Chapter 4–The Sports and Politics Cocktail–Drinking from the Olympic Fire Hose

1. Romano, David Gilman. "The Politics of the Olympic Games." From the Penn Museum's "The Real Story of the Ancient Olympic Games." (n.d.) Retrieved December 14, 2007, from http://www.museum.upenn.edu/new/olympics/olympicpolitics.shtml.

2. Multiple sources: Nisetich, Frank J. "Olympian 1.8–11: An Epinician Metaphor." *Harvard Studies in Classical Philology,* Vol. 79, (1975), pp.55–68. Publisher: Department of the Classics, Harvard University. Retrieved December 15, 2007, from Stable URL: http://www.jstor.org/stable/311128 and retrieved December 15, 2007 from http://www.museum.upenn.edu/new/olympics/olympiccommercialism.shtml.

3. Multiple sources: Burton, Rick. "Olympic Games Host City Marketing: An Exploration of Expectations and Outcomes." *Sport Marketing Quarterly,* Volume 12, Number 1, 2003, pp.37–47, and Official website of the Olympic Movement. (n.d.) "117th IOC Session Candidate Procedure for the 2012 Olympic Games." Retrieved January 23, 2008, from http://www.olympic.org/uk/news/events/117_session/candidature_uk.asp.

4. Official website of the Olympic Movement. (n.d.) Retrieved February 27, 2008, from http://www.olympic.org/uk/games/index_uk.asp.

5. Ibid.

6. Wolk, Martin. "Games hold allure for would-be host cities." August 30, 2004. Retrieved November 2, 2007, from http://www.msnbc.msn.com/id/5481584.

7. Elberse, Anita; Catherine Anthony and Joshua Callahan. "The Vancouver 2010 Olympics." Case 9-507-049. p.21. Revised October 5, 2007. Harvard Business School. ©2007 President and Fellows of Harvard College.

8. Zarnowski, Frank C. "A Look at Olympic Costs." *International Journal of Olympic History.* (1993) pp.16–26. Retrieved on December 21, 2007, from http://www.la84foundation.org/index/JOHIndex.html.

9. Brunet, Ferran. "An economic analysis of the Barcelona '92 Olympic Games: resources, financing and impacts." (1995) p.10. This document has been published as part of the book by Miquel de Moragas Spá and Miquel Botella (eds.) (1995), *The Keys of Success: the social, sporting, economic and communications impact of Barcelona '92.*

10. Ibid. p.13. Brunet noted the table was supplemented with additional data from the IOC, the SOOC, and the COOB '92.

11. Multiple sources: Burton, Rick. "Olympic Games Host City Marketing: An Exploration of Expectations and Outcomes." *Sport Marketing Quarterly*, Volume 12, Number, 1 2003, pp.25–31; IOC, Auditor-General's 2002 Report to Australian Parliament, Vol. Two, Burton (2002); Associated Press (2002c): Boeck (2002); Repanshek (1995), Burton (2002) p.41.

12. Ibid. The 1992 Olympics in Barcelona generated a $3 million profit for the Olympic organizing committee but left $6.1 billion in debt for government and public entities. The Spanish government assumed $4 billion in debt and the city/provincial government carried the additional $2.1 billion. The cost of the Barcelona Games can be broken down as follows: Olympic organizing committee, $1.4 billion; Spanish government, provincial government, city of Barcelona, and private investors for Olympic-related projects such as roads, airports, sports facilities, $9.3 billion. Of the $9.3 billion, private investment provided $3.2 billion, with public money providing $6.1 billion.

13. Elberse, Anita Catherine Anthony and Joshua Callahan. "The Vancouver 2010 Olympics." Case 9-507-049. p.16. Revised October 5, 2007. Harvard Business School. ©2007 President and Fellows of Harvard College. Originally adapted from IOC reports and Holger Preuss,. *The Economics of Staging the Olympics: A Comparison of the Games 1972-2008*, 2004. The 1980 Games in Moscow, USSR, are excluded for lack of data.

14. Multiple sources: "Games of the XXI Olympiad Montréal 1976 Official Report." pp.54–62 Legal Deposit Quebec National Library 2nd Quarter, 1978. Retrieved November 3, 2007, from http://olympic-museum.de/o-reports/report1976.htm; "Olympic Games may be close to being buried." *The Peterborough Examiner*. Retrieved April 27, 2008, from http://www.peterboroughexaminer.com/PrintArticle.aspx?e=993090; Guayar, Michel. "Legacy of the Olympic Games in Montreal-An Introduction." April 27, 1996. Retrieved November 3, 2007, from http://www.montrealolympics.com/mg_legacy.php.

15. Brunet, Ferran. "An economic analysis of the Barcelona '92 Olympic Games: resources, financing and impacts". (1995) p.11. This document has been published as part of the book by Miquel de Moragas Spá and Miquel Botella (eds.) (1995), *The Keys of Success: The Social, Sporting, Economic and Communications Impact of Barcelona '92*; Morrow, Lance. "Feeling Proud Again." *Time Magazine* 'Man of the Year' 1984. January 7, 1985. Retrieved December 14, 2007, from http://www.time.com/time/magazine/article/0,9171,956226,00.html.

16. Riding, Alan. "Rivalry in '92 Barcelona Olympics Starts Early." September 26, 1989. *The New York Times*. Retrieved December 11, 2007, from http://query.nytimes.com/gst/fullpage.html?res=950DE4D71F3DF935 A1575AC0A96F948260.

17. "Olympics: A Pre-Olympic Gold Drain as Budget Surplus Dwindles." January 25, 1994. *The New York Times*. Retrieved December 11, 2007, from http://query.nytimes.com/gst/fullpage.html?res=9405E6D71130F936A15752 C0A962958260.

18. Longman, Jere. "Atlanta Games, a celebration for 197 Nations, Close." August 5, 1996. *The New York Times*. Retrieved February 6, 2007, from http://query.nytimes.com/gst/fullpage.html?res=9B0DEED81E3FF936 A3575BC0A960958260&sec=&spon=&pagewanted=all.

19. Longman, Jere. "Olympics: Nagano 1998; Cold Shoulder Turns Into Warm Embrace." February 6, 1998. *The New York Times*. Retrieved December 11, 2007, from http://query.nytimes.com/gst/fullpage.html?res=9B0DE2D8123D F935A35751 C0A96E958260.

20. Multiple sources: Armstrong, David. "Reinventing the Rings—Sydney Olympics Depends Less on Commercial Sponsorship, More On Responsible Financing." January 10, 1998. *The Sydney Examiner*. Retrieved December 12, 2007 from http://olympics.ballparks.com/2000Sydney/index.htm. Landler, Mark. "Sydney 2000; Sydney Anticipates Long-Term Boon." October 3, 2000. *The New York Times*. Retrieved December 12, 2007, from http://query.nytimes.com/gst/fullpage.html?res=950CE2DD133DF930A35753 C1A9669C8B63.

21. Authorstream.com. Winter Olympics 2010 presentation. Slide 6. Retrieved January 9, 2008. from http://www.authorstream.com/presentation/HannahBanana-64394-2010-vancouver-olympics-sports-mkting-pres-education-ppt-powerpoint.

22. Multiple sources: "Beijing to unveil Olympics budget in May." March 6, 2008. Retrieved March 11, 2008. from http://news.xinhuanet.com/english/2008-03/06/content_7734331.htm; "China invites the world to Olympics." August 8, 2007. Retrieved January 6, 2008, from http://www.chinadaily.com.cn/olympics/2007-08/08/content_6017952.htm; Zubkov, Vasily. "How Much Will Beijing Pay for the Olympics." May 28, 2007. Retrieved January 7, 2008, from http://www.spacedaily.com/reports/How_Much_Will_Beijing_Pay_For_The_Olympics_999.html.

23. Van Riper, Tom. "Host City Curse." February 8, 2006. *Forbes*. Retrieved January 11, 2008, from http://www.forbes.com/2006/02/08/host-city-olympics_cx_tvr_0208olympiccity.html.

24. "The 2010 Winter Olympics and Paralympic Games." (n.d.) *City Mayors Sport Report Vancouver*. Retrieved March 3, 2008, from http://www.citymayors.com/canada/vancouver_olympics.html.

25. Elberse, Anita; Catherine Anthony and Joshua Callahan. "The Vancouver 2010 Olympics." Case 9-507-049. p.10. Revised October 5, 2007. Harvard Business School. ©2007 President and Fellows of Harvard College. Originally adapted from IOC reports and Holger Preuss, *The Economics of Staging the Olympics: A Comparison of the Games 1972-2008*, 2004.

26. Timmons, Heather. "Corporate Sponsors Nervous as Tibet Protest Groups Shadow Olympic Torch's Run." March 29, 2008. *The New York Times*. Retrieved March 29, 2008, from http://www.nytimes.com/2008/03/29/business/worldbusiness/29torch.html.

27. Official website of the Olympic Movement. (n.d.) Retrieved December 29, 2007, from http://www.olympic.org/uk/games/index_uk.asp.

28. "Beijing officials say air quality improved during trial Olympic traffic ban." August 21, 2007. *International Herald Tribune*. Retrieved December 2, 2007, from http://www.iht.com/articles/ap/2007/08/21/sports/AS-SPT-OLY-Beijing-Car-Ban.php.

29. Elberse, Anita; Catherine Anthony and Joshua Callahan. "The Vancouver 2010 Olympics." Case 9-507-049. p.12. Revised October 5, 2007. Harvard Business School. ©2007 President and Fellows of Harvard College. Originally adapted from IOC reports and Holger Preuss, "The Economics of Staging the Olympics," 2004.

30. Ibid.

31. Multiple sources: Nel-lo, Oriol. "The Olympic Games a a tool for Urban Renewal: The Experience of Barcelona '92 Olympic Village." (1997) pp.2–9. This document has been published as part of the book by Miquel de Moragas Spá and Miquel Botella (eds.) (1997), *Olympic Villages: A Hundred Years of Urban Planning and Shared Experiences*: International Symposium on Olympic Villages, Lausanne 1996; Baliko, Jennifer. "Turin's turnaround Olympic Games spark an industrial city's makeover." *The Daily Herald*. December 5, 2005. Retrieved January 14, 2008 from http://goliath.ecnext.com/coms2/gi_0199-5070752/Turin-s-turnaround-Olympic-Games.html.

32. Brunet, Ferran. "An economic analysis of the Barcelona '92 Olympic Games: resources, financing and impacts." (1995) p.7. This document has been published as part of the book by Miquel de Moragas Spá and Miquel Botella (eds.) (1995), *The Keys of Success: the social, sporting, economic and communications impact of Barcelona '92*.

33. Tschang, Chi-Chu. "An Olympic Glitch in China." November 12, 2007. *BusinessWeek*. Retrieved December 5, 2007, from http://www.businessweek.com/magazine/content/07_46/c4058040.htm.

34. Morrow, Lance. "Feeling Proud Again." *Time Magazine* 'Man of the Year' 1984. January 7, 1985. Retrieved December 14, 2007, from http://www.time.com/time/magazine/article/0,9171,956226,00.html.

35. Multiple sources: Davidson, Thomas. *Journal of the American Geographical Society of New York*, Vol. 12, (1880), pp.217–233. Publisher: American Geographical Society. Retrieved November 23, 2007, from Stable URL: http://www.jstor.org/stable/196526 ; University of Pennsylvania Museum of Archaeology and Anthropology. (n.d) "The Games." Retrieved November 11, 2007, from http://www.museum.upenn.edu/new/olympics/olympicorigins. shtml.

SECTION II
When Things Go Well...

Chapter 6–The Global Stage
1. Olympic Marketing Fact File 2008 Edition, p.24. Retrieved February 23, 2008 from http://www.olympic.org.
2. Official website of the Olympic Movement. (n.d.) Retrieved January 24, 2008 from http://www.olympic.org/uk/organisation/facts/broadcast_uk.asp.
3. Olympic Marketing Fact File 2008 Edition, p.23. Retrieved February 23, 2008, from http://www.olympic.org.
4. Ibid. p.26.
5. Ibid. p.32–37.
6. Auditor-General's Report to Parliament 2002 Volume Two. April 22, 2003. Auditor General New South Wales. Archived Auditor's report, p.10–11.
7. Multiple sources: "Athens Olympics cost may top $14.6 billion." November 18, 2004. *USA Today*. Retrieved December 1, 2007, from http://www.usatoday.com/sports/olympics/athens/news/2004-11-18-cost_x.htm; "Athens Olympics Seen Costing More Than Double Initial Target." August 25, 2004. *Reuters/FoxNews*. Retrieved December 1, 2007, from http://www.foxnews.com/story/0,2933,130057,00.html.
8. "Beijing 2008 Olympic Budget Unveiled." February 24, 2001. *People's Daily*. Retrieved December 11, 2007, from http://english.peopledaily.com.cn/200102/24/eng20010224_63279.html.
9. Forney, Matthew. "Beijing Bags It." July 15, 2001. *Time*. Retrieved December 11, 2007, from http://www.time.com/time/arts/article/0,8599,167611,00.html.
10. "Olympics Budget Rises to £9.3 billion." *BBC News*. March 15, 2007. Retrieved December 15, 2007, from http://news.bbc.co.uk/2/hi/uk_news/politics/6453575.stm.
11. Olympic Marketing Fact File 2008 Edition, p.24. Retrieved February 23, 2008, from http://www.olympic.org.
12. Ibid. p.25.
13. Author's note: Watching the 2004 Olympic Games in Athens from Singapore, where I had just moved a few months before, was a great example of regional programming preferences. While each day's broadcast brought coverage of the various sports, much of the Olympics' coverage centered on badminton and table tennis, two enormously popular sports in Asia. The fans of these sports are no less passionate than those of the more recognized swimming, track and field, gymnastics, and basketball events (among dozens of sports). Indeed, Singaporeans in 2004 watched with rapt attention the fortunes of Li Jiawei, their women's table-tennis sensation. She finished fourth, just out of the running for a medal, but her performance endeared her to Singaporeans and the television coverage of her throughout the Olympics captured the collective attention of this small city-state. The local media featured extensive profiles of her athletic achievements, her family, and her long-term ambitions, giving Li Jiawei a more personal appeal.

Chapter 7–Olympic Halo Effect: Long Term and Short Term
1. Davis, John. *Measuring Marketing: 103 Key Metrics Every Marketer Needs*. (Singapore: John Wiley & Sons (Asia) Pte. Ltd., 2006), p.253.
2. Multiple sources: Foster, George, and Victoria Chang. "Visa Sponsorship Marketing." Case: SPM-5 p.15. Stanford University Graduate School of Business ©2003; "Olympics, What Olympics? Sponsors, What Sponsors." Performance Research Independent Studies. Performance Research conducted 509 pre-event (January 12–13, 1994) and 268 post-event (February 28, 1994) random nationwide telephone interviews. The margin of error is + 1%. Retrieved November 6, 2007 from http://www.performanceresearch.com/olympic-sponsorship-lillehammer.htm.

3. "Top 100 Global Brands Scorebocard." Interbrand and *BusinessWeek*. August 6, 2007. Retrieved August 23, 2007, from http://bwnt.businessweek.com/interactive_reports/top_brands/index.asp.
4. Multiple sources: Douglas, Susan P. Samuel C. Craig; and Edwin J. Nijssen. "An International Brand Architecture: Development, Drivers and Design." (1999) Retrieved November 12, 2007, from http://pages.stern.nyu.edu/~sdouglas/rpubs/intbrand.html; "Samsung-The Top Brand in the World." (n.d.) Retrieved January 16, 2008, from http://www. 123helpme.com/view.asp?id=47241; "Samsung Extends Sponsorship of Olympic Games Until 2016." April 24, 2007. *Sport Business*. Retrieved November 6, 2007, from http://www.sportbusiness.com/news/161740/samsung-extends-sponsorship-of-olympic-games-until-2016.
5. Davis, John. *Measuring Marketing: 103 Key Metrics Every Marketer Needs*. (Singapore: John Wiley & Sons (Asia) Pte. Ltd., 2006), p.66 and 71.
6. Multiple sources: Worthington, Kamala. "AmEx Won't Be the Only Loser as Credit Card Deliquencies & Defaults Skyrocket." January 15, 2008. Gerson Lehrman Group. Retrieved January 27, 2008, from http://www.glgroup.com/News/AmEx-Wont-Be-the-Only-Loser-As-Credit-Card-Delinquencies—Defaults-Skyrocket-20731.html; Foster, George, and Victoria Chang. "Visa Sponsorship Marketing." Case: SPM-5 p.14-15. Stanford University Graduate School of Business ©2003.
7. Ibid. Visa Sponsorship Marketing.
8. Multiple sources: Wilson, Richard. "Nokia and Samsung see strong mobile phone sales." January 25, 2008. *Electronics Weekly*. Retrieved January 30, 2008, from http://www. electronicsweekly.com/Articles/2008/01/25/43001/nokia-and-samsung-see-strong-mobile-phone-sales.htm; Winter, Holly. "Gartner Says Worldwide Mobile Phone Sales Increased 16 Percent in 2007." February 27, 2008. Retrieved March 16, 2008, from http://www.gartner.com/it/page.jsp?id=612207.
9. Ansoff, H.I. "Strategies for Diversification." *Harvard Business Review*, 35(2), September-October (1957).
10. Ibid.

Chapter 8–David vs. Goliath–Those Delightful Surprises

1. Multiple soures: Official website of the Olympic Movement. (n.d.) Retrieved December 1, 2007, from http://www.olympic.org/uk/athletes/profiles/bio_uk.asp?PAR_I_ID=16525; "Whatever Happened to Vera Caslavska (TCH)?" (n.d.) Retrieved December 7, 2007, from http://www.gymnpics.com/gymnasticgreats/wag/caslavska.htm.
2. Multiple sources: Swift, E.M. "A Reminder of What We Can Be." *Sports Illustrated*. February 21, 1994. Retrieved October 9, 2007, from http://sportsillustrated.cnn.com/features/cover/news/2000/02/17/a_reminder_of_what_we_can_be/; "Do You Believe in Miracles?" (n.d.) Retrieved October 17, 2007, from http://www.miracleonice.us/; Official website of the Olympic Movement. (n.d.) Retrieved October 18, 2007, from http://www.olympic.org/uk/athletes/profiles/bio_uk.asp?PAR_I_ID=109240.
3. Multiple sources: Lowitt, Bruce. "Do You Believe in Miracles?" December 26, 1999. *St. Petersburg Times*. Retrieved October 30, 2007; Video footage on Youtube.com features multiple samples of the famous Al Michaels' sportscast in which he clearly, excitedly calls the end of the U.S.–Soviet hockey game. Retrieved December 14, 2007, from http://www.youtube.com/results?search_query=miracle+on+ice&search_type=.
4. "Flying High." September 3, 2007. *The Guardian*. Retrieved November 21, 2007, from http://film.guardian.co.uk/news/story/0,,2161238,00.html.
5. Ibid.
6. "Eddie the Eagle: 20 Years On." February 13, 2008. *BBC Gloucestershire*. Retrieved December 12, 2007, from http://www.bbc.co.uk/gloucestershire/content/articles/2008/02/13/eddie_the_eagle_feature.shtml.

7. Interview by Jonathan Sale. "My First Job: Eddie the Eagle, the Olympic ski-jumper, was a plasterer." December 13, 2007. *The Independent*. Retrieved January 5, 2008. from http://www.independent.co.uk/student/career-planning/getting-job/my-first-job-eddie-the-eagle-the-olympic-skijumper-was-a-plasterer-764891.html.
8. Dodd, Mike. "Jamaican bobsled team story continues to inspire." February 23, 2006. Retrieved December 12, 2007, from http://www.usatoday.com/sports/olympics/torino/sliding/2006-02-23-jamaica-brazil-bobsled_x.htm.
9. Multiple sources: "Winter Olympics; Russia Surprises Russians." February 28, 1994. *The New York Times*. Retrieved October 23, 2007, from http://query.nytimes.com/gst/fullpage.html?res=9D02E1DB143AF93BA15751C0A962958260; "Fall of the Soviet Union." Coldwar.org. (n.d.) Retrieved October 24, 2007, from http://www.coldwar.org/articles/90s/fall_of_the_soviet_union.asp.

SECTION III:
When Things Go Wrong...

Chapter 10–Marketing Challenges

1. Multiple sources: Borza, Eugene N. "Athenians, Macedonians, and the Origins of the Macedonian Royal House." *Hesperia Supplements*, Vol. 19, Studies in Attic Epigraphy, History and Topography. Presented to Eugene Vanderpool (1982), pp.7–13; Official website of the Olympic Movement. (n.d.) Retrieved December 4, 2007, from http://www.olympic.org/uk/games/ancient/athletes_uk.asp.
2. Multiple sources: Strenk, Andrew. "What Price Victory? The World of International Sports and Politics." *Annals of the American Academy of Political and Social Science*, Vol. 445, Contemporary Issues in Sport (Sep., 1979), pp.128–140. Publisher: Sage Publications, Inc., in association with the American Academy of Political and Social Science. Retrieved December 2, 2007, from Stable URL: http://www.jstor.org/stable/1042961; "Emperor Nero–Olympic Champion." January 2, 2001. Retrieved December 11, 2007 from http://www.bbc.co.uk/dna/h2g2/A493689; Benario, Herbert. W. "Nero (54-68 AD)." (2006) Retrieved December 15, 2007, from http://www.roman-emperors.org/nero.htm.
3. Andrews, Peter. "The First American Olympics." May/June 1988, Volume 39, Issue 4. *American Heritage Magazine*. Retrieved October 30, 2007, from http://www.americanheritage.com/articles/magazine/ah/1988/4/1988_4_39.shtml.
4. Kuriloff, Aaron. "25 great hoaxes, cheats and frauds in sport." April 17, 2005. Retrieved December 22, 2007, from http://proxy.espn.go.com/oly/columns/story?id=2039471.
5. Brennan, Christine. "TV ratings slip as figure skating loses its edge." (n.d.) *USAToday*. Retrieved March 29, 2008, from http://www.usatoday.com/sports/columnist/brennan/2008-01-23-skating_N.htm.
6. "Three-year ban for skating judge." April 30, 2002. *BBCSport*. Retrieved January 7, 2008 from http://news.bbc.co.uk/sport2/hi/other_sports/1959181.stm.
7. Multiple sources: Starr, Mark. "Scoring Without Scandal?" February 27, 2006. *Newsweek* and *NBCSports*. Retrieved November 30, 2007, from http://www.msnbc.msn.com/id/11347377/site/newsweek/. Thomson, Candus. "Revised system born in scandal." February 1, 2006. *The Baltimore Sun*. Retrieved December 9, 2007, from Readers may find the International Skating Union website, www.isu.org, worth visiting for additional detail on the new scoring system.
8. Clendenin, John A, and Stephen A. Greyser. "Tarnished Rings? Olympic Games Sponsorship Issues." Case 9-599-107. pp.1,5. Revised August 4, 2004. Harvard Business School. ©1999 President and Fellows of Harvard College.
9. Ibid.p.6.
10. Ibid.
11. Ibid.

12. Multiple sources: "S.L. bid scandal leads to Olympic reforms." (n.d.) *Deseret News*. Retrieved February 1, 2008, from http://deseretnews.com/oly/view/0,3949,30000166,00.html; "Samaranch leaves mixed Olympic legacy." (n.d.) *CNN.com*. Retrieved February 1, 2008 from http://edition.cnn.com/SPECIALS/2001/olympicbid/samaranch.profile.html; "Bribery scandal dulls Olympics' century-old shine." (n.d.) *CNN.com*. Retrieved February 1, 2008, from http://edition.cnn.com/SPECIALS/1999/olympic.probe/overview.

13. Wallechinsky, David, and Jaime Loucky. *The Complete Book of the Winter Olympics Turin 2006 Edition*. (Toronto: Sports Media Publishing, Inc., 2005), pp.8–9.

14. "Kwan Withdraws from Olympic Winter Games." February 12, 2006. *U.S. Olympic Committee Report*. Retrieved December 21, 2007, from http://www.usfigureskating.org/Story.asp?id=33082.

15. Rovell, Darren. "There will be some awkward moments for Coke, Visa." February 13, 2006. *ESPN.com*. Retrieved December 21, 2007, from http://sports.espn.go.com/oly/winter06/figure/columns/story?id=2328319.

16. "Protestor Ruins Marathon." August 29, 2004. *BBCSport*. Retrieved December 22, 2007, from http://news.bbc.co.uk/sport2/hi/olympics_2004/athletics/3610598.stm.

17. Majid, Kashef; Ramdas Chandra and Annamma Joy. "Exploring the Growing Interest in the Olympic Winter Games." *Sport Marketing Quarterly*. Volume 16, Number 1, 2007. p.31.

18. Multiple sources: Crouse, Karen. "Scrutiny of Suit Rises as World Records Fall." April 11, 2008. *The New York Times*. Retrieved April 12, 2008, from http://www.nytimes.com/2008/04/11/sports/othersports/11swim.html?_r=3&ref= sports&oref=slogin&oref=slogin&oref=slogin; "Critics: Swimsuit 'technological doping.'" April 30, 2008. *CNN.com*. Retrieved April 30, 2008, from http://edition.cnn.com/2008/TECH/04/11/lzr.record.breaking.ap.

SECTION IV:
Winning Marketing Gold: Work Like Crazy

Chapter 12–Sponsorships

1. "Are the Olympics Worth it?" April 11, 2008. *Portfolio.com*. Retrieved April 11, 2007, from http://biz.yahoo.com/portfolio/080411/dcr4cd9f7d57c5d5ab192b141a0270d32ed.html?.v=2.

2. Olympic Marketing Fact File 2008 Edition, p.5. Retrieved February 23, 2008, from http://www.olympic.org.

3. Ibid.

4. Ibid. p.18.

5. Ibid.

6. Ibid. p.38.

7. Ibid.

8. Ibid.

9. Ibid.

10. Multiple sources: Lieberman, David. "*USA Today* CEO Forum: GE sees growth opportunites." *USA Today*. (n.d.) Retrieved February 27, 2008, from http://www.usatoday.com/money/companies/management/2007-12-13-immelt-ge_N.htm; Madden, Normandy. "Sponsoring the Games: Marketing plans shaping up." February 14, 2007. *AdAge*. Retrieved January 3, 2008, from http://www.plasticsnews.com/china/olympics/english/headlines2.html?id=1175176784; "Kodak Ends Olympic Sponsorship After Beijing Games." October 16, 2007. National Press Photographers Association. Retrieved December 14, 2007, from http://www.nppa.org/news_and_events/news/2007/10/kodak.html; "Coca Cola extends Olympic Sponsorship." August 1, 2005. *Atlanta Business Chronicle*. Retrieved December 1, 2007, from http://atlanta.bizjournals. com/atlanta/stories/2005/08/01/daily4.html; "Olympic Sponsor-Omega Contract Extended to Include the London 2012 Olympic and Paralympic Games." May 16, 2006. 2010 Commerce Centre BC Olympic and Paralympic

Winter Games Secretariat. Retrieved November 30, 2007, from http://www.2010 commercecentre.com/news.aspx?articleID=85; "Manulife-Sinochem announces long-term partnership with Olympic Taekwondo Gold Medalist, Luo Wei." September 29, 2006. Retrieved Dcember 5, 2007, from http://www.manulife. com/corporate/corporate2.nsf/public/china092906.html; "McDonald's signs eight-year Olympic deal to include Turin, Vancouver Games." June 7, 2004. *Ski Racing*. Retrieved December 12, 2007, from http://www.skiracing.com/index.php?option=com_content&task=view&id=1581&Itemid=38; "Atos Origin Becomes Worldwide Partner of the International Paralympic Committee." January 28, 2008. Atos Origin. Retrieved February 4, 2008, from http://www.atosorigin.com/en-us/Newsroom/en-us/Press_Releases/2008/2008_01_29_01.htm; "Case Study: Samsung has the WOW factor-September 2005." (2005) *Sport and Technology*. Retrieved December 4, 2007, from http://www.sportandtechnology. com/features/0298.html; McDonald's website. Retrieved January 22, 2008, from http://www.mcdonalds.com/corp/values/balance/physical_activity.html.

11. Foster, George, and Victoria Chang. "Visa Sponsorship Marketing." Case: SPM-5 p.3. Stanford University Graduate School of Business ©2003.

12. Official website of the Olympic Movement. (n.d.) Retrieved October 14, 2007, from http://www.olympic.org/UK/organisation/facts/programme/sponsors_uk.asp.

13. Ibid.

14. Olympic Marketing Fact File 2008 Edition, p.10. Retrieved February 23, 2008, from http://www.olympic.org.

15. Ibid. p.11.

16. "2006 FIFA World Cup™ broadcast wider, longer and farther than ever before." February 6, 2007. Retrieved December 10, 2007, from http://www.fifa.com/aboutfifa/marketingtv/news/newsid=111247.html. Note that the Olympics changed their tracking of viewing audience from cumulative viewing audience to cumulative viewing hours in 2000. The last Olympiads that tracked cumulative viewing audiences were the 1996 Atlanta Olympics (cumulative viewing audience of 19.6 billion) and Nagano in 1998 (cumulative viewing audience of 10.7 billion); see Olympic Marketing Fact File 2008 Edition, p.24. These figures compare to cumulative viewing audiences of 24.7 billion for the 1998 World Cup and 28.8 billion for the 2002 World Cup, respectively.

17. Speech by David Haigh at BrandFinance Forum in Asia, March 2008, Singapore Management University.

18. "Top 100 Global Brands Scorebocard." Interbrand and *BusinessWeek*. August 6, 2007. Retrieved August 23, 2007, from http://bwnt.businessweek.com/interactive_reports/top_brands/index.asp.

19. Visit the BrandFinance website to see various brand surveys and results. http://www.brandfinance.com/docs/global_brands_survey.asp.

20. Official website of the Olympic Movement. (n.d.) Retrieved January 28, 2008, from http://www.olympic.org/uk/organisation/facts/introduction/index_uk.asp.

21. Martínez-Jerez, Asís F, and Rosario Martínez de Albornoz. "Hala Madrid: Managing Real Madrid Club de Fútbol, the Team of the Century." Case 9-105-013. p.4. Revised June 8, 2006. Harvard Business School. ©2004 President and Fellows of Harvard College.

22. "Starbucks, Fair Trade, and Coffee Social Responsibility" guidelines, published 03/07/06. Visit http://www.starbucks.com/aboutus/csr.asp for more information.

23. Taylor, Humphrey. "Widespread Belief that Super Bowl Players Use Steroids." *Harris Poll #6*. January 30, 2004. Retrieved January 17, 2008, from http://www.quickin sights.com/harris_poll/index.asp?PID=435.

24. Bajaj, Vikas, and; Peter Edmonston. "ETrade struggles to avert big write-down as shares tumble'." November 13, 2007. *International Herald Tribune*. Retrieved November 15, 2007, from http://www.iht.com/articles/2007/11/13/business/etrade.php.

25. Berger, Warren. "Hot Spots!". (n.d.) *Wired*. Retrieved December 14, 2007, from http://www.wired.com/wired/archive/8.02/commercials_pr.html.

26. Kronick, Scott, and Dalton Dorne for the Ogilvy Group. "Going for an Olympic Marketing Gold." (n.d.) *The China Business Review*. Retrieved April 16, 2008, from http://www.chinabusinessreview.com/public/0501/ogilvy.html.

27. Clifford, Stephanie. "Coca-Cola Faces Critics of Its Olympics Support." April 17, 2008. *The New York Times*. Retrieved April 18, 2008, from http://www.nytimes.com/2008/04/17/business/17coke.html?_r=1&partner= rssnyt&emc=rss&oref=login.

28. Ibid.

29. "Partnership History." (n.d.) Coca-Cola corporate website. Retrieved January 30, 2008, from http://www.thecoca-colacompany.com/heritage/olympicgames_partnership.html.

30. "The Real Thing: Coca-Cola Extends Sponsorship of Olympic Games Through 2020." August 1, 2005. *BrandWeek*. Retrieved December 10, 2007, from http://www.brandweek.com/bw/news/recent_display.jsp?vnu_content_id=1001001168.

31. According to BrandFinance, Coca-Cola's brand value in 2007 was $43 billion and Interbrand calculated a brand value of $65 billion. The difference is due to different methodologies. Readers are encouraged to visit www.brandfinance.com and www.interbrand.com for more information.

32. "The Olympic Games." Coca-Cola corporate website. Retrieved January 30, 2008, from http://www.thecoca-colacompany.com/heritage/olympic games.html.

33. Ibid. http://www.thecoca-colacompany.com/heritage/olympicgames_ difference.html.

34. Multiple sources: "New Environmental Champion Torchbearers around the World Prepare to Carry Flame as Coca-Cola Extends Sustainability Platform to Olympic Torch Relay." March 24, 2008. *MSNMoney*. Retrieved March 27, 2008, from http://news.money central.msn.com/ticker/article.aspx?Feed=BW&Date=20080324&ID=8374833&Symbol =US:KOltip Collier, Joe Guy, and Craig Simons. "Coke takes neutral stance on Olympic protests." April 13, 2008. *The Atlanta Journal-Constitution*. Retrieved April 15, 2008, from http://www.ajc.com/business/content/business/coke/stories/2008/04/12 cokeolympics_0413.html.

35. Official website of the Olympic Movement. (n.d.) Retrieved January 28, 2008, from http://www.olympic.org/uk/organisation/commissions/marketing/full_story_uk.asp?id=2375.

36. "The Olympic Games." Coca-Cola corporate Web site. Retrieved January 30, 2008, from http://www.thecoca-colacompany.com/heritage/olympic games.html.

37. Multiple sources: "The Olympic Games." Coca-Cola corporate website. Retrieved January 30, 2008, from http://www.thecoca-colacompany.com/heritage/olympicgames.html; Official website of the Olympic Movement. (n.d.) Retrieved January 30, 2008, from http://www.olympic.org/uk/games/index_uk.asp; Wallechinsky, David, and Jaime Loucky. *The Complete Book of the Winter Olympics Turin 2006 Edition*. (Toronto: Sports Media Publishing, Inc., 2005) Wallechinsky, David, and Jaime Loucky. *The Complete Book of the Summer Olympics Athens 2004 Edition*. (Toronto: Sports Media Publishing, Inc., 2004)

38. Foster, George, and Victoria Chang. "Visa Sponsorship Marketing." Case: SPM-5 p.3. Stanford University Graduate School of Business ©2003.

39. Ibid.

40. Visa corporate website. Retrieved January 16, 2008, from http://www.corporate.visa.com/md/fs/sponsorships/sponsorships.jsp.

41. Foster, George, and Victoria Chang. "Visa Sponsorship Marketing." Case: SPM-5 p.15. Stanford University Graduate School of Business ©2003.

42. Davis, Robert T. *Marketing in Emerging Companies*. (New York: Perseus Books., 1984). Author's note: this book was written by my dad, Bob Davis, who was the Sebastian S. Kresge Professor of Marketing at Stanford Graduate School of Business until his death in 1995.

43. Foster, George, and Victoria Chang. "Visa Sponsorship Marketing." Case: SPM-5 p.4. Stanford University Graduate School of Business ©2003.

44. Ibid. pp.5–6.

45. Olympic Marketing Fact File 2008 Edition, p.10. Retrieved February 23, 2008, from www.olympic.org.

46. Visa revenues retrieved April 22, 2008 from: http://finance.yahoo.com/q/ks?s=V.

47. Multiple sources: Foster, George, and Victoria Chang. "Visa Sponsorship Marketing." Case: SPM-5 p.1-15. Stanford University Graduate School of Business ©2003; Read, Madlen. "Visa IPO Could Be Largest in US History." February 25, 2008. *Associated Press*. Retrieved March 15, 2008, from http://biz.yahoo.com/ap/080225/visa_ipo.html; Visa corporate website. Retrieved March 15, 2008, from http://www.corporate.visa.com/md/st/main.jsp; Woolsey, Ben. "Credit card industry facts and personal debt statistics." (2006–2007) *CreditCards.com*. Retrieved March 17, 2008 from http://www.creditcards.com/statistics/credit-card-industry-facts-and-personal-debt-statistics.php; "Top 10 IPOs by Deal Value." March 19, 2008. *Associated Press*. Retrieved March 24, 2008, from http://biz.yahoo.com/ap/080319/ipo_glance.html?.v=1.

48. Foster, George, and Victoria Chang. "Visa Sponsorship Marketing." Case: SPM-5 p.14. Stanford University Graduate School of Business ©2003.

49. Multiple sources: Ibid. p.5; Saeger, Becky. "Visa Has What it Takes at The Olympics." *Marketer's Forum*. April 2002, Volume 6, Number 3, p.30.

50. Teopaco, John, and Stephen A. Greyser. "John Hancock Sports Sponsorship: 1993-2000 and Beyond." pp.3–4. Case: 9-599-027. December 30, 1998. Harvard Business School. ©1998 President and Fellows of Harvard College.

51. Ibid.

52. Ibid.

53. Ibid. (adapted from pp.4–5).

54. Ibid. p.4.

55. Ibid. pp.5-7.

56. Ibid. p.7.

57. Ibid. p.4.

58. Foster, George, and Victoria Chang. "Visa Sponsorship Marketing." Case: SPM-5 p.16. Stanford University Graduate School of Business ©2003.

59. Teopaco, John, and Stephen A. Greyser. "John Hancock Sports Sponsorship: 1993-2000 and Beyond." pp.9. Case: 9-599-027. December 30, 1998. Harvard Business School. ©1998 President and Fellows of Harvard College.

60. Ibid. pp.8–9.

61. "Manulife Financial becomes Worldwide Life Insurance Partner of the Olympic Games." August 31, 2004. Manulife Press Release. Retrieved December 23, 2007, from http://www.manulife.com/corporate/corporate2.nsf/Public/hongkong083104.html.

62. Based on two meetings: Speech by David Shaw, Director of Brand/Asia Pacific for Lenovo at BrandFinance Forum in Asia, March 2008, Singapore Management University; and a meeting with David Shaw on April 17, 2008.

63. Quelch, John, and Carin-Isabel Knoop. "Lenovo: Building a Global Brand." p.12. Case: 9-507-014. Revised October 19, 2006. Harvard Business School. ©2006 President and Fellows of Harvard College.

64. Ibid. p.1.

65. Spencer, Jane. "Lenovo CEO has Global Ambitions." November 17, 2006. *The Wall Street Journal*. Retrieved November 2, 2007, from http://online.wsj.com/public/article/SB116370857929525438-gdYjYdeCw1OMKJvw5R4LRPuKTkc_20061128.html?mod=regionallinks.

66. Hamm, Steve; Pete Engardio and Frederik Balfour. "Big Blue's Bold Step Into China." December 20, 2004. *BusinessWeek*. Retrieved November 5, 2007, from http://www.businessweek.com/magazine/content/04_51/b3913045_mz011.htm.

67. Speech by David Shaw, Director of Brand/Asia Pacific for Lenovo at BrandFinance Forum in Asia, March 2008, Singapore Management University.
68. Nystedt, Dan. "Acer Eclipses Lenovo, Takes Aim at Dell." October 26, 2007. *PCWorld*. Retrieved November 15, 2007, from http://www.pcworld.com/businesscenter/article/138973/acer_eclipses_lenovo_takes_aim_at_dell.html.
69. Multiple sources: "Lenovo Wins Two Gold Awards at IDEA 2006." July 19, 2006. Retrieved November 16, 2007, from http://www.lenovo.com/news/us/en/2006/07/idea06.html; speech by David Shaw, Director of Brand/Asia Pacific for Lenovo at BrandFinance Forum in Asia, March 2008, Singapore Management University.
70. Multiple sources: "Lenovo Delivers Top Performance at Winter Olympics." February 17, 2006. *XTVWorld*. Retrieved December 27, 2007, from http://press.xtvworld.com/article9640.html; meeting with David Shaw on April 17, 2008; Quelch, John, and Carin-Isabel Knoop. "Lenovo: Building a Global Brand." Case: 9-507-014. Revised October 19, 2006. Harvard Business School. ©2006 President and Fellows of Harvard College; Frommer, Dan. "Wiring the Torino Olympics." January 10, 2006. *Forbes*. Retrieved December 28, 2007, from http://www.forbes.com/2006/01/09/winter-olympics-technology-cx_df_0110 olympics.html.
71. "Lenovo Delivers Top Performance at Winter Olympics." February 17, 2006. *XTVWorld*. Retrieved December 27, 2007, from http://press.xtvworld.com/article9640.html.
72. "Lenovo Lands Perfect Score at Winter Olympics." March 2, 2006. *XTVWorld*. Retrieved December 27, 2007, from http://press.xtvworld.com/article-print-9908.html.
73. IGRS definition: retrieved January 23, 2008, from http://www.igrs.org/en/contentmanage/detail.asp?ChannelIndex=Resources&channelid =110140110&subchannelid =&keyword= &id=494&exid=&yr=&mt=&epid.
74. Quelch, John, and Carin-Isabel Knoop. "Lenovo: Building a Global Brand." p.20. Case: 9-507-014. Revised October 19, 2006. Harvard Business School. ©2006 President and Fellows of Harvard College.
75. Ibid. p.10.
76. Ibid. p.17.
77. Based on two meetings: speech by David Shaw, Director of Brand/Asia Pacific for Lenovo at BrandFinance Forum in Asia, March 2008, Singapore Management University; and a meeting with David Shaw on April 17, 2008.
78. Quelch, John, and Carin-Isabel Knoop. "Lenovo: Building a Global Brand." p.11. Case: 9-507-014. Revised October 19, 2006. Harvard Business School. ©2006 President and Fellows of Harvard College.
79. Hamm, Steve. "A Torch Lights the Way for Lenovo." August 3, 2007. *BusinessWeek*. Retrieved November 30, 2007, from http://www.businessweek.com/innovate/content/aug2007/id2007083_498676.htm.
80. "Lenovo Champions." (2008). Retrieved April 14, 2008, from http://2008.lenovo.com/.
81. Pettey, Christy. "Gartner Says Worldwide PC Market Grew 13 Percent% in 2007." January 16, 2008. *Gartner*. Retrieved January 24, 2008, from http://www.gartner.com/it/page.jsp?id=584210.
82. Ibid.
83. Ibid.
84. Ibid.
85. Multiple sources: "Top 100 Global Brands Scorebocard." Interbrand and *BusinessWeek*. August 6, 2007. Retrieved August 23, 2007, from http://bwnt.businessweek.com/interactive_reports/top_brands/index.asp; "Olympics Hot Sheet-Samsung Ready for 2008 Games." September 9, 2004. *China Daily*. Retrieved January 9, 2008, from http://www.buyusa.gov/china/en/hs040909.html.
86. Davis, Matthew. "Games' Eagle-eyed Sponsor Police." August 14, 2004. *BBCNews*. Retrieved January 17, 2008, from http://news.bbc.co.uk/2/hi/europe/3565616.stm.

SECTION V:
Training for Olympic Marketing Victory

Chapter 14–Customers
1. Adapted from: Sanjay Dhar, James H. Lorie Professor of Marketing, University of Chicago Graduate School of Business.
2. Ibid.
3. Ibid.

Chapter 15–Creative Execution
1. See Youtube.com for samples of Outpost.com's television commercials, including the gerbil commercial referenced in this section. www.youtube.com.
2. Regan, Keith. "Goodbye COOL-Fry's Electronics Completes Outpost.com Acquisition." November 9, 2001. *E-Commerce Times*. Retrieved November 26, 2007, from http://www.ecommercetimes.com/story/14700.html?welcome =1209974781.
3. Mark Twain (Samuel Clemmons). (n.d.). *Senior Magazine*. Retrieved December 3, 2007, from http://www.seniormag.com/whitt/mark_twain.htm.
4. Raine, George. "Visa is putting new life in advertising theme, It's Everywhere You Want to Be ends after 20 years." February 8, 2006. *San Francisco Chronicle*. Retrieved February 5, 2008, from http://www.sfgate.com/cgi-bin/article.cgi?file=/chronicle/archive/2006/02/08/BUGIIH4FD21.DTL &type=business.
5. Multiple sources: McDonald's corporate website, Olympics section. Retrieved April 3, 2008, from http://www.mcdonalds.com/corp/news/corppr/2005/CPR_11032005.html; Lenovo corporate website, Olympics section. Retrieved April 11, 2008, from http://2008.lenovo.com/en-us/; Panasonic corporate Web site, Olympics section. Retrieved April 3, 2008 from http://panasonic.net/olympic/; Johnson & Johnson corporate website, Olympics section. Retrieved April 2, 2008, from http://www.jnj.com/connect/caring/initiatives/; Samsung corporate website, Olympics section. Retrieved March 30, 2008, from http://www.samsung.com/global/experience/beijing2008/index.html; Visa corporate website, Olympics section. Retrieved April 12, 2008, from http://sponsorships.visa.com/olympic/main.jsp?src=home; Atos Origin corporate website, Olympics section. Retrieved April 3, 2008, from http://www.atosorigin.com/en-us/olympic_games/; Kodak corporate website, Olympics reference. Retrieved April 2, 2008, from http://www.kodak.com/eknec/PageQuerier.jhtml?pq-path=2/8/12409&pq-locale=en_US&_requestid=220; Manulife corporate website, Olympics. Retrieved April 11, 2008, from http://www.manulife.com/corporate/corporate2.nsf/Public/hongkong082007.html; Omega corporate website, Olympics section. Retrieved April 3, 2008, from http://www.omegawatches.com/index.php?id=1065; Coca-Cola corporate website, Olympics section. Retrieved April 12, 2008, from http://www.thecoca-colacompany.com/heritage/olympicgames.html.
6. To read about the mascots and their histories, visit the official website of the Olympic Movement at http://www.olympic.org/uk/games/index_uk.asp.

Chapter 16–Marketing Communications
1. Davis, John. *Measuring Marketing: 103 Key Metrics Every Marketer Needs*. (Singapore: John Wiley & Sons (Asia) Pte. Ltd., 2006), p.183.
2. Ibid. p.185.
3. Ibid. p.188.
4. Multiple sources: Foster, George, and Victoria Chang. "Visa Sponsorship Marketing." Case: SPM-5 p.31. Stanford University Graduate School of Business ©2003; "By the Numbers 2003." (2003) *Street and Smith's Sports Business Journal*, Retrieved November 27, 2007, updated with data from: "Isilon to Provide Clustered Storage for NBC's Coverage of the Beijing Olympic Gamess," Retrieved April 16, 2008, from http://biz.yahoo.com/prnews/080415/aqtu131.html?.v=41; "Reality Shows Put Big Dent in Winter Olympics Ratings." March 1,

2006. *The New York Times*. Retrieved March 2, 2008, from http://www.nytimes.com/2006/03/01/sports/olympics/01olymps.html?_r=1&oref=slogin; Murrah, Ken. "An experiment that worked." August 29, 2004. *Yahoo!Sports*. Retrieved March 2, 2008, from http://sports.yahoo.com/olympics/athens2004/news?slug=km-tv0829&prov=yhoo&type=lgns.

5. Hanna, Julia. "Authenticity over Exaggeration: The New Rule in Advertising." December 3, 2007. Harvard Business School Working Knowledge. http://hbswk.hbs.edu/item/5812.html.

6. Bhargava, Rohit. "Analysis: The Top 10 Most Underappreciated Metrics to Track in 2008." December 18, 2007. *DigitalMediaWire*. http://www.dmwmedia.com/news/2007/12/18/analysis:-top-10-most-underappreciated-metrics-track-2008.

7. "Advertising boom in developing ad markets compensates for credit-crunch gloom in the West." March 31, 2008. p.1. ZenithOptimedia. http://www.zenithoptimedia.com/gff.

8. Ibid.

9. Ibid. p.3.

10. Ibid. p.2 (adapted).

11. Vanier, Fiona. "World Broadband Statistics: Q4 2007. March 2008." http://point-topic.com/home/press/dslanalysis.asp, p.13.

12. Ibid.

13. "Study: Brands Must Adapt to Shifting Media Habits of Users." (2007). *Media-Screen*. http://www.marketingcharts.com/topics/blogs/study-brands-must-adapt-to-shifting-media-habits-of-users-369.

14. Ibid.

15. Data from speech made by Mitch Joel, CEO of Twist Image and 6 Pixels of Separation, in a July 2007 presentation made to Singapore Management University's conference called PodCamp 2007. Cited source was Arbitron & Edison Media Research 2007.

16. Multiple sources: "Mobile Music, Games and TV to Generate US$34 Billion by 2010." March 2008. *Juniper Research*. http://www.cellular-news.com/story/29857.php; "Mobile Entertainment Markets: Opportunities & Forecasts (Second edition) 2007-2012." pp.5–6. *Juniper Research*. http://www.juniperresearch.com.

17. Data from speech made by Mitch Joel, CEO of Twist Image and 6 Pixels of Separation, in a July 2007 presentation made to Singapore Management University's conference called PodCamp 2007. Cited source was Arbitron & Edison Media Research 2007.

18. Verna, Paul. "Podcast Advertising: Seeking Riches in Niches." January 2008. *eMarketer*. http://www.emarketer.com/Reports/All/Emarketer_2000474.aspx?src=report_head_info_sitesearch.

19. Multiple sources: Data from speech made by Mitch Joel, CEO of Twist Image and 6 Pixels of Separation, in a July 2007 presentation made to Singapore Management University's conference called PodCamp 2007. Cited source was Arbitron & Edison Media Research 2007; Vogelstein, Fred. "How Mark Zuckerberg Turned Facebook Into the Web's Hottest Platform." September 6, 2007. *Wired*. http://www.wired.com/techbiz/startups/news/2007/09/ff_facebook; "Social Networking Goes Global." July 31, 2007. Comscore Press Release. http://www.comscore.com/press/release.asp?press=1555; Charny, Ben. "Even with slowing growth, YouTube still No.1" March 21, 2007. *MarketWatch*. http://www.marketwatch.com/news/story/even-slowing-growth-youtube-remains/story.aspx?guid=%7B98FB4A03-0B53-4CFB-BA2D-716D2B59CAAB%7D.

20. "North American Technographics Media and Marketing Online Survey Q3 2007." (2008). Forrester. http://www.forrester.com/rb/consumertechno.jsp.

Chapter 17—Is Your Company in Shape for Olympic Marketing?

1. Adapted and augmented based on information from George Foster, Stephen A. Greyser, and Bill Walsh. *The Business of Sports: Text and Cases on Strategy and Management*. ©2005 South-Western College Pub; Section 6: Sports Marketing: Advertising, Sponsorship, and Endorsements, p.237.

INDEX